The Cashless Society

The
Cashless
Society

ROBERT A. HENDRICKSON

DODD, MEAD & COMPANY
NEW YORK

ISBN: 0–396–06538–4

Library of Congress Catalog Card Number: 72–3928

Printed in the United States of America
by The Cornwall Press, Inc., Cornwall, N. Y.

To Rob and Eleanor

Contents

Introduction   9

1. A QUESTION OF MONEY   25

2. A CADE IN THE AGE OF CREDIT   34

3. A NATURAL HISTORY OF CREDIT CARDS   45

4. THE DARKER SIDE OF THE CREDIT CARD   66

5. LIVING WITH COMPUTER DATA BANKS   82

6. BREAKING OUT OF THE PAPER COCOON   100

7. THE LAWLESSNESS OF MONEY   111

8. THE ILLUSION OF MONEY AS CASH   134

9. THE REALITY OF MONEY AS CREDIT AND DEBT   155

10. RECONCILIATION TO A NEW RESOURCE   173

11. AN ECONOMY OF CASHLESS EQUILIBRIUM   200

12. THE CASHLESS SOCIETY   223

Bibliography   247

Introduction

Wealth is not without its advantages and neither, of course, is money. But the assumption that cash and money are practically the same, or at least interchangeable, has for too long gone unexamined. So has the proposition that, if cash and money are not exactly synonymous, the more nearly they approach equivalence the better. Cash money is said to be ready money, cash on the barrelhead, the "good" money that, according to Gresham's law, is supposed to be driven out by the "bad." A thesis of this study is that none of these axioms except the first is so. A corollary is that this is not necessarily a bad thing, and that the sooner we understand this and act upon an understanding of these facts, instead of illusory axioms, the better for our money, political economy and society.

A curiosity of modern economic life is the role of change: small change in cash coins like quarters and nickels and shillings and pence, and large change in cash paper currency like dollars and pounds and francs, for which credit in the form of checks and promissory notes may ultimately be exchanged.

Such exchange in the form of cash money is a conspicuous presence in the life of contemporary society. Amid the general glut, to an individual who has none, it becomes more painfully conspicuous still. Yet the general absence of money as cash is a conspicuous feature of utopias of the future as well as golden ages of the past. Without it the high civilization of ancient Egypt left monuments behind that still have the power to stun us with their nobility and grandeur. In their scale of values, Athenian Plato and Spartan Leonidas alike would rank it low, although quite likely it meant a good deal more to the slaves and helots of their day than has come down to us in the writings of psychologically secure sages and economically well-entrenched pharaohs and kings.

Looking ahead from the 1880s, Edward Bellamy, in *Looking Backward*, envisaged the year 2000 A.D. as a golden age for the United States metaphorically but not monetarily. As much as anything else, this was the result of eliminating all transactions in gold backed money between one person and another. The demonetization of money, of money as cash, of money thought of as intrinsically commodity money, as cash money with gold backing, would bring about a golden age, according to Bellamy, because it would cause people to be less materialistic in their dealings with the natural world and with one another. In short, the demonetization of gold would lead to the demonetization of mankind.

But according to most futurists, all that is necessary is to wait out a short term in the current cycle of human history, perhaps no more than a quarter of a revolution, and a cashless society will inevitably befall us. Without further conscious human effort, without application of additional intellectual energy, and without the deliberate guidance of human foresight, the advent of a cashless society requires little more from us than a moderate amount of time and patience. By their lights it should not be necessary to dally here upon the disappearance of money as cash because this is a development that is automatic and inevitable.

In the rich literature of political economy the area of money as cash likewise turns out to be a rather surprising pocket of poverty. A characteristic attitude of political economists toward it has been one of benign neglect. John Stuart Mill's insouciant comment on money in *Principles of Political Economy* is typical: "There cannot, in short, be intrinsically a more insignificant thing, in the economy of society, than money; except in the contrivance for sparing time and labor."

But Mill's dictum does not really disturb our conviction that few things, intrinsically, are more significant than money as cash. The exception Mill makes of "the contrivance for sparing time and labor" only reassures us of the rightness of this impression. Money as cash does not seem to be going out of style. Money, and particularly money as cash, remains for most of us a subject of extraordinary, if not painful, significance.

If Edward Bellamy was right, we have only a little more than a quarter of a century to wait before a cashless society catches up with us, and we with it. That will be the day, when we simply cash in all our cash. But if Utopians and futurists join political economists in extending the blessings of benign neglect to the subject of money as cash, does this mean that a book called *The Cashless Society* can be no more than descriptive of a future that is inevitable in any event without it?

I think not.

This study describes the kinds of conscious human effort and intellectual energy and understanding that must be brought to bear to foster evolution in the direction of the kind of cashless society that sages like Bellamy and Mill have depicted as scenes of true human fulfillment. It considers the consequences of failure to bring the deliberate guidance of human foresight to bear in directing the evolution of society toward a cashlessness that is fundamental and not superficial. And this is something more than receiving a free credit card in the mail from a third or fourth bank.

It is also a thesis of this study that the further proliferation of a cash and carry society throughout the world will contribute materially to the forces that the Club of Rome has identified as leading toward a future condition of human society that may well be nasty, brutish, and short.

If utopians and futurists are right in assuming that a historical cycle is moving us inevitably toward a cashless society without further effort on our part, a lot of recent United States statistical facts stand stubbornly in the way. Curiously enough, in 1972 the United States had more cash around than ever before. The amount of paper money and coin in circulation, excluding amounts held by the United States Treasury and Federal Reserve Banks, had risen sharply over the previous ten years and stood at a record high of $61 billion. In per capita terms, currency outstanding amounted to $292 for each man, woman and child in the nation compared with only $182 per capita in 1960, between $14 and $22 during the period from 1892 to 1917, and between $27 and $46 during the period from 1918 to 1939.

Even after allowing for increases in population and inflation, real per capita holdings of cash are now more than 50 per cent higher than they were in 1939. More than $13 billion in $100 bills was outstanding in 1972, more than double the amount in 1960. Ironically, all this is at a time when checks and credit cards and innumerable other forms of credit are instantly available, and more widely used than ever before.

A sharp rise in coins has also occurred, both in subsidiary coins like dimes, quarters, half-dollars and dollars, and minor coins like pennies and nickels as well. Coins outstanding now are valued at $6.7 billion, well over double the amount of coins circulating in the early 1960s. An estimated $2.3 billion of silver coins has disappeared into private hoards since 1965. The commemorative Kennedy half-dollar and the Eisenhower silver dollar are in demand everywhere. Thousands of people have suddenly taken up numismatic pursuits for knowledge, fun, and profit.

Facts are stubborn things, said Oliver Wendell Holmes. The cyclical historical trend toward a cashless society that most utopians and futurists have assumed was automatic, and most political economists have treated as not mattering very much whichever way it goes, is in danger of being submerged by tides of money as cash which are rising at a quickening rate everywhere across the Western world.

Well, what is so bad about cash, anyway? Look at the convenience. With a cashless society, without coins, how would we pay local sales taxes at ever higher rates? How would we have quarters and dimes to throw by the sackful into toll collection baskets as we speed through toll bridges, tunnels and turnpikes? What would we drop in collection boxes on buses where local systems require exact change from riders so the driver will not be a target for robbers? What would we use in vending machines for everything from combs and candy, to soup to nuts? They accounted for more than $6.2 billion in sales in 1970, double the volume as recently as 1963. With inflation, and the price of practically everything higher these days, how would we carry on business with less paper money, instead of more? We must carry more cash money than ever before just to pay for our morning paper, for the bus, subway or taxi, to buy lunch, get a haircut, a pack of gum or cigarettes, to cover all the routine day-to-day expenses we normally pay in cash. Without cash, what could we hoard in safe deposit boxes, jelly jars, in mattress ticking or mouldering chests buried under the magnolia trees?

Narcotics agents in New York seized a green suitcase containing almost $1 million in crisp packets of new $100 bills from two men who were charged with a conspiracy to distribute heroin. Without cash, what would airline managements use to pay off hijackers' ransom demands? How would politicians' payoffs be transported secretly to Swiss banks? Would the pushers or the hijackers or the co-conspirators find their game worthwhile if the only medium they had to play it with was credit, and no cash in bills and coin?

13

John Stuart Mill (of whom the reader has not yet heard the last) wrote:

If we did not have such a thing as money the principal inconvenience would be the lack of a common measure for values of different kinds. If a tailor had only coats, and wanted to buy bread, or a horse, he would have a hard time figuring out how many loaves of bread he ought to get for a coat, or how many coats he should give for a horse.

The lack of a common measure for values of different kinds would certainly be a serious inconvenience, but the lack of money as a store of value and a hoard of cash for all the uses suggested above would be no less serious. Or would it?

Once we have run over the usefulness of coin and small paper currency, we have said most of what there is to say in favor of cash. When we look at the way we really live we realize that at least in terms of amount, most of what we use for money is credit. The illusion of money as cash is so powerful that we can hardly bring ourselves to believe that this is so. But why, indeed, if you are not engaged in illegal enterprises, hold cash that can be lost, stolen, burnt up or otherwise destroyed, which earns you no return, and which you find so devilishly hard to account for when it is gone? Substitutes for cash, in the form of checks, credit cards, charge accounts, travelers' checks and letters of credit are abundantly available, safer than cash, and cheaper for large transactions because a cost inherent in using large amounts of cash is the possibility of loss, theft or destruction. Do you just like to flash a big roll? You can wrap a $10 bill around a cucumber.

It seems ridiculous when we are as conscious of inflation as we are these days, that, with plenty of opportunities for getting high rates of interest on savings accounts, still higher rates on practically risk-free market investments with capital growth besides and large amounts of credit which does not tie up large amounts of non-interest-bearing, inflation eroding cash, we still hold so much money in cash, and more every day. So this book looks at the credit on which a typical member of the American corporate state spends his cashless days, at the money substitutes for cash found in the natural history of credit cards, at ways of reducing the volume of paper in the economy by eliminating the checks, stock certificates and other forms of hoardings which surround so much of our everyday lives, and shut so much of the time of our life off from the living of it.

Money as cash is bait for crimes against our persons and for large-scale frauds whose perpetrators often cannot be proven guilty under existing rules of legal evidence. Such frauds extend to the cash purchase of political and economic influence, which threatens the ultimate integrity of our free political system itself. Political leaders and economic advisers relate contemporary political issues in political economy to the familiar polarities suggested by Jeffersonian and Hamiltonian traditions. All too often this comes across as rather simplistic talk about whether a particular policy tends to favor "the little man" or "the big interests." This study assumes as a fact of contemporary life the reality of the American corporate state as it exists in the troubled world of the late twentieth century. The large question of whether money as cash is a prerequisite of the pursuit of happiness in political and economic freedom within the American corporate state is explored, as is the question of the elimination of money as cash in a rational civil service state.

The Tragedy of the Commons describes the situation in a picturesque little old New England village where every man is allowed to graze his cows free on the village common. Each one gains an individual advantage in increasing the number of his cows, but if everyone does so the common is destroyed.

So a license fee of $10 per cow is imposed to inhibit the growth of the herds grazed on the common of pasture, and for a while this works well. The proceeds are used for village restoration, and as years go by the village grows ever more quaint and picturesque.

Introduction

But the $10 grazing fee seems no more than a joke to the rich New Yorkers who have been buying up the village's lovely old white clapboard Federal houses for second (or third or fourth) homes. They still insist on grazing cows on the common to enhance the picturesqueness of their scene. So by the late 20th century, the common has been destroyed anyway.

This is an example of an N-person game. It begins as a game in which many people compete for a few scarce resources. Individual rationality becomes collective irrationality. The aggregate sum of money available to the farmers in the early economy of the village is finite, and limited, much as it is in the set used for playing the famous old parlor game of Monopoly. Only a fixed amount of money comes with each Monopoly set. It is divided up pro rata among the players under the direction of a banker, who exercises strict control of all cash issuance and withdrawal. Money is merely the medium with which the game is played, like the dice, the colored counters and the little wooden blocks that are houses, mansions and hotels. The $10 grazing fee originally served as an effective curb on collective irrationality because it had a rational relationship to the limited amount of money available for all purposes to the farmers who made up the economy that surrounded the village green.

But when the rich New Yorkers arrive and buy up the old Federal houses, the $10 fee is no longer a limit; it becomes a license. It is a license to destroy the common, and so the common is destroyed. The comparison of the village economy with the Monopoly set falls apart. The impact of the ungovernable weight and mass of late 20th century money as cash has destroyed it.

Many axioms of economics which we still try to apply to our late 20th century lives were derived by Adam Smith, Karl Marx and hosts of other political economists from engaging vignettes of 18th and early 19th century life like *The Tragedy of the Commons*. The impact of the late 20th century money turns them inside out, as when the limit on grazing turns out

16

to be a license to destroy the common of pasture. The charm of these old vignettes, the certitudes of the old economic axioms derived from them and the illusion of money as cash screen us from a more accurate perception of the late 20th century reality.

The cashless society refers to the newer perception that in a world of finite natural resources, we can no longer ignore the fact that the weight and mass of late 20th century money as cash is a force that is potentially infinite, and has the capacity for infinite destructiveness. It is potentially all the paper money in all the Monopoly sets ever manufactured, put to use in one game, without the game's banker or most of the other players realizing what has happened.

With money as cash, no banker can distinguish the paper money that belongs in his set from the paper money that some of the players have brought in from theirs. The rules of the game are based on definite relationships between costs and rents. They are skewed by all the new cash. The situation is hopeless. The biggest cheater will probably win the game, and ruin it.

In the cashless society, if the game is ever going to make sense again, the banker will have to have a way to separate the money that originally belonged in his Monopoly set from the money from all the other sets, and to control the infusion of different kinds of money into the game, or exclude them from it. A mechanism for the rational exercise of control by the banker must exist. Just how the banker would exercise control, whether he would inject more money into the bank, or distribute more to the poorer players than to the richer to keep them going, is beyond the scope of this book.

No mechanism for exercising any ultimate control over money as cash now exists in the world. An important thesis of this study is that without such a mechanism our late 20th century cash and carry society is living dangerously, and that we should apply serious human effort to create such a mechanism soon. A mechanism through which rational human policy decisions can be brought to bear on the massive, irrational and eccentric forces of late 20th century money as cash may as well be called by the name of a cashless society as any other. Cashlessness would seem almost certain to be its most significant characteristic.

The original Utopia was an imaginary island which Sir Thomas More depicted as enjoying a perfect social, legal, economic and political system. It has come to seem if anything even more utopian than when he first described it in 1516. Neither it nor any other Utopia deals satisfactorily with the question of growth.

A paper, prepared by The Conference Board for the 1972 White House Conference on the Industrial World Ahead, projected that the gross national product of the United States would reach a total of more than $2.4 trillion by 1990 from the level of about $1.1 trillion in 1972. The rise in gross national product per worker is expected to go from $12,500 in 1970 to $22,500 in 1990 in 1971 prices. In a major speech at the Conference, Secretary of the Treasury John B. Connally called the idea of zero growth "a misguided concept." He went on: "Never has growth been more important. You can never feed the poor or ease the lives of the wage-earning families, ameliorate the problems of race or solve the problems of pollution without real growth."

On the other hand, about the same time, a report of the Club of Rome, entitled *The Limits of Growth*, prepared by scientists using world system models developed at the Massachusetts Institute of Technology, disclosed that every model they had built assuming continuation of present world trends, and the prevailing official philosophy of growth, ends in collapse. According to these econometric models, Utopia will not be reached by the year 2000. It will be still farther beyond our reach, if indeed we survive until then. The econometric model builders see the real issue as whether life will be recognizably similiar to the life we live at present, or whether on the other hand there will be no human life at all.

Barry Commoner, in his new book *The Closing Circle*, puts the issue in moving words:

> The world is being carried to the brink of ecological disaster, not by a singular fault, which some clever scheme can correct, but by the phalanx of powerful economic, political and social forces that constitute the march of history. Anyone who proposes to cure the environmental crisis undertakes thereby to change the course of history.*

What does the great debate about growth have to do with the cashless society? Just this: money as cash, money freely disposable, transferable and investable as capital, is one of the main forms of fuel for continuous economic growth. Its absence is characteristic of no-growth economies.

In a world of sharpening divisions between rich and poor people, developed and underdeveloped countries, multi-national corporations and national aspirations, and outward looking and xenophobic countries, individual economic decisions in the marketplace, expressed through money transactions—spending, saving, buying, selling, borrowing—motivated by individual self-interest, no longer necessarily activate an invisible hand that guides all society toward the common good. Adam Smith's 18th century vignette which depicted the operation of market forces in a small national economy of small individual and corporate units is simply crushed by the weight and mass of the gigantic economic forces which now bear down upon it. One of these forces is the brute power of unimaginable sums of money as cash.

If the market no longer governs these immense forces, then something else has to be invented that will. The prospect of a cashless society offers a promising but somewhat neglected approach to a structure and method of governance for the economic system which might serve to replace the old concept of

___
* Barry Commoner, *The Closing Circle*. New York: Knopf, 1971.

an invisible hand operating through unitary decisions in free markets for the general good.

The Club of Rome's study retells a French children's riddle about a pond with a water lily in it. The water lily doubles in size every day. In thirty days it will cover the entire surface, killing all the creatures in the pond. The owner wants to avoid that, but he sees no hurry: he will cut the plant back when it covers just half the pond. When will that be?

The answer is the 29th day. He has only one day, just that one, to save the lives of all the creatures in his pond.

According to the makers of econometric models, man's impact on the earth grows exponentially like the water lily: doubling every so often. A population curve rising at a rate which means doubling every thirty-three years, means that there would be twice as many people living in the year 2000 as now; industrial production likewise would grow exponentially, as would demands for food and natural resources. So would pollution and destruction of water, earth and air.

Money as cash, particularly U.S. dollars freely created, and recreated over and over again from the same base as Eurodollars, and other forms of money and capital reserves, slosh freely around the globe. It is like fertilizer sprinkled randomly on the lily pad. On the 29th day when the lily pad covers half the pond, the farmer will have to work fast and stop everybody from putting on more fertilizer to keep the pad from covering the whole pond the next day. But if, as it turned out, the pond was the world and the 29th day was tomorrow, the farmer would have no shears and no way to stop the spreading of fertilizer. So, of course, all of the creatures would die the day after tomorrow.

A cashless society under the control of an international reserve system might some day serve as one kind of economic shearing mechanism. It might also provide a means for control, cancellation or recall of random broadcasts of economic fertilizer, or the withholding of fertilizer from overdeveloped areas to spread on those that were underdeveloped or not developed at all. Or, indeed, on other ponds. These economic shears could probably be no less effective than existing national political, legislative, judicial and international organization shears, and might well be much sharper.

Growth, and no-growth, and indeed shrinkage in lieu of growth, are going on all the time around the edges of the metaphorical world lily pad. Even if it is true that the margins of the pond are not impervious to extension by opening up new bays and channels through technology, and even if one concedes the unreliability of econometric models which extrapolate geometric progression from existing numbers in all variables, there is no conclusive evidence that such studies are entirely wrong. And the consequences if they are more or less right, even though the probability is small, are sufficiently grave to require acceptance of the proposition that limits must eventually be recognized and, once recognized, must somehow be enforced. Such limits would, in turn, eventually impose a stationary state on the economy considered in global terms, although individual national and local economies might grow or shrink so as to leave the aggregate total in balance overall. This might be called the social economy of equilibrium.

To conceive of such a social economy arising some day in the future by good luck, or accident, or Act of God, without the application of conscious human effort, is a thing much harder to imagine than the alternative: total self-destruction of the system by bad luck, accident, or Act of God or man, given the same nonapplication of human understanding and effort. But one of the more promising directions in which to press human effort and understanding is toward a cashless society.

To speak of a social economy of overall equilibrium reminds us lightly of the young people in blue jeans who reached the blessed state of Consciousness III described in *The Greening of America.*

21

Introduction

Professor Charles A. Reich announced on its first page that

> There is a revolution coming. It will not be like the revolutions of the past. It will originate with the individual and with culture, and it will change the political structure only as its final act. . . . It promises a higher reason, a more humane community, and a new and liberated individual.

No real revolution occurs except by evolution. The kind of post-revolutionary state Professor Reich so winsomely describes is, of course, a cashless society. Among its features would be a minimum income level without any obligation to work, maintenance of a higher income level with a job, an allocation of credit without need for cash and coexistence of all within and not outside the structure of the corporate or civil service state. Although the conventional wisdom of the Huxleys, Orwells and Vonneguts is to the contrary, this would bring with it an era of political freedom more extensive and humane for more people than any country has yet experienced, and could spread to other countries of the world as well. In this light the cashless society might be seen as the indispensable technical prerequisite, the economic underpinning, for the social economy of overall equilibrium, whether or not overalls were still in vogue.

John Stuart Mill put the big questions:

> Towards what ultimate point is society tending by its industrial progress? When the progress ceases, in what condition are we to expect that it will leave mankind?
>
> Destruction of the globe? Or a Utopia at least no worse than the one we live in now?

And once again he answers them as well as anyone else:

> It must always have been seen, more or less distinctly, by political economists, that the increase of wealth is not boundless: that at the end of what they term the progressive state lies the stationary state, that all progress in wealth is but a postponement of this, and that each step in advance is an approach to it.
>
> Only when, in addition to just institutions, the increase of

mankind shall be under the deliberate guidance of judicious foresight, can the conquests made from the powers of nature by the
intellect and energy of scientific discoverers, become the common property of the species, and the means of improving and
elevating the universal lot.

Money as cash is a conspicuous presence in the life of contemporary society. There is more coin and paper money currency in circulation than ever before. For Americans, and
people in most other Western countries, there is also more
money as credit and debt outstanding than there ever has been
before, and the credit and debt overtop the cash by more than
ten to one. Credit and debt are more easily obtained than ever
before, and more easily turned into cash, which can in turn be
turned into still more credit and debt. More kinds of cash and
credit money transactions are possible than ever before, more
ways of circumventing limits exist than ever before, and aggregates of money at large in society are at higher per capita levels
and growing faster than they ever have been before. If wealth
is not without its advantages, why is it that in this economic
redoubt surrounded by these rising ranges of money, we feel
so much more psychologically and economically insecure than
philosophers and kings and pharaohs of cashless societies of
the past?

The answer, I believe, is that we sense that we cannot continue living with the unlimited growth of the two kinds of
money side by side—money as cash and money as credit and
debt. The proliferation of money as cash once was limited by
the amount of the physical commodity—gold, silver or copper
—from which it was minted. It is limited no more now that
the amount of paper currency that can be manufactured and
imprinted with digits is unlimited. Money as credit once was
under the control of human discretion and judgment through
the London guild of goldsmiths, or the astuteness of private
bankers, or their legitimate successors. The gold standard, the
gold exchange standard and the Bretton Woods agreement

23

vastly extended the parameters subject to presumed control, but these institutions at least served as tangible symbols that sustained the general assumption that judicious application of human wisdom to monetary aggregates existed and was indispensable. But since 1968 United States political leaders have treated all such institutions as dispensable.

The conscious repudiation of these tangible symbols of human governance of monetary aggregates, whenever their purposes have seemed to conflict with the national interests of an individual country, has left the Western world with neither institutional symbol nor rational basis for the assumption that any mechanism did or should exist for bringing the judicious application of human foresight to bear on worldwide aggregates of money.

The argument here is that we cannot have it both ways: while strict limits exist on everything else on the globe, money cannot continue to exist without them. If it is allowed to continue to exist in the form of money as cash, no rational imposition of any kind of limit is possible. Only with the disestablishment of money as cash, and the introduction of a cashless society, can the judicious application of human foresight be brought to bear effectively against the increasing danger to society of the lawlessness of money as cash.

Under the governance of an international reserve system a cashless society could serve as a reasonable way of imposing limits, as well as a means of fostering desirable growth where need for growth existed. This is probably as much as could be claimed by way of necessity for a cashless society, if not, indeed, too much. In any case it would be enough to concern a study so entitled.

1.

A Question
of Money

In all Western countries where free enterprise, individual initiative, private property and competitive markets are basic principles of polity, we live our adult lives in the ambience of money, or the lack of it. An old-fashioned Indiana farmer may own his section and a quarter in fee, and raise all the beans, corn, eggs and fowl his family needs to eat, and power his generator and pump with a windmill, but he must pay his school and property taxes with cash money. The hippie in his commune needs cash to buy food with his food stamps.

The ambience of money impinges on every aspect of our lives. We take it for granted. We feel its omnipotence through our skins, but find it not much easier to understand than it is for a fish to understand the ocean. Money itself, as distinguished from its ambience which surrounds us, cannot be taken for granted. Most of us think about it practically all the time.

Aspects of our feelings about money are complex and purposefully hidden. We flaunt our sexual drives like plumes, but hide money drives by all kinds of body language and cover stories. In business life, as in stud poker, a benign expression innocent of greed is a great advantage. Society rewards a philanthropist with its highest praise, and a miser with awful opprobrium. Yet these may be no more than the conventional reactions to the same person at different times in his life: John D. Rockefeller and Andrew Carnegie came to avarice early and almsgiving late. At expensive French restaurants, arcane rituals are involved in merely turning up the check.

Few have described the ambience of money as cash better than Thoreau in "Economy," the first chapter of *Walden*:

> Some of you, we all know, are poor, find it hard to live, are sometimes, as it were, gasping for breath. I have no doubt that some of you who read this book are unable to pay for all the dinners which you have actually eaten, or for the coats and shoes which are fast wearing or are already worn out, and have come to this page to spend borrowed or stolen time, robbing your creditors of an hour. It is very evident what mean and sneaking lives many of you live, for my sight has been whetted by experience; always on the limits, trying to get into business and trying to get out of debt, a very ancient slough . . . always promising to pay, promising to pay, tomorrow, and dying today, insolvent; seeking to curry favor, to get custom, by how many modes, only not state prison offenses; lying, flattering, voting, contracting yourselves into a nutshell of civility, or dilating into an atmosphere of thin and vaporous generosity, that you may persuade your neighbor to let you make his shoes, or his hat, or his coat, or his carriage, or import his groceries for him; making yourselves sick, that you may lay up something against a sick day, something to be tucked away in an old chest, or in a stocking behind the plastering, or, more safely, in the brick bank; no matter where, no matter how much or how little.

When Thoreau was at Walden, the population of the commonwealth was sparse. Fertile open land and clear ponds at the margins of town seemed free for the taking and squatting. As a man, or at least as the hero of his own literary creation, Thoreau possessed many of the natural skills of a caveman, Indian and Eagle Scout, few of the lusts, desires and drives that rile the rest of us, and the incalculable advantage of a

Harvard education in the classics. Yet he could only sustain his personal example of doing without money for less than two years, and he never repeated it. Reading "Economy" today reminds us how much more nearly impossible it would be in our day to clamber outside the ambience of money than it was in his.

Even in the woods at Walden, Thoreau could not wholly escape the ambience of money. Nor was there any way he could show the world how to live without money, except in money terms. The first year he calculated his net income at $8.71½, plus produce on hand of the value of $4.50. In terms scarcely different from those a contemporary member of the Concord Rotary Club might use, he concluded: "I believe *that* was living better than any farmer in Concord that year." The second year, however, $25.21¾ showed up on the deficit side of his account, "this being very nearly the means with which I started." But, on the whole, not so bad, he thought, because it covered, "beside the leisure and independence and health thus secured, a comfortable house for me as long as I choose to occupy it."

On welfare these days one does not fare as well. In 1970, a graduate student working toward a doctorate in clinical psychology at Berkeley with a $2400 fellowship and a $1000 loan grant, living in a communal boarding-house, applied for food stamps. "I've been living off stuff like candy bars," he said. "If I didn't have the food stamps I wouldn't be able to eat, and I couldn't possibly keep up my work."

The caseworker in the county welfare department office granted his application. She explained why her office was swamped with similar applications: "The recession is having an effect. People just can't make it, that's all."

Unduplicatable experiments in trying to clamber outside the ambience of money are common throughout American history. Brook Farm, Elbert Hubbard's East Aurora and Robert Owen's New Harmony are familiar examples. There are said to be more than 2000 urban and rural communes in the United States to-day. The practical reason for experiments in communal living is that they are the only way to live more or less within the law, more or less outside the ambience of money. Ten unrelated people knock down the interior walls of a frame house and make community rooms where they live as one family. They split a single rent and they share one bathroom, automobile, telephone, television set and radio ten ways. This obviously re-duces the amount of money each of the ten needs. In economic terms, most communes are dismal failures. But for those whose consciences, moral standards or lack of cunning render them unqualified for living outside, or competing within, the free enterprise, individual initiative, private property and free mar-ket system, there are few practical alternatives to the commune. On welfare these days, no one fares as well as Thoreau did at Walden.

The literature of academic economics does not dispute Thoreau's thesis that life without money is possible. Standard definitions admit the possibility of society being organized so as to get along entirely without it.

Professor Paul A. Samuelson's standard text, *Economics*, de-fines the subject matter as follows:

> Economics is the study of how man and society *choose, with or without the use of money*, to employ scarce productive re-sources, which could have alternative uses, to produce various commodities over time and distribute them for consumption, now and in the future, among various people and groups in society.*

Note how this smoothly concedes the possibility of man and society organizing existence "without the use of money."

Another definition holds that economics is the study of those activities which, *with or without money*, involve exchange transactions among people: the study of how men choose to

---

* Paul A. Samuelson, *Economics*. New York: McGraw-Hill, 1970.

use scarce or limited productive resources (land, labor, capital goods such as machinery, technical knowledge) to produce various commodities (such as wheat, beef, overcoats, concerts, roads, yachts) and distribute them to various members of society for their consumption; the study of men in their ordinary business of life, earning and enjoying a living, and the study of how mankind goes about the business of organizing its consumption and production activity.

Still another says simply that economics is the study of wealth, without insisting on wealth being money as cash.

With the alternative possibilities of human society being organized either with, or without, the use of money thus conceded and counterpoised, it comes as something of a surprise that innumerable volumes of economic literature go on to study the first possibility, and very few the second. Societies organized without the use of money, cashless societies, are left to the literary dreamers of utopian dreams. Academic economists do not even bother to explain what "without the use of money" means. Practical men, not futurists castellating dreams of cashlessness on future clouds, like the rest of us, are enveloped by the ambience of money. So the road toward the cashless society remains a road not taken.

Much professional economic writing on the subject of money is not about money as most of us understand the word. Rather, it deals with social and political consequences which flow from the way money moves in the economy of Western countries, but not about money itself. Such literature has more to do with the plight of the victims of the flood, and the rescue efforts, than it does with the tidal wave itself.

For example, the name of Professor Milton Friedman, one of the most influential of living economists, stands for the proposition that "only money matters." But when Professor Friedman and his followers of the monetarist school say that "only money matters," they are not talking about the essential nature of money, the thing itself. Nor are they arguing the question whether or not money is essential to the operations of society. They assume that it is. When they say "only money matters," they mean that governmental monetary policy, not taxes, interest rates, subsidies, trade regulation or other governmental fiscal policies, is of primary significance in national economic management. They mean that governmental manipulation of money aggregates is what really matters when it comes to solving supposed social problems by economic measures in a free society where resources are assumed to be relatively scarce. When it comes to policy for moving the economy from poverty into prosperity, or from deflation to inflation and back, they say, with an expansiveness that is illusory, that "only money matters."

To economists who insist that "only money matters," money itself seems to be something like quicksilver in a thermostat: an element that serves to measure the temperature and, if necessary, activate a switch. Alcohol or something else might serve the same function, but the element is of no particular consequence in itself. This is conventional wisdom of economics.

> It must be evident, however, that the mere introduction of a particular mode of exchanging things for one another, by first exchanging a thing for money, and then exchanging the money for something else, makes no difference in the essential character of transactions.
>
> There cannot, in short, be intrinsically a more insignificant thing, in the economy of society, than money, except in the character of a contrivance for sparing time and labour. It is a machine for doing quickly and commodiously what would be done, though less quickly and commodiously, without it: and like many other kinds of machinery, it only exerts a distinct and independent influence of its own when it gets out of order.*

So money as a thing in itself remains as elusive as quicksilver is when it escapes from the thermometer of its thermostat.

---

* John Stuart Mill, *Principles of Political Economy*, Volume II, 5th ed. London: Parker, Son and Bourn, 1862, pp. 8-9.

There is another gap in the way the literature of economics deals with money. None of the standard definitions of economics call for human society necessarily to be organized in such a way as to preserve free enterprise, individual initiative, private property or free markets, any more than they insist on the use of money. All the definitions apply equally well to societies organized along socialist or communist lines. But once the definition is out of the way, most economic literature of the West, at least, tacitly assumes free markets and money as cash.

Mill and followers of his tradition stand for free enterprise, private property and free markets as basic conditions for the successful organization of human society, while Marx and his disciples deny the legitimacy of these premises and call for state ownership of property and controlled markets. Each competing polity has had great champions. The literature of each side is counterpoised on the scales somewhere near a balance. One emphasizes political controls and coercion as the means for attaining desired social ends; the other stresses the vital importance of freeing markets and money from controls. Both traditions assume that society will use some form of money, if only as a medium of exchange. Both treat money itself as the more or less inevitable setting for everything else, as in the simile of the ocean where the fish swims.

So when Mill says that "there cannot be intrinsically a more insignificant thing in the economy of society than money," he is both wrong and right. Wrong because, at least to practical men in Western societies, there is hardly anything that is intrinsically more significant in the economy than money; right because everyone assumes its importance and takes it for granted, and so we need talk no more about it than the air we breathe.

Political and social questions seeking solution sooner or later have to come to grips with the ambience of money in the form of the oft-repeated questions: How can we afford it? Where is the money coming from?

31

All political and social problems are thus steeped in the ambience of money. Without money, they are insoluble. Without it, we are insolvent. Control of money thus seems to be an ultimate way to deal with social and economic problems.

But the inherent nature of money, the stuff itself, remains as elusive as ever. It is not necessarily the neutral, natural and inevitable ambience of our lives that it seems to be. The definitions of economics readily admit the possibility that men and society may choose to live without it altogether. For a while, at least, communes get by with very little, as Thoreau did at Walden. Great societies have existed without it in the past, some do today, and there seems no reason why others could not do so in the future. The peculiar characteristics of money itself, and its overwhelming pressure on our lives, hides from us the fact that money itself, not the lack of it, may be at the root of many of our social and political ills. In its various peculiar guises, money shapes society and molds our characters. The way we think about money, more importantly the way we don't think about money, may be the greatest obstacle of all to solving the social and political problems that we claim we cannot solve because of lack of money. Perhaps if we did not put the question of money before the question of solving the problem itself, we could get on sooner with the solution. A horse wearing blinders cannot see any way to get around the fence directly ahead of him. Take away the blinders and the solution is clear—there is an open gate off to one side. If we were not distracted from solving social and political problems by a different question, the question of money, we might be using the same time and skill to solve the problem itself.

The literature of economics has exhaustively analyzed the social and political means by which money is regulated and distributed among members of society. Many ideal social and political solutions have been put forward, but none has been universally adopted. Ideological clashes between proponents of ideal systems make a significant contribution to the troubles of the world. But the extent to which social ills arise from unnecessary assumptions about the nature of money as cash, as distinguished from the way money as cash is regulated and distributed, remains largely unexamined. For example, in the practical conduct of daily life, charge accounts and credit cards have already carried us far beyond the idea of money as cash. How, for example, does this omnipresent fact fit in with our hitherto unexamined assumptions about the nature of all money as cash?

2.

A Cade in the Age
of Credit

Britain and the United States have had remarkable luck in escaping the kind of social revolution and class warfare fought along economic lines that are so bloody a part of the history of countries like France and Russia. Cavaliers and Roundheads squared off on questions of dynasty and religion; Colonials and Loyalists centered their quarrel on taxation and legislation. The summer of 1450, when Jack Cade and "infinite numbers" with him seized Westminster Bridge for a few days, was probably as close to economic class warfare as Anglo-Saxons ever came.

According to Shakespeare's report in *Henry VI*, Jack Cade, the clothier, bricklayer or whatever—no one is even sure of his trade—rallied "infinite numbers" of other brave minds and hard hands round himself at Blackheath: George Bevis and John Holland, Dick the Butcher, Smith the Weaver, the Clerk of Chatham, who was good at accounts, and Best's son, the tanner of Wigham.

"Be brave then," cried Cade, "for your captain is brave, and vows reformation."

Cade's manifesto was as broad as it was brief:

> There shall be in England seven halfpenny loaves sold for a penny; the three-hooped pot shall have ten hoops, and I will

make it a felony to drink small beer. All the realm shall be in common, and in Cheapside shall my palfrey go to grass. And when I am king, as king I will be,—

ALL: God save Your Majesty!

CADE: I thank you, good people: there shall be no money; all shall eat and drink on my score; and I will apparel them all in one livery, that they may agree like brothers and worship me, their lord.

DICK: The first thing we do, let's kill all the lawyers.

CADE: Nay, that I mean to do.

"When I am king, as king I will be, there shall be no money." Jack Cade's call for the abolition of money is a key plank in his platform for social revolution and reform. Another is that: "All the realm shall be in common."

A third is: "All shall eat and drink on my score; and I will apparel them all in one livery."

This is the great dramatist's concise way of expressing the undying socialist dream of a state which guarantees food, clothing and all the other necessities of life to all its citizens without work and without money. The state guarantees that they will never be in want for the necessities of life, and will not be held accountable for what the government supplies. Once this happens, it logically follows, as Cade promises, "that they may agree like brothers." Shakespeare's treatment does not ask us to take any of this very seriously.

The commerce of buying and selling, of exchanging goods and labor for each other's money that sets man against man and brother against brother, shall be no more. What Cade did not realize was that abolishing cash money would not abolish trade and commerce among men, and that trade and commerce would grow a thousandfold by using credit money instead of cash.

By the late 20th century, Cade's revolution had been swamped by evolution. There was very little cash money, but more commerce and trade among men and women than ever.

It had not been necessary to kill all the lawyers, because they were on both sides of all revolutionary and evolutionary movements at the same time, and tended to cancel each other out. Hardly anybody used cash, but commerce and trade flourished in an ocean of credit and debt.

John Cade, age 30, is a direct lineal descendant of Jack Cade. His daily life in the seventh decade of the 20th century is largely cashless. Of money transactions in his life, nine out of ten are cashless, and on the basis of the amounts of money involved, 99 per cent are cashless. His day illustrates an American social revolution along economic lines that has already taken place. There has been no violence, and no one has taken it very seriously.

John Cade happens to be employed as an associate lawyer in the law firm of Holland & Bevis, 41 Wall Street, in New York, N. Y. There are still a great many lawyers left unkilled, but there is practically no cash money in their lives. Nearly everybody eats and drinks on somebody else's score, as often as not the Diners' Club.

John is awakened at 7:00 A.M. by the alarm bell of the $12.95 traveling clock which he bought by clipping, filling out and sending in a coupon from *Signature*, the Diners' Club magazine. He still owes two $4.15 monthly payments on the clock, which include interest on the unpaid balance calculated at 18 per cent per annum. Since he does not yet own the clock, he suppresses his urge to hurl it to the floor, and calmly switches off the alarm. He gets out of bed and mounts the Exercycle he also ordered by mail from *Signature* in a weak moment, after allowing himself to pause one day to read an ad which asked: "Are your friends by-passing you?" It had answered its question thus: "Keep on your toes with the new Exercycle exerciser."

Sitting on his backside pedaling fiercely, Cade reflects that it is not the machine, it is six months' payments to go, including the 18 per cent interest on the unpaid balance, that keeps him on his toes. Under his punishing pedaling, the machine rattles, shimmies and shakes, so he slows his pumping and dismounts hoping it will not fly apart before all his payments are in.

He shaves with his $36.95 electric razor, brushes his teeth with his $25.75 electric toothbrush, tickles his gums with his $46.15 water toothpick and puts on his $195 (plus sales tax) glen plaid suit, all of which he bought with his credit cards. Sooner or later, and usually as much later as possible, he will pay for them by check, or else his bank will pay for them by charging the bills against his checking account. He goes to the kitchen of his $375-a-month apartment, pours himself a cup of coffee from his $34.95 electric coffee pot, has some toast which pops up out of his $22.65 electric toaster, butters it with some $.95-a-pound butter from his $285 (plus sales tax) refrigerator, beats three eggs in his $89.95 blender, cooks an omelette on his $325 electric range and tries not to think of all the payments, plus interest on unpaid balances and sales taxes, which he owes on this commonplace constellation of conveniences. He has never paid cash for any of it.

He goes back to the bedroom and kisses his still sleeping wife Elizabeth a perfunctory goodbye. After all, even if she does not get up to cook his breakfast, she does make it possible for him to file a joint income tax return at a slightly lower rate than he would pay if filing separately, and is good for one personal exemption. Knowing that currency is useless on the bus because the bus driver will not accept it nor make change, out of a box on his bureau he takes two transit tokens.

It is October 1 and payday. But Holland & Bevis does not pay him any cash or check money for the past month's services. The bookkeeper hands him a credit memorandum slip showing that the firm has credited his bank account with his monthly salary of $1400, after deducting withholdings of estimated United States, New York State and New York City income taxes, plus Social Security tax, New York State disability tax, New York State unemployment insurance tax, his contribution to the firm's group insurance policy coverage, Blue Cross, Blue Shield and his contribution to the firm's profit-sharing plan.

There are also deductions for his personal long distance telephone calls, his share of personal postage and other personal office expenses not chargeable to clients. He has canceled his participation in the Series E bond purchase program and the Christmas Club, so there are no deductions for these. Even with these savings unsaved, the balance of his salary that remains his is not far above zero. The year he started work at Holland & Bevis, the firm's computer had transmitted his weekly wage (after offsets) to the bank at 4:30 P.M. each Friday afternoon. But since then, after the firm renewed its office lease from the bank in its building, it must deposit his and all other employees' salaries in the bank at the end of each day.

When the bank receives the credit to Cade's account, it pays any standing orders due for payment that day. It is now exactly 14 days after the telephone company's computer sent its bill to the bank's computer, so the bank now pays the telephone bill. The telephone company had notified Cade by mail that in the event he wished to question the bill and stop payment, he had to do so within 14 days, and he had done nothing. Both the telephone company and the bank's salesman were enthusiastic about this kind of "management by exception." Cade's apartment rent is paid by computer credit to the landlord's account and the forty-third instalment on his home video terminal is credited directly to the bank which has factored the seller's receivables.

Cade's wife Elizabeth has been on a deferred spending spree and there is a long list of bills due against her credit card. The Central Comprehensive Computerized Credit Card Clearing Corporation (known as the seven C's) has been on the line and has debited Cade's account for the total, so the Cades are now overdrawn by $70. The bank's computer looks at their savings account. At the end of August, the bank's computer had cut the current balance in their checking account back to $500 and put the excess into their savings account, in accordance with a pre-programmed arrangement. This had brought the savings account balance $1000 over $5000, so the $1000 had automatically been spent to buy mutual fund shares from the bank.

Although the Cades' checking account is now overdrawn, their credit rating was good when the computer looked it up and they had no bills to pay next week. A bank loan of $100 for two weeks would cost less than the loss of interest they would incur on a transfer from the savings account back to the checking account. So the bank covered the overdraft by an immediate loan. The bank did not even bother the Cades about the overdraft. Its computer simply adds and subtracts all debits and credits and prepares to record them on the next monthly statement it sends them. If the Cades do not agree with the statement, if they can figure it out, they must notify the bank within two weeks; otherwise, the computer printout stands.

When the bank statement arrives, John and Elizabeth go through it. The local supermarket computer has her regular order on its files and telephones her each week to confirm it. The computer reads out her order over the telephone and then asks for her account number, and "YES" or "NO," two of the very few words it understands. John lets Elizabeth check out the supermarket bills and he checks the department store items. The last time Elizabeth was there they had a special sale of classic clothes from Peck & Peck which she had let the saleslady talk her into buying. All Elizabeth had to do was put her credit card in the Touch-Tone telephone and key in two numbers—her own and her bank account—she did not have to spend any money.

But Cade is not yet in the clear. He checks out the "automatic" deductions from what the bank still, ironically, describes as "his" bank account: premium payments on his bank life insurance, electric and gas utility bills, interest on a secured loan which he took out to buy a vacation cottage in Vermont and repayment of a chattel mortgage on a loan he took out to buy his car.

Dispatched to Washington next morning to file a registration statement with the Securities and Exchange Commission, he charges his air shuttle ticket on his air travel card, charges a Hertz car at Washington National Airport and calls Elizabeth on his A.T.&T. telephone credit card. The operator reports back a busy signal. Not having time to sit through his wife's regular morning chat with her mother, he gives up, but later places the call through his hotel switchboard operator. It is not charged to his credit card, so an extra fifty-cent phone service charge is added to the hotel bill. He charges the whole bill to his American Express credit card when he checks out, so he doesn't even notice the extra telephone charge on it.

After checking out next morning, Cade tries to pay for a copy of *The Washington Post* at the hotel's magazine stand with a twenty-dollar bill he has been carrying around in his pocket for days, without being able to get rid of it. The newsdealer noisily objects to changing such a large bill, but finally gives Cade $19.75, all in coins. Too cowed to object to being short-changed ten cents, Cade buys a package of Life Savers, has a shoeshine, takes a taxi back to Washington National and the Eastern shuttle to New York, where a police strike is going on. Cade is glad he has no more than enough cash in his pocket to pay his fare home from the airport, plus tip.

He turns in his trip expense voucher to Holland & Bevis's bookkeeper and attaches written receipts or duplicate credit card vouchers to it which back up all his expenses except the $20 bill. The bookkeeper scowls at this item, looks at Cade suspiciously, shrugs and says, "This cash item will have to be approved and countersigned by the managing partner."

Cade says, "The hell with it."

The bookkeeper smiles smugly and turns back to posting the journal.

Under our tax laws there is no way Cade can escape from keeping written vouchers and records to substantiate every cent he spends. Ordinary and necessary expenses incurred in carrying on a trade or business, including traveling expenses, are deductible as a general rule, but the deduction may be disallowed if the expenditure cannot be substantiated by written vouchers. No problem arises with expenditures charged to credit cards but there is no written record of cash transactions. For business purposes, the penalty for use of cash is to risk loss of tax deductions for items which pass unquestioned when charged to credit cards.

Holland & Bevis has a computerized time-record-keeping system that can tell the senior managing partner whether Cade's trip to Washington, and the rest of his work during the month, have resulted in a profit or loss to the firm. Each day, Cade records for programming in the firm's computer the number of hours and minutes he has worked for each client. The number representing this time is multiplied by his own hourly time charge factor of, say, $50 per hour, and the product is subtracted from the sum which the firm bills the client. The billing may be either more or less than Cade's "time charge." Looking at the computer's printout, the senior managing partner can quickly find out whether Cade's work has brought profit or loss to the firm. All his human effort has been translated into dollar terms, but no money in the traditional cash sense has changed hands. When Jack Cade cried, "There shall be no money," he was calling for a new and greater freedom. This is not exactly the kind of social revolution he had in mind.

Back at home, pressed for time, Cade puts his checkbook on the dinner table and starts filling in check stubs, writing out checks, inserting checks in envelopes, sealing and addressing the envelopes and paying unprogrammed bills that have come in on the first of the month: extra groceries, laundry service, dry cleaning, a new suit, daughter's piano lessons, son's guitar lessons, school bills for both, American Express, Diners' Club and Mobil Oil. There's a bill from Master Charge for a new vacuum cleaner Elizabeth has bought. The automatic bank loan that covered his checking account overdraft is nowhere near enough to cover them all. So an additional 18 per cent or so of interest will accrue on the outstanding balance he cannot pay.

In different months, he uses different methods of "aging" these liabilities. Sometimes, he pays the ones with the highest interest charges on unpaid outstanding balances first. One month, he stands on the top step of the fire escape and throws all the bills down the stairs and pays the ones on the bottom step first, the ones on the next step next, and so on, until all the money in the checking account is gone. The next month, he throws them down the steps again, but pays the ones that land on the top step first, and works his way down till he again runs out of money, or rather, credit. In still other months, he arranges them alphabetically, paying his way down from A to Z, or rather, from A to K, which is where his credit usually runs out; and the next he works from Z to A, or rather, from Z to S, when the money runs out sooner than usual. Such are the revolutionary freedoms of computerized cashless society.

Next month, things will be better. One of Cade's own clients has paid a substantial fee to the firm. The partners, after reviewing the time charges and finding that the fee was larger than Cade's time charges, voted Cade one third of it as additional special compensation, so for the first time in months he will be able to pay a bill at the foot of the stairs.

But this additional fee does not get him out of the woods with all his creditors. He is in deeper with the biggest of all: his government, or rather, his governments. Cade spends a couple of hours computing amended declarations to Federal, New York State and New York City estimated income tax returns to avoid penalties and interest for underpayment. He writes out checks for the additional taxes, fills in the stubs, and mails them to Andover, Massachusetts, Albany, New York, and the City Collector in self-addressed return envelopes on which is imprinted the stern injunction: DO NOT MAIL CASH.

If Cade could bill the government, or rather, the governments of the United States, New York State and New York City, at the same $50-an-hour time-charge rate that Holland & Bevis bills his time to clients, the three governments would owe him $100 just for making this amendment to his declarations. The uncompensated time he spends figuring out how much more to assess himself to pay these greedy governments ruins his disposition, his dinner and Elizabeth's as well. If he could likewise charge his creditors at his regular rate for all the time he spends each month checking bills, credit card statements, writing out checks and addressing, stamping and mailing envelopes, it might come to as much as six hours more, or $300 a month. Not only does he feel he is a captive of his creditors, he also feels smothered to death by all this paper work.

The telephone suddenly rings. Cade's mother-in-law is calling with more than her usual array of problems. Apparently her local credit-rating computer, which has long since been supplied with a correct knowledge of her name, address, previous addresses, employment past and present, length of service, her late husband's name, outstanding debts, the length her accounts have been active, her outstanding loans, name of bank, children, their numbers and ages, her telephone number, annual income, make of car, insurance and assurance coverages, legal judgments, criminal record and machine aptitude scores, has goofed. It has given her an omega-minus credit rating. She demands that Cade institute a libel suit against the computer the following morning. Cade wearily agrees to do so, telling her that he will put in a count for slander as well as libel, since the credit bureau's computer uses a voice response unit, as well as a printout.

Before Cade falls asleep over his nightly glass of beer, Elizabeth asks, "John, why were you so disagreeable at dinner?"

Cade's checking account, checkbook, token coins, his many separate credit cards, and all the credit "float" they create, his complex tax returns and amendments and all the paper work and figure juggling all of these require are all too familiar a part of the world of a responsible citizen of the 1970s. What Cade may not comprehend is that he is stumbling along a road partway to a cashless society, and suffering from the worst of both the old world and the new. So Cade worries about the negative cash balance in his checking account, and about how inevitably when he earns more he owes more.

What he and the rest of us may be forgetting is that the application of a little imagination to the problems of credit standing and credit cards might be the way out of the present morass toward the freedom and peace of mind that is one promise of a rational cashless society. Without being any more portentous about it than Shakespeare was, the time seems ripe for us to take Jack Cade's platform for middle class social revolution a little more seriously. Especially since, without a shot being fired, it seems to be almost over before anyone noticed it had begun. That the revolution, or at least a quarter revolution, has happened is certain, but whether it should be scored as won or lost remains to be seen.

3.

A Natural History of Credit Cards

When they are examined at all, credit cards are regarded by scholars of economics and sociology as little more than superficial symptoms of the times. Credit card commercials do nothing to improve their low estate with scholars, or rouse interest in serious study of the new money. The copy is catchy and full of low comedy images: if you had no credit cards the wad of bills you would have to carry on a two-week trip to a strange town would puff out your wallet to the shape of a pickle. Pickpockets lounging in the lobby would squint cheerfully as you registered at the front desk.

The spectacular success of ad campaigns pitched to these emotional levels distracts attention from the service or product, whichever it is, at the intellectual level. Aggressive promotions promote withdrawal symptoms in sensitive promotees. So credit cards remain in limbo, seemingly beyond the pale of fit subject matter for serious works of scholarship. They are considered purely technical, or organizational developments, like television or the Peace Corps. They are dismissed as not leading toward new perceptions of reality, nor involving new methods of analytical operation, nor opening up new sectors of knowledge.

In any age, one good way to distinguish a great idea for

social change whose time has come from hundreds of contemporaneous ideas that are also-rans is that the big one manages to find itself a memorable tangible symbol: a hammer and sickle, a cross, a crescent. If the effect works in reverse, that is, if a memorable tangible symbol will carry a broad movement for social change behind it, then the movement toward the cashless society has to be one of the most important of the twentieth century. It has appropriated to its own use the twentieth century's symbol par excellence, the credit card.

— Credit cards are called by other more or less interchangeable names: charge card, money card, bank card and "the new money." They might with more justice have been called "debt" or "debit" cards, but the phrase has a dour ring. This being America, and given a choice, such a lack of positive thinking would have been unthinkable.

Credit cards are, of course, instantly recognizable for what they are. Stiff, shiny two-by-three-inch rectangular embossed cards, they happen to be made out of the characteristic material of the age: plastic. They carry the name, usually the signature, often a magnetic tape voice print, sometimes a photograph, of the holder, the name of the issuer and a mysterious series of code numbers. Meaningless to humans, the code numbers and the magnetic tapes communicate volumes beyond the power of words to the characteristic machine of the present age: a computer.

Credit card issuers generally are satisfied to go on promoting business as usual, with more volume, and more often. Still, the rest of us cannot quite get over the feeling that there is a deeper significance to the increasing credit card cashlessness of society than the slick clamor of the commercials lets us in on. The search for the origins of this remarkable institution, or whatever it is, begins not with history, sociology or economics, but with popular utopian literature of the 19th century.

Like coin money, noncommodity paper money, the gold

standard, the gold exchange standard, the Eurodollar market and practically all other great inventions of economics, credit cards were not invented by an economist. A lawyer and journalist, Edward Bellamy, first applied the term "credit card" to a tangible physical object closely resembling the thing we know as a credit card today.

In Mr. Bellamy's best seller, *Looking Backward: 2000–1887*, published in 1887, Mr. Julian West falls asleep on May 30, 1887 and awakens in 2000 A.D. in the Boston home of Dr. and Mrs. Leete and their beguiling daughter Edith.

Dr. Leete tells Julian how American society of the last year of the 20th century gets along entirely without money in two paragraphs that cover a mind-boggling stretch of economic evolution:

> "A credit corresponding to his share of the annual product of the nation is given to every citizen on the public books at the beginning of each year, and a credit card issued him with which he procures at the public storehouses, found in every community, whatever he desires whenever he desires it. This arrangement, you will see, totally obviates the necessity for business transactions of any sort between individuals and consumers. Perhaps you would like to see what our credit cards are like."
>
> "You observe," Dr. Leete pursued as Julian was curiously examining the piece of pasteboard Dr. Leete gave him, "that this card is issued for a certain number of dollars. We have kept the old word, but not the substance. The term, as we use it, answers to no real thing, but merely serves as an algebraical symbol for comparing the values of products with one another. For this purpose they are all priced in dollars and cents, just as in your day. The value of what I procure on this card is checked off by the clerk, who pricks out of these tiers of squares the price of what I order."

Unlike the innumerable credit cards issued by all manner of private firms to all sorts of heterogeneous collections of people today, in *Looking Backward* a single credit card was issued by the government each year to each individual in society. You did not get a bill at the end of the month or, indeed, ever. The card represented an annual credit the government extended to each individual which enabled him to satisfy his yearly wants, as long as the holder did not exceed its limits. This meant that all economic transactions occurred between individuals and the government. It eliminated the need for economic transactions between one private person or firm and another. At one stroke, it also eliminated the need for money except as a measure of value. When he said, "We have kept the old word, but not the substance," Dr. Leete meant that they had kept the word money but not its substance, which was cash. What Dr. Leete calls money is only a medium of exchange, with no basis or exchange value in cash or gold or any other commodity of any kind. In the 1970s we have adopted Mr. Bellamy's phrase credit card, and its physical manifestation, but we have not yet exactly "obviated the necessity of business transactions of any sort between individuals and consumers."

Obviously, Mr. Bellamy's idea of a credit card was not the same thing we identify as a credit card in the 1970s. But then Mr. Bellamy was writing about the cashless society of the year 2000. His basic vision of the credit card proved quite prescient. More than a quarter of a century is left until the rest of Mr. Bellamy's vision is proven wrong, or right.

Nobody invented the credit cards we use today; like Topsy, and most other great economic inventions, they "jes' growed." But in less than twenty years, they have passed from the status of an insignifiant convenience to an important new part of our lives. Few of us could live the way we do today without them. They are so commonplace and familiar it is hard for us to see them as symbols of anything but themselves, and their holders' credit standing.

They were not invented, but without much fanfare they

have indisputably arrived. They serve as a fixed starting point, an institutional benchmark, for this survey of all the relationships between people and money in present-day society. They serve as a symbolic centerpiece for the cashless society which is only now beginning to emerge from the imprinter.

At the start of the twentieth century, a few hotels began to issue credit cards to their most favored regular patrons. By 1914, large department stores and chains of gasoline stations were also issuing credit cards. In those days, credit cards were instant symbols of the holder's prestige. Merchants issued them only to their most valued customers. They were more convenient to use than cash, and they made it much easier for good customers to spend more.

"A regular charge customer buys two and a half to three times more in a year than the average cash customer," Edward V. Donnell, president of Montgomery Ward, was recently quoted as saying. He added, "I'd estimate that sales of appliances, furniture, tires and other expensive items would drop 35 percent to 50 percent if credit were suddenly discontinued."

To the card issuer, as long as the card stays in the hands of the holder to whom it has been issued, the card provides a quick, simple and convenient means of establishing that the holder has qualified for credit. Cards make it unnecessary for the holder to carry large sums of cash on his person. But as they provide cashless safety, they increase risks of other kinds of petty crime: over-extension of buying and loss of the card itself.

Some years ago, the Gallup polling organization conducted a survey for the American Express Company called "Careless Americans—A Report on How People Lose Cash." The survey found that in the adult U.S. population of 106.4 million persons, as of September, 1961, about nine million five hundred thousand had lost cash totaling more than seven hundred million dollars during the year. In other words, about one out of eleven adult Americans, nine per cent of the population, had lost an average sum of $75 during the year. Of those who lost cash, 90% reported no recovery.

The Gallup pollster would ask people: "Thinking back to the loss that created the most difficulty for you, would you tell me how much cash you lost that time and exactly how or why you lost it?" Some of the answers are one-line short stories:

"I was working on a bulldozer and my pocketbook fell out of my pocket."

"Seven hundred dollars was put in a bathtub. Dirty clothes were put on top of it—I went out to eat and when I returned it was gone."

"Lost about thirty dollars from a little car bank. It disappeared from the house, bank and all."

"I pulled out a diaper to wipe the baby's nose and evidently pulled money out which was loose in my purse."

"My pocket was picked on the subway when I was on my way to the hospital to be operated on."

"$19.75 at a church supper. I left the money in my purse while I waited on tables. It was all gone when I locked up my purse."

"Between $60 and $80. A substitute iceman took wallet when no one was in house."

"Son stole money and ran away from home."

"Don't know. First it was there and then it wasn't."

This American Express survey made better selling points for their Travelers Cheques than it did for their credit cards. When you lose cash your loss is only what you had to begin with, and no more. But when you lost a credit card (in the days before legislation which limited liability), there could in theory be almost no limit to your liability. The finder or thief of your credit card could run up charges against you to the maximum limits of your credit rating allowed by the card issuer.

The character of the loss and of the crime or accident

50

which causes the loss are different, depending on whether you lose cash or a credit card. If you carry cash, and you are robbed, it is usually at gun point or knife point. The experience is a dangerous one, and psychologically traumatic. Usually it is difficult to identify and recover the cash, and a nuisance to help the police identify and prosecute the robber. The robber for cash is a dangerous person. The thief who takes a credit card out of your wallet, for example, while it is lying on your bureau when you are in the motel bathroom, is less of a threat to your safety, the charges he runs up can be verified and losses can be covered by insurance. The thief and the money are easier to trace and find.

If everyone carried credit cards and no one carried cash, crimes against the person might almost entirely disappear.

During World War II, the use of credit cards virtually ceased because of government restrictions on consumer spending and credit. But after the wartime restrictions were lifted, most issuers reinstated their credit card plans. In 1947, railroads and airlines began to issue their own travel cards.

The Universal Air Travel Plan (UATP) is a typical cooperative credit card venture in which most of the major airlines have participated. Air travel cards issued by airlines which participate in UATP all look alike, but the cardholder's identification number has a two-letter prefix that shows which airline originated the card. Since the cards are primarily for the accommodation of businessmen, each company must pay a deposit of $425 to open an account, and can then issue as many cards to its employees as it wishes. The deposit bears interest, but the interest is computed in such a way that the more the card is used, the less interest the cardholder receives on the deposit. All UATP member airlines honor the cards of member airlines, and each bills its cardholders for all trips charged on its card, including flights made on other lines which honor the card. The cardholder receives one monthly bill which is payable within ten days. There is no centralized accounting system, but there is a clearing arrangement through which the member airlines periodically clear their interline UATP charges in a manner similar to bank clearings.

Practically all the major oil companies issue credit cards without charge. There are interchange agreements between some companies, under which one will honor the cards of another, usually in areas where the two companies are not in direct competition with each other.

Oil companies constantly expand the uses which may be made of their cards beyond oil and gas, to cover hotels, restaurants and many kinds of appliances. In 1967, oil companies found that the average credit card purchase at gas stations was nearly $5.00, while the average cash sale was less than $3.00. No oil company executive doubts that holders of its credit cards are likely to have more minor repairs made and more frequent oil changes than cash customers. Traditionally, charge-offs for losses on unpaid accounts have been about one half of one percent, but more recently the loss ratio has risen to nearer one percent.

By 1949, the Diners' Club was promoting a new kind of credit card: instead of receiving the card free, you paid an annual fee; instead of itself providing you with the goods or services which were charged on the card, the Diners' Club acted as a credit reference agency, and saw to it that charges made on Diners' Club cards in restaurants which had joined Diners' Club and displayed its decal symbol in the window would be honored promptly and without default. It was not long before the Diners' Club extended its plan to cover not only restaurants but also general travel and entertainment purchases. American Express Company, Carte Blanche and others soon followed with their own "two party" plans.

More recently, products and services with no real relationship to travel and entertainment have been added to the innumerable things which can be purchased with so-called "travel and entertainment" cards. Single party card issuers like oil companies are also selling all kinds of other products unrelated to oil and gas by way of their credit cards. In fact, many are using their cardholder lists as mailing lists for mail order catalogue sales.

American Express Company describes its "travel and entertainment" card as "the new money." Its advertising is at pains to show why this "new" money is not just a substitute for the old cash money. From the cardholder's point of view, it is something entirely new and different, much better, safer and more desirable than the old cash money ever was or could be. As the company's advertising never fails to point out, you can run out of cash at embarrassing times, but the limits to what you can charge on your credit card are much more flexible.

If you lose your cash, perhaps hundreds or even thousands of dollars, you're out of luck. With credit cards, under recently enacted legislation, and depending on the contractual relationship between the issuer and the holder, monetary losses from wrongful charges by a thief or finder of the card are limited to $100, $50 or $25, depending to some extent on the promptness of notification of loss which is given to the company. All issuers of credit cards feel that there should be some minimum amount of loss imposed on the cardholder where his card is wrongfully used, so that he will have an economic incentive to take good care of his card, to keep it in a safe place and not be careless with it and allow it to be stolen.

When you travel from one country to another, you have to stop at currency exchange windows at the border stations and exchange one country's cash money for another's through official money-changing facilities of airports, banks and hotels. This is usually a time-consuming and expensive procedure, and an exchange fee, or a discount, is usually charged. On travel and entertainment credit cards, travelers' expenses incurred in French francs, British pounds or German marks, may all be charged on the same card and billed to the holder as a total in one currency. The card issuer takes care of the currency exchange problems by billing in one currency at official exchange rates for the several different currencies which have been used.

If you need cash in a strange city, but no one there will take your personal check, usually a company office or a bank can be found that will honor an American Express or Diners' Club card and give travelers' checks or cash in a local currency in exchange.

On rare occasions you may want to take a client or a friend out to dinner and have him be your guest, but for some reason you are unable to be there with him in person. With a travel and entertainment credit card, you can arrange for your guest to be your guest even if you are not there, and you can pay his bill and have it put on your account. Of course, if you travel and stay in a different place each night, and eat at different places during the day, you would either have to carry an unwieldy amount of cash to cover your expenses, or write dozens of separate checks to pay your bills if, by some rather remote chance, your checks were honored at all. But on your credit card, all of the bills would be consolidated into one bill, with one check to write for payment at the end of the month. Travel and entertainment card companies provide for borrowing and making payments even when you do not have enough money in your bank account to cover all the bills.

Single party credit card plans, such as cards issued by department stores and oil companies to their customers, are primarily intended to sell the products of that company, and to keep the customer coming back to the store or gasoline company whose card he has, and away from all competitors. This was also originally true of other kinds of cards for specific limited purposes, such as cards issued by hotel chains, individual restaurants, specialty stores and car rental agencies. The main purpose of such single party cards is simply to move goods and hold on to good customers.

Dual party credit card plans of the kind established by the Diners' Club and American Express Company represented an important evolutionary step in the natural history of credit cards. The card issuer signs up restaurants and hotels and merchants who display its decal sign, and then issues credit cards to as many credit-worthy cardholders as can be found to purchase cards. The issuer charges $10, $15 or $20 a year to each cardholder for the privilege of having a card.

From a legal point of view, issuers of dual party cards like the Diners' Club think of themselves as operating as an "old line factor." That is, when the cardholder charges a restaurant meal to his Diners' Club card, the restaurant owner holds the diner's account receivable. All the Diners' Club does, in its view, is purchase the account receivable which its cardholder created at the restaurant from the restaurant owner at a discount. By issuing the Diners' Club card to its cardholder, Diners' Club shows that it has approved in advance the cardholder's credit rating and agrees to stand behind the receivable. Holding the cardholder's signed dinner check, the restaurant owner knows in advance that he will be able to "factor" the account receivable by "selling" it to the Diners' Club. This view of the legal relationships is the conventional view of card issuers. It provides them with maximum insulation, under the "holder in due course" doctrine, from liability to cardholders on claims that the restaurant owner, for example, served a "lousy" lunch.

Since the potential liability of issuers of travel and entertainment cards extends much higher than the $15 or $20 annual charge for the card, they usually apply the highest credit standards. A minimum annual income of $10,000 is usually required. Because of higher credit standards, they are able to offer higher credit limits. The cardholder customer is expected to pay his bill within a specified grace period. Under deferred payment plans for air and sea travel, credit is extended for as much as twelve to twenty-four months, and interest is charged on the cardholder's unpaid balance. Fly now, pay later, is a memorable catch phrase of the cashless society.

Under joint arrangements between travel and entertainment card issuers and banks, instant money is available to cardholders through revolving bank credits. Plans such as American Express' Executive Credit simply allow the cardholder to tap the bank's credit resources for revolving credit and cash advances up to prearranged credit limits of $5000 or $20,000. Since travel and entertainment cardholders may obtain extended payment privileges anyway without signing up with a bank, and since customers who meet strict credit requirements are not very likely to borrow through their credit cards on any extended scale, the volume of credit under plans of this type has been relatively low. Banks join with the travel and entertainment card issuer to finance these plans more as a customer service than for the earning power of the credit they generate.

Banks moved into credit card operations on their own rather late in the game, but bank credit and charge card plans are now of greater importance than all other kinds. The Franklin National Bank of Franklin Square, New York, started the first of the present-day bank credit card programs in August, 1951, and swung into full-scale operation in April, 1952. In the next two years, fewer than 100 banks, and those mostly small ones, started credit card plans. They had high hopes of big profits—but about half of those who started them discontinued them in a short time: dreams of profits turned into nightmares of losses.

Starting a bank credit card program proved to be far more costly than most banks had foreseen. They had to buy additional equipment, hire new people and persuade the public to use the cards as often as possible. They had to persuade skeptical merchants to honor them. Advertising expenses were heavy, and the banks simply lacked experience with all the "nitty gritty" involved in this new form of lending. Many banks gave up their plans. According to a report of the Federal Reserve System, of the nearly 200 banks which had credit card plans in force in 1967, only 27 had started their plans before 1958.

The watershed year was 1958, when Bank of America National Trust and Savings Association of San Francisco, the world's largest privately owned bank, and The Chase Manhattan Bank in New York introduced credit card programs. Naturally, other large banks quickly introduced charge card plans, and by the end of 1959 more than forty banks, most of them in New York and on the west coast, were offering plans. In all, 235 plans were first established during the two-year period, 1958–1959.

Both Bank of America and The Chase Manhattan Bank lost money in the early years of their plans, primarily because of their inability to generate sufficient volume. Large, highly competitive New York department and specialty stores would not readily yield up their own well-established credit facilities to banks. In 1962, Chase sold its credit system, which eventually became the Unicard system. Such unfortunate experiences probably discouraged many smaller banks from entering the field.

Until about 1965, bank credit card programs were confined to a single local area where the bank which sponsored the plan did business. But since then the banks have developed regional groupings and national groupings. BankAmericard, Master Charge and Interbank Cards are used all over the country. These interregional groupings are set up in a number of different ways. Under a typical plan, there is a principal bank in a region which issues the cards, operates a central accounting system and carries any revolving credit that is generated. Agent banks who are members of the same system sign up local merchants for the plan. When purchases are made by the credit card, the merchants forward the sales slips to the agent banks, and the agent banks forward them on to the principal regional bank. Sometimes the agent banks share in the revolving credit as well; sometimes they also issue cards in their own name through the principal bank. By the beginning of the 1970s, almost all of the large banks in the country were offering one form or another of credit card plans, and several of the plans linked banks across state, regional and national boundaries.

Once the bugs were worked out, bank credit and charge card plans opened up a number of new ways for banks to make money. By signing up merchants who must maintain demand deposit accounts with the bank which sponsors the charge plan, the bank gains more deposits. Each new merchant must pay the bank an initiation fee and rent an imprinter. The merchant must turn over his sales tickets to the bank. The bank does not pay him face value for them; it discounts them for him at rates of between 2.5 and 7 per cent, depending on the size of purchases, his volume and so forth. So the bank earns discounting income from the merchant. Bank charge cardholders do not necessarily have to make deposits with the bank which issues the card, and they do not have to pay an annual fee for the card, as they do for travel and entertainment cards. But the bank's credit card provides a ready means of soliciting demand and time deposit accounts from cardholders. It is a contact for selling other bank services to the cardholder. When he is looking for a consumer loan, for example, a cardholder will probably turn first to the bank which issues his charge card. Consumer loans are generally the most profitable kind of bank loans.

The merchant also benefits from his charge card relationship to the bank. He deposits his sales slips at the bank and the bank credits his account with the amount of the sales slips, less the bank's discount. In this way the merchant reduces the capital he has tied up in credit. When the bank discounts the merchant's sales slips, the discounting is generally "without recourse." Thus, when the merchant collects the amount of his sales slip from the bank, he no longer has to worry about the legal costs of collecting delinquent bills.

The charge card plan eliminates the overhead the merchant would incur if he maintained his own charge accounts.

In one survey, it was estimated that bank charge plans cost a merchant forty to eighty per cent less than maintaining his own private charge department. A merchant who is too small to maintain his own charge department obtains the benefits of one through a bank charge plan, and becomes more competitive with larger merchants who can afford the overhead of maintaining their own charge departments. Banks advertise in such a way as to benefit the merchants who are members of their plans, and such advertising encourages customers to look for merchants who accept the bank's credit cards. Merchants believe that credit cards tend to make customers more susceptible to impulse buying, and most customers can confirm the truth of that belief. The decal symbol of the bank's credit card in the merchant's window leads him to hope, and the customer perhaps subconsciously to feel, that some of the bank's supposed prestige and substantiality rubs off on him.

On a bank charge card, if the charge is not paid within the period of grace, a finance charge is added at a relatively high rate of interest, usually 1.5 percent per month or an effective rate of 18 percent per year. A cardholder in high income tax brackets may not feel the burden of 18 percent interest too much. If he is in a 50 percent tax bracket and can deduct this interest, his effective rate of interest will be only 9 percent; and if he also pays state and city income taxes and deducts the interest there as well, his effective rate may be still less.

Inflation is also a factor for the higher-bracket credit card charger. If the current rate of inflation is one-half of one percent per month, or 6 percent per annum, as it has often been during recent years, the charger is able to pay back the credit extended to him in depreciated money. On an annual basis, 6 percent may be regarded as having been subtracted from his effective annual rate of interest by inflation. Thus, depending on one's own position in society, the 18 percent interest rate may not be as outrageously usurious as it sounds. You might even be able to invest the money you delayed paying to the credit card issuer in a stock or tax-exempt security which appreciated at the rate of 10 percent per annum, and be well ahead of the bank's monthly credit card service charge.

Travel and entertainment card issuers do not impose the monthly charge on the same basis. But the fixed sum per annum for the "convenience" of the card may result in a percentage cost for convenience higher than the bank's rate for its extended credit, if the travel and entertainment card is seldom used.

When the credit card charge is not paid immediately, and instead a finance charge is imposed and paid, the credit card assumes a function well beyond merely serving as a convenient substitute for cash money; it becomes an important financing device. A typical bank charge plan provides that if payment is made within a limited period—30 days, for example—there is no financing charge. Thus, when payment is made within this period of grace, the credit card serves as a "medium of exchange" and to a considerable extent merely replaces money or cash, at least from the standpoint of the use that the holder of the card makes of the card. It is a "convenience" to have a card to make the charges on, rather than to have to carry the necessary cash to cover the charges. But if payment is not made within the period of grace, and the automatic service charge is imposed, the relationship is clearly one of debtor and creditor in an important financing arrangement.

It has been estimated that 40 per cent of credit card users pay their bills during the period of grace before any interest charge accrues. Those who do use the credit feature usually pay rather promptly and banks have found that repayment experience is comparable to experience in other kinds of consumer credit repayments. Bank credit cards generally maintain credit user limits for individuals which are related to the size of the deposits they maintain.

Bank check-credit plans developed independently of bank credit card plans. Both credit card and check-credit plans involve the extension of a prearranged line of credit to an individual cardholder or checking account customer upon demand. The difference between the two is that bank credit cards are not tied directly to any one individual's checking account. They involve a three-party arrangement among: (1) the cardholder, (2) the bank, and (3) the merchant.

Bank check-credit plans, on the other hand, are two-party arrangements: the bank links the extension of the line of credit to the individual's checking account. There is no formal arrangement between the bank and any merchant. In a check-credit plan, there is no embossed plastic card, only a prearranged privilege to make what in effect are legally permitted overdrafts against the depositor's checking account.

The First National Bank of Boston introduced the first check-credit plan in 1955. From a bank's point of view, check-credit plans are an alternative to bank credit card plans that are far less costly to operate. Overdraft banking by means of check-credit plans make it possible to handle small loans at a profit. By lending small amounts automatically through overdrafts on checking accounts, or utilizing overdraft lines of credit for direct lending, the bank eliminates the need for reviewing and evaluating each loan application. Overdraft banking provides greater opportunity for flexibility and growth than do either special check-credit accounts or bank credit cards. The overdraft privilege also enhances the customer appeal of checking accounts. It eliminates the embarrassment of bouncing returned checks. A simple overdraft account provides the means for greater customer acceptance of payment plans which are automatically billed to his account. This, in turn, reduces check processing and is a long step toward a checkless society. Indeed, widespread introduction of overdraft banking would open up the use of credit in many places where no bank credit card or charge card has yet penetrated.

It has been estimated that at the beginning of the 1970s there were more than 50 million bank credit cards in circulation as against 5 million five years before. In 1969, a total of $5 billion of goods and services were charged to bank credit cards, more than double the two billion dollars of 1968. About $2.7 billion of credit was outstanding on these cards. In 1969, more than three million American Express cardholders charged about $1.8 billion worth of goods and services, two million Diners' Club cardholders charged about $1 billion worth and 650,000 Carte Blanche cardholders charged about $200 million worth.

Montgomery Ward claims 13.5 million credit card users, Esso 45 million, BankAmericard and Master Charge claim about 30 million each and Texaco 38 million.

It is said that more than 40 million people have two or more oil company credit cards. Airlines are estimated to have about five million cards outstanding, and untold millions of other credit cards are available from uncounted numbers of merchants. Most of us are aware from personal experience that we carry many more credit cards than we need, but these numbers are nonetheless overwhelming.

Total sales through use of BankAmericards, in 1970 in the United States alone, were $2,773,584,654 compared to $1,768,-516,000 in 1969, an increase of 57 per cent. That year, the number of merchant locations which accepted BankAmericards increased from 518,320 to 679,518, an increase of 31 per cent. The number of cards outstanding rose slightly, from 25,775,000 to 25,958,000. The significance of these figures is that even though there was only a small increase in the number of cards outstanding, and a somewhat greater increase in merchant locations, as time goes on the dollar sales volume of credit card purchases increases at a much faster rate. This suggests that the total dollar volume of credit card purchases is increasing dramatically in relation to dollar volume of purchases by cash or through ordinary checking accounts.

You can now use your credit cards to pay for tooth extractions, tombstones, taxi rides, driving lessons, diamonds, dog kennel fees, ambulance service, apartment rent, auto license fees, music lessons, movie admissions, rented cars, savings bonds, scuba diving instruction, church tithes, college tuition, garbage removal and psychiatric care. New York City's offtrack betting corporation has issued credit cards for betting on horse races in an effort to draw business away from illegal bookmakers.

Late in 1970, there was about $123.7 billion of consumer credit outstanding, including $99 billion of installment credit and $23 billion of noninstallment credit. The amount of credit outstanding on credit cards is a significant part of these totals. Even with gross national product above the one trillion dollar mark, it is obvious that credit under credit cards accounts for a significant part of the total. This growth is all the more striking when one recalls that bank credit cards did not come into wide use until the decade of the 1960s, and into extensive use only within the last five years of that decade.

The credit card revolution has extended the availability of unsecured credit to purchase volumes of consumer goods and luxuries far beyond the circle of the affluent members of society to the middle-income and lower-income members of society who once had little or no access to credit of any kind. Now, practically anyone who is able to maintain a bank balance has access to some form of credit card credit. Some who even have negative bank balances enjoy extensive credit card credit. The credit card society makes the affluent society still more affluent.

There are no free gifts. All this easy affluence is not without its costs. Department stores, oil companies and other issuers of one-party credit cards have known for a long time that a purchaser who does not have to pay cash but can buy on credit will spend predictably larger sums of money. Instead of buying the cheapest suite of living-room furniture because its price is within the limits of the cash he has with him, a customer will buy a medium- or high-priced set if he can defer payment and pay on time. With a travel and entertainment credit card, he will go to the more expensive restaurants, order more expensive dinners from the bill of fare, buy a better wine, pencil in a larger tip for the waiter and select a more expensive Havana cigar. The only one in the establishment who suffers is the hat-check girl, who is usually still stuck with a quarter tip paid in cash.

— Credit standing and other benefits of credit cards and check credit are not bestowed by the banks and American Express Company and the rest of the issuers out of benevolent altruism. The Diners' Club is not a friendly sodality of hail-fellows-well-met, nor a convivial band of brothers, nor, indeed, a particularly exclusive club. If you do not pay your dues and your house charges in such a club, you are not just posted on the bulletin board and then dropped, you are also hounded by bill collectors, visited by a process server and hauled into court.

Noting that personal bankruptcies increased in each of the last six years of the 1960s in the United States District Court for the Southern District of New York, Referee Roy Babbitt remarked in May of 1971:

— "There are more bankruptcies in good times because of Americans' spending mentality, and the blandishments of credit cards and television, which tells of all the goodies in the world. No guy is going to tell his children, 'We've got to save up the money for a new TV.' It's just not done that way any more."

He added sympathetically, "You really can't blame a guy who uses a credit card that the bank sends him."

Landon L. Chapman, a bankruptcy lawyer in Chicago, added:

"Ten or twelve years ago individuals filing bankruptcy were mostly Negroes. Now they are about half blacks. Where consumer frauds were the big factor a decade ago, now much of the trouble is from credit cards." (*The New York Times*, May 9, 1971)

The 50 per cent-bracket taxpayer is likely used to handling credit. Not so the 25 or 30 per cent bracket taxpayer, whose first heady experience with unsecured credit is often a bank charge card which arrived free and unsolicited in the mail with his name on it. It is all too easy for him to incur more debt than he can possibly repay, and to allow the outstanding balance of his debt to increase rapidly at 18 per cent per annum interest to a point where he simply no longer can handle his mounting burden of debt. The low-bracket taxpayer is exposed to great temptation to spend more than he knows how to repay. The wages of his sin are dire: garnishment, repossession, legal judgments, foreclosure, seizure of property and personal bankruptcy. Worst of all is the probability that his default will be recorded against his credit rating in a remote credit-rating bureau. If this happens he will, in practical effect, be ostracized, exiled and banished from any future membership in the cashless society.

4.

The Darker Side of the Credit Card

Does the issuer of a credit card have a moral or legal obligation to protect holders of the card from unscrupulous merchants? From bad food and liquor, from other tempting merchandise? From running up more debts than they can pay? From the excesses of their own appetites?

Chapter 2 did not tell all that John Cade did when he took his business trip to Washington. When he had completed filing the Registration Statement with the Securities and Exchange Commission, the rest of the evening stretched invitingly before him. After consultation with the bellhop, and the purchase of a map, he decided to take a trip to Baltimore.

In a venerable area of that city known as "the strip," where the bellhop had told him to look, he saw an American Express Company decal emblem on the window of a bar. Assuring himself by the decal that the place was respectable, he went in to look for a drink of unimpeachable quality. A bar girl invited him to join her table and he politely accommodated her wish. She ordered a bottle of champagne. Hardly had the waiter popped the cork than she promptly knocked it off the table, spilling the whole bottle. Cade gallantly ordered a second bottle. Jacques Boinet champagne retails at $5 a bottle, about as cheap as champagnes go. Cade's bill for both bottles came to $56. Owing to the heady atmosphere, no doubt, he charged the whole thing on his American Express credit card. This report is silent as to what transpired during the rest of the evening. In any case, no further charges were recorded by American Express.

In the cold light of dawn he awakened in dismay. He wrote to American Express. He was shocked that it would lend its name and decal to such a place. He insisted indignantly that he would not pay his bill. He addressed his letter to the attention of the person whose name was described on its billings as the individual in charge of his account. The named individual turned out to be fictitious. The only reply Cade received were computerized form letters, polite but firm, all to the same effect: "Thanks for the information, but pay up."

Time went by, and in due course Cade received an American Express renewal card for 1971. He ripped it up in disgust and sent the little pieces back to the company saying he had discontinued his membership. He received a bill charging him the renewal fee of $15, plus $56 for the Jacques Boinet champagne. In a separate envelope, he received a polite form letter asking him please to reinstate his membership.

The dunning letters grew fiercer. He received a bill for a battery he had purchased two years before. Another said that legal action would be taken against him. In desperation, Cade wrote to the Better Business Bureau. It acknowledged his letter, but he heard no more. He wrote to the counsel of the United States Senate Permanent Investigations Subcommittee, and received no reply.

He wrote to the office of the Attorney General of Maryland. The Attorney General replied, pointing out that under Maryland law the use of "female sitters" was illegal. He reassured Cade that: "We have a statute that prohibits use of 'female sitters' employed for the purpose of soliciting customers to purchase drinks and who thereafter receive a commission or salary based upon the amount spent by the customer."

The Baltimore Police Department had, in fact, received similar complaints from customers about "being taken." But these customers were too shy, or embarrassed, or married, to press such complaints with vigor.

Cade's expensive evening raises three questions which occur to all credit card holders. Should not credit card issuers share liability for gouging or overcharging or other practices that go on in establishments operated by the merchants who display their decal? Should the card issuer cut off relations with a merchant where gouging or racketeering is carried on? Should the card issuer be required to cooperate with local police in prosecuting the local merchant, or else make him take its decal off the door?

Most credit card issuers deny that they have any responsibility to card holders, local police or merchants where their display decal shows that their credit cards are honored. In the issuer's view, all legal rights of action are Cade's alone. He can sue the bar, or the B-girl, or testify as a witness for the Baltimore police.

Cade's case did not resolve any of these questions. In the end he offered to send a check for the $56 worth of Jacques Boinet champagne to American Express, made out to the American Cancer Society. American Express replied that they would not take him to court for the amount due, accepted the check, turned it over to the American Cancer Society and closed out Cade's account.

If he had paid his bill at the Baltimore bar in cash, Cade would have had no large, solvent creditor like American Express as a "sitting duck" against which to assert his claim. He would have had to sue the bar and the B-girl in Baltimore, at great cost of time, money and embarrassment. On the other hand, if he had not seen the American Express decal emblem on the window of the Baltimore bar, it is possible that he would not have ventured in, whatever the bellboy in his Washington hotel had told him. He might even have asked the price of the champagne before the B-girl ordered it.

Should not the credit card issuer be held responsible when its name lends an impression of probity to a swindle?

Not long ago, Elizabeth Cade and thousands of other New Yorkers received letters on the letterhead of "Riccar Sewing Machine Center" which prominently displayed decals of the Master Charge and Unicard bank credit card systems. The letter was as follows:

> YOU WERE SELECTED AT RANDOM FROM ALL THE PEOPLE IN YOUR AREA TO RECEIVE A 1969 DE LUXE TWIN-NEEDLE, ZIG-ZAG SEWING MACHINE AND A HANDSOME WALNUT CONSOLE WITH BUILT-IN CONTROLS TO MONOGRAM, APPLIQUE, OVERCAST, MAKE BUTTONHOLES, BLIND HEM, DARN, EMBROIDER, ETC. AT NO CHARGE.

The letter went on to explain that the recipient should bring the letter to the office of the center, and receive a 1969 model 108 sewing machine, "Nationally advertised at $239, at no charge." According to the letter, the only requirement for receiving the machine was to purchase a ten-year service instruction contract amounting to $8.95 a year.

The sad truth was that the letter was not sent to a small list of winners, but to thousands of names on a mailing list. The machine was not a $239 machine but sold for $41 wholesale, or $52 retail. The ten-year "service" contract represented a sales price of $90. A year later the company went out of business. Hundreds of people who had accepted the machines were still entitled to nine more years of service, and still had nine years of $8.95 annual charges against their Master Charge cards. No bank was prepared to supply the promised repair service or sewing instructions, but they were prepared to insist that the cardholder pay the bank all remaining installments. Unpaid installments are still accumulating interest at 18% per annum.

But, Elizabeth says, the decal of the credit card issuer appeared on the letterhead. John saw it on the window of the Baltimore bar. Does not the decal imply quality of service? Does it not warrant that the merchant is reliable and induce you to become the victim of a fraud? No, never, nothing of the kind, say the issuers. The decal is not the "Good Housekeeping Seal of Approval." It is only a notice to let you know that inside the establishment goods and services can be charged on your credit card for your convenience and benefit.

Holders of United California Bank's credit cards purchased Filter Queen Vacuum Cleaners from salesmen who pointed out that these vacuum cleaners not only did a superior job of removing lint, dust, dirt and debris from places difficult to reach, but that when there was no dirt around these vacuum cleaners were still useful because they could be used as air conditioners. Notwithstanding this appealing feature of its product, and the ingenuity of its salesmen, the company went out of business. Purchasers of Filter Queens sued United California Bank in a class action. Since United California Bank was not only the card issuer, but also happened to be the financing agent of the Filter Queen Company, the plaintiffs had good reason to believe their suit would prevail. As a general rule, the card issuer is not liable to a merchant's customer if the card issuer has no separate connection with the merchant who sells the appliance. But recently adopted state and Federal Truth in Lending legislation has limited the number of situations in which the credit card issuer can avoid responsibility for defective goods or services by pleading the "holder in due course" defense against the cardholder.

Then there was the time that John and Elizabeth Cade's apartment was broken into when they were out of town on a two-week Bermuda vacation. The thief stole a Bloomingdale's credit card and ran up charges of $2460 before they returned. The store sued Elizabeth, claiming that she had agreed to pay for all purchases made on her card unless the store had received notice of the loss. Cade defended the claim, and the judge backed him up: Elizabeth was not responsible for the purchases because she did not even know her card had been stolen.

The judge found that Elizabeth had a duty to exercise reasonable care of her charge card, but that the store had a "concurrent obligation to protect its customers from the imposition of unjust charges." He also found that the fine print in the credit card agreement did not expressly provide that the cardholder was responsible for purchases on the card if she was not aware that it was stolen.

Yet an earlier case in the New York Supreme Court had held in favor of an oil company which sued a cardholder who had refused to pay bills which were run up on a card which he had lost. Oil companies, hotel chains and other convenience card issuers hailed the decision as a precedent for future cases involving the use of cards by others than the one to whom they were issued.

The rationale of such cases is that the person who makes the loss possible must suffer the loss, so the cardholder is responsible for all purchases made on his credit card until he gives notice to the issuer. They illustrate only a few of the innumerable possible kinds of credit card losses and frauds. There are other common situations that all credit cardholders should watch out for.

For example, when you are making a credit card purchase, the sales clerk can imprint the impression of your card on a duplicate blank sales slip. The clerk returns your card and the duplicate sales slip to you. Later, when another customer makes a cash purchase, he bills the second customer's purchase on the duplicate sales slip he has stamped with your card, forges your signature, and pockets the cash. Sometimes a clerk will "palm" the card you hand him, and hand you back a different card, one that has expired or one that is on the "hot cards" list. If you happen to notice the switch, he will quickly hand you back your own card with profuse apologies for his "carelessness." Or sometimes the clerk will simply change the figures on your sales slip and help himself to the extra items that make up the difference, hoping you will not notice.

What if Elizabeth receives a bill prepared by a computer which contains inaccurate charges? Or charges for goods she never receives? Or charges for someone else's goods? She or Cade send in a corrective explanation, but receive a series of unresponsive form letters printed out by a computer. Should they give up in disgust? Will their credit cards be revoked, and their credit rating fall to omega-minus? Will they find themselves outcasts in the cashless society? Of course not. Federal Trade Commission regulations require a credit card issuer to defer further billing to the cardholder whenever there is a disputed charge, unless the issuer explains the reason for the disputed charge in a responsive way.

The patience of many credit card holders with card issuers is beginning to wear thin. Many of their complaints find their way into letters to the Federal Trade Commission. Unfortunately, the cardholder's grievance and the real merit of his case often get lost in his frustration. He will politely beg the Commission staff member to excuse the writer for troubling him to read it, and then berate the staff member whom he has never met for some situation or other over which the Federal Trade Commission has no jurisdiction. Complaints to the Commission about deceptive credit card practices are said to be second in number only to complaints from people who send in money for pornographic books which they never receive.

One of the chief complaints is that where the bank charge card establishes a revolving charge account, and the holder does not pay his bill until the end of a month, the bank will compute its finance charges on the previous month's (or opening) balance in the account, without any offset for the payment the customer has made. So full particulars of all interest charged must be shown on the bill. In addition to interest, the Federal Trade Commission Act, the Truth in Lending Act and various state consumer protection laws permit the bank issuer-creditor under this kind of arrangement to impose a minimum finance charge of up to 50 cents for each billing period without including such charge in the annual percentage interest charge.

Where a customer makes an excess payment on his account, the issuer is required to return the payment to him, or post a credit to his account which is clearly stated on his billing. The billing must also state clearly the name and number of the person to communicate with or complain to about the billing.

The Federal Trade Commission has also sought to remedy an abuse known as the "shrinking billing period." Where there is a revolving charge, this means that each month the issuer shrinks the period of time between the billing date and the date within which payment must be made before interest charges accrue, so that eventually the holder's bill may show he has run up interest even before he receives the bill in the mail. The Truth in Lending Act outlaws this practice and requires full disclosure of the actual amount of interest charges and credit terms.

State usury laws are sometimes brought to bear to limit the amount of interest which may be charged on revolving credit balances. Other local legislation limits the liability of the cardholder for lost or stolen cards, forbids the mailing of cards on an unsolicited basis and requires that all cards issued must be issued only upon written request. Such laws, of course, effectively prohibit new issuers from entering the bank credit card field, because all such programs are prohibitively costly, and generally produce large losses until substantial numbers of cards are in frequent use.

What is to be said on the card issuer's side of these complaints? Banks are not lacking in funds with which to pay fees of lawyers to defend them, particularly where opportunities to earn 18% per annum on money loaned are at stake. Lawyers are not lacking in ingenuity to protect banks' interests. But then, candidates for office are not lacking in desire to please consumers by attacking banks and demanding application of ancient usury laws to recover excessive exactions of interest. Holders of cards may be carried away by thoughts of owning beautiful antiques at bargain prices, perhaps acquired during the euphoria of a vacation in a faraway place, and quick to forget their own imprudence when they return home. No merchant is sorry to make a sale. The powerful drive of human greed is present on all sides of these questions.

Multi-party or compatible credit card plans like Master Charge involve a bank which issues the card to its customer, a merchant who often has no direct relationship to the bank which issues the card and the holder of the card. For example, the holder of a Master Charge card who lives in New York, and has received his card from a bank there, buys an antique Chinese vase at a bargain price in San Francisco while on vacation there. He pays for it with Master Charge. When he takes the vase back to New York, and proudly shows it to a friend who works at Parke-Bernet Galleries, the friend takes one look and tells him that it is not worth even one-tenth what he paid for it. The New Yorker tells his local bank he will not pay his Master Charge bill. He is, of course, simply going back on the deal.

The fine print on the back of his Master Charge card agreement provides that "any dispute with the seller shall be settled between holder and seller and shall not affect indebtedness due to bank hereunder." The fine print also says that the bank is not responsible for goods or services acquired through purchases, or for any seller's refusal to honor a card, and that "use of a card constitutes the holder's consent to the bank's acquiring his indebtedness due to the seller." But the courts have often refused to honor such fine print. Where the issuer of the credit card in fact has a "close connection" with the seller, the courts have permitted the cardholder to recover his loss from the card issuer without making him go back and sue the distant seller first. But no such "close relationship" existed here.

Bank credit cards replace any number of separate merchants' cards, so a bank charge card reduces not only the amount of cash you have to carry, but also the number of other credit cards you must keep. A bank charge card also reduces the number of checks you have to write. They increase your ability to shop at numerous stores for the lowest prices and best values. They permit you to open a line of credit with a bank and borrow from it. Ease of bank borrowing increases the likelihood of borrowing, and reduces the likelihood that you will need installment credit plans of department stores or other credit card issuers. The automatic loan feature of the bank charge card eliminates the time-consuming paperwork of filling out credit applications whenever you make time purchases, and ordinarily you have twenty-five days to pay the bank without a service charge.

Credit cards affect competition among all suppliers of installment credit, and change their relative shares of the market. Large department stores, sales finance companies and consumer finance company credit operations are vulnerable to bank competition because bank charge plans will improve the relative competitive position of commercial banks in the consumer credit field.

Credit cards make it possible for small retailers who cannot afford to extend credit to customers, cannot afford to finance charge accounts and cannot maintain the expense of a charge account billing department to compete on a more equal footing with large retail stores which maintain their own charge accounts and billing services. In a society where the trend is increasingly toward large firms, bank charge cards provide a way for small firms to survive through reducing the high cost of credit elements in their retail service mix.

One critic of bank credit cards recently charged that bank credit cards would permit banks eventually to dominate and control the entire retail segment of the nation's economy. Credit rates, the criteria for granting credit, collection procedures, even the existence of credit as an activity of institutions other than banks, are all being challenged by the expansion of bank credit cards and related systems.*

Credit card plans also affect the extent of inter-bank competition. Large banks will be able to compete effectively among themselves, but smaller banks are at a disadvantage. Customers of small banks without credit cards will switch to larger banks which offer card plans. Small banks may sign up to join the card plans of larger banks, or join other small banks to set up joint plans. In either case, individual banks will lose part of their independence. Large and ambitious banks can use credit card plans as a step toward eventual take-over of smaller banks.

Credit cards are such a commonplace phenomenon of modern American life that one would expect the law to have worked out simple, clear and consistent rules to govern the legal relationships they create. Nothing could be further from the fact. Under the jurisprudence of some states, they have been found to create a debtor-creditor relationship, in others a debtor-factor relationship and in still others a letter of credit relationship.

Issuers, cardholders and merchants, as well as courts, judges, legislatures and professors of economics are in total conflict over the legal rules that ought to apply to credit cards. The truth of the matter is that they are a new phenomenon that cannot be successfully poured into any one of these traditional legal molds.

One way of looking at the relationship between the credit card issuer and the cardholder is that of lender and borrower. The credit card issuer lends money to the cardholder and charges him interest at a fixed rate, usually 1.5 per cent per month, or 18 per cent per annum, on the unpaid balance outstanding, beginning after a limited period of grace, such as 20 or 30 days after the holder has used his card to make a purchase

---

* *The New York Times,* January 13, 1971.

76

and incurred the obligation to pay for it. But if the relationship is in fact one of lender and borrower, should not the laws against usury apply?

Most states' usury laws make interest charges of more than 8 per cent or so per annum illegal, with certain exceptions, such as obligations of corporations, secured obligations and small consumer loans. So how can the card issuer legally charge you 18 per cent? Pope Alexander III (1159–1181) is said to have declared that credit sales at a price higher than the cash price should be considered usurious and added that "God will judge beyond the form of the contract." The Attorney General of Minnesota, Douglas Mead, who also happened to be the Republican candidate for Governor at the time, filed suit against three Minnesota banks who were participants in the Master Charge Credit Card system on grounds that they were violating Minnesota's usury law that limits annual interest to 8 per cent by adding the 1.5 per cent per month charge to billings not paid within a specific time. Many similar lawsuits have been brought in other states. There is no doubt card issuers are in trouble under the usury laws in any state where enabling legislation has not been adopted.

Most credit card issuing companies refuse to admit that their relationship to the holder of their card is like that of a lender to a borrower. On the contrary, they contend it is like that of a debtor to a creditor. It arises by prearrangement when the cardholder, in effect, opens an account with the issuer by acquiring a card. This contemplates the cardholder's making purchases from merchants, and the merchant's assigning his debt to the card issuer, which becomes his creditor. The issuer and the merchant have a contractual relationship by which the issuer purchases the merchant's accounts receivable (consisting of the cardholder's charges), without recourse and at a discount. The name of the cardholder (the debtor) and the amount of the credit (within limits) must be approved by the card issuer (in legal terms, the "factor") before the merchant extends the credit to the debtor. The credit card itself is the evidence of advance credit approval granted by the issuer. The issuer's contract with the cardholder expressly provides that the cardholder will not seek to recover for claims against the merchant by refusing to pay the bill from the card issuer. For example, the American Express cardholder agreement provides:

> 5. Amexco shall not be liable for any act or omission of any establishment, including without limitation, any refusal to honor the card or any defect or deficiency in the goods or services. Member will handle any claim or dispute directly with the establishment and will not withhold payment from Amexco on account of any such claim or dispute.

But legal conflict is not limited to just the above two views of credit card relationships.

A third legal analysis compares a credit card to a letter of credit. The holder of a BankAmericard, for example, in theory agrees to assume responsibility to pay for credit which the bank extends on the basis of the card. A BankAmericard holder may enter any retail establishment which accepts BankAmericards, make a purchase and present his card for payment. If the purchase exceeds the coded limit shown on the card, the merchant must obtain the bank's approval by telephone before accepting the payment. The bank in effect assumes responsibility for the credit which the merchant has extended on the basis of the credit card.

These three conflicting legal theories illustrate how state laws, federal laws, federal regulations promulgated by the Federal Trade Commission and court decisions overlap and conflict. Federal legislation preempts the area of state legislation in an ill-defined and inconclusive manner.

In January, 1971, a *Journal of Commerce* survey reported an alarming drop in the number and volume of retailers who would accept credit cards. This trend was particularly noticeable in the Far West, where the pattern of heavy usage of bank credit cards had first become established. The reason seemed to be that, during the recession year of 1970, as profit margins declined, merchants became more and more reluctant to accept the banks' discounts on their credit card business. Buyers who were becoming increasingly price-conscious would come to the small merchant, make a purchase and give him a choice: put the purchase on the credit card, or else accept cash, and give the buyer a five percent discount. Many merchants chose the cash, and kept the discount within the buyer-seller "family," instead of yielding it up to the bank. Some merchants added a five percent credit charge to the bill of the customer who used a credit card.

The drop in credit card acceptance was, of course, more noticeable among small firms than large. One reason for this was that the banks give larger retailers a substantially lower discount rate on credit card sales than they give to smaller merchants. Another is that large merchants simply do not bargain with customers.

The legislation, regulation and judicial decisions which establish the legal framework within which all forms of credit cards are used are piecemeal, tangential, narrow in scope and uncertain of objective. Much of the regulatory activity adversely affects most consumers by raising credit costs all round, limiting the number of cardholders and making credit more expensive. The paper work involved in complying with much of the well-meaning legislation increases all the costs for all. These costs probably far exceed the cost of the occasional abuses which much of the well-meaning legislation and regulation is designed to prevent.

Cardholders, issuers, merchants, official and self-appointed consumer advocates, lawyers, judges and candidates for political office have been dealing with credit cards in contradictory and conflicting ways that serve their own immediate interests, without concern for the larger interests that are at stake.

79

They have been trying to deal with credit cards by working within traditional legal concepts invented for dealing with coin and cash money, and coin and cash money credit instruments, paper currency, promissory notes, "notes accountable," bills of exchange, bank deposits, loans, purchases and the like. What all these large interests have failed to do is recognize credit cards for what they are: an entirely new and different institution. They are not only that; they are more than that. They are also a means of social regulation and social control. What the legislature, judges, issuers, merchants, holders and financial institutions must do is recognize the credit card for the new and different thing it is, and seek to legislate and judge it in ways consistent with a broad public interest in the new institution.

It is obvious that credit and charge cards have a pervasive influence on all our lives and society at large, not all for good, not all for bad. But they have an impact, nevertheless, of enormous importance, and with enormous potential consequences that remain almost entirely unrealized and ignored.

Are credit cards the new money? Is the cashless society merely a pretentious name for the kinds of charge account transactions we have always known, embellished by a two-by-three-inch embossed plastic card overprinted with computer language? Is it just another name for a plastic cosmetic job on the coin and cash money society we already know so well?

The answer ought to be a negative one. Certainly credit cards are a medium of exchange which have many of the qualities of coin and cash money, but they also have many other and different characteristics and possibilities which are far more significant. It is these significant differences that make them a new order of things from the old order of things, money as cash.

If this important distinction is not drawn, and these unrealized and unexplored possibilities for economic and social progress remain hidden behind the cosmetic plastic of two-by-three-inch cards, we will all be losers—cardholders, merchants and issuers as well, even bank issuers. Shortsighted consumerist legislation, bank-oriented special interest legislation, special private deals between small holders, sharp practices and simple frauds will curtail the usefulness of credit cards and raise the costs of doing business with them, to the point where the remarkable growth trends in credit card usage of the past will be reversed. If such a reversal should take hold, it would be a long step away from the world of *Looking Backward.*

Patience and a sense of humor will be required. As long as cardholders are human beings, and issuers must deal with them through computer systems, we will have to learn to cope with pre-programmed aggravations.

When Elizabeth Cade found out that none of the tellers or anyone in the bank was going to service her Riccar sewing machine, she stopped paying the annual installments that were still due. Here is the letter she received shortly thereafter on the letterhead of a firm of bank collection attorneys:

Dear Customer:

Could you please recommend to us a good lawyer in your community? It may be necessary for us to sue you.

5.

Living with Computer Data Banks

Not long after Elizabeth had stopped payment on her ten-year service contract for the "free gift" Riccar sewing machine she had won, she received another letter, this one on the letterhead of the Credit Bureau of Greater New York:

FINAL NOTICE

The files of the Credit Bureau are available to stores, banks and financing institutions throughout the United States. Pay your bill forthwith in the interest of having your credit record appear as favorable as possible.

The latter form letter contained blank spaces filled in to show the amount it claimed Elizabeth owed, but there was no return address on the dun. All it said was: "Please send payments to Riccar 1971, Inc."

Elizabeth showed the letter to John when he came home from the office and he was furious.

"I'm taking this straight to the Consumer Frauds Bureau of the New York State Attorney General's office," he announced, with the precision of a TV spot identifying the sponsor's product, and a fine professional air of righteous indignation.

Elizabeth sighed, "Even when I can't stand you, I'm glad I'm married to a lawyer."

The Assistant Attorney General in charge of Consumer Frauds pulled out a file of letters like the one Elizabeth had received, leaned back in his chair and said to John Cade:

"The Credit Bureau of Greater New York sells those letters to stores all over town. The stores just fill in the blanks, put in their name, your name, the amount they say you owe and mail them out by the thousands."

"Can't you do anything about them?" John asked.

"We've got a consent judgment enjoining the Credit Bureau from selling those letters. The big stores that have been using them have given us their 'assurances of discontinuation.' We've got them from Lord & Taylor, Gristede's, Gimbel's, Plymouth Shops, Brooklyn Union Gas Company, Time Inc. and Doctors Hospital, to drop a few of the bigger names with the most prestige."

"But Riccar! Don't forget about Riccar!" John insisted.

"Of course not," the Assistant Attorney General snapped with annoyance. "It's practically the only one I ever hear about."

"Oh, by the way," he added, "you needn't worry about yourself. We now have a New York City law that prohibits a credit bureau or store from sending a threatening credit letter to a debtor's employer, unless the creditor has a court judgment and permission to attach the employee's salary."

"That's reassuring," John said.

Elizabeth and John were suffering the experience of many being dunned for a debt they felt they did not owe because they had been defrauded by Riccar's advertising, including the credit card emblems that lent credibility to it. Their nonpayment of the dun had brought them into contact, and disfavor, with the credit information and rating system on which our increasingly cashless economy is based.

The next time Elizabeth presents her credit card to charge a purchase, and the clerk checks it in one way or another against a list of numbers of lost or stolen or discredited cards, the credit decision on her has to be yes or no, and it has to be quick. If it is negative, she has no right of appeal and no way to argue with a computerized credit rating bureau that may be a thousand miles away.

Credit rating and verification systems are the central nervous system of the cashless society. They are complex marvels of technical ingenuity. At the nerve end of contact between customer and sales clerk, they operate quickly, simply and ruthlessly.

American Express, for example, has an Audio Response Computer System. When a card is presented to an airline ticket counter or a hotel clerk and credit authorization is required for a bill above a certain limit, the clerk contacts the computer in New York by means of a Touch-Tone card dialer telephone. He puts in his own employee identity card and pushes buttons to identify the customer's card number and the amount. The computer checks a file of two million or more accounts for "lost, stolen or canceled" cards and then checks the cardholder's credit rating. It also scans the data bank for any unusual spending pattern. When a card has been stolen, the records usually show a spending spree: purchase of many expensive things within a short period of time. If the computer for some reason cannot give a "spoken" approval immediately, it transfers the call to a "credit authorizer" and displays the account record for the credit authorizer to refer to in making his decision.

Another prototype for a national credit verification system is National Data Corporation's nationwide system for twenty-six major oil companies. One service handles Mobil Oil Corporation customer reservations for about 3500 hotels and motels. Another handles impatient motorists as they sit beside the gas pump, eager to be speeding down the throughway. At a Mobil station anywhere in the continental United States, when you buy a tankful of gas and present your credit card to the attendant, he can call in the number on your card. In twenty seconds, he is told whether or not it is valid.

84

One feature of the card verification system is an "early warning" feedback of suspicions of fraud. When the gas station attendant phones in the amount you are charging on your card, the total is stored in a central computer. If this and other purchases on your card add up to more than your preset limits, the computer will note this and warn the attendant that something suspicious may be happening. He is alerted to check you for a possible stolen card.

How does the credit authorizer recognize an acceptable credit risk? This is a big question mark in back of every last plastic credit card. It is the big question mark behind every credit transaction of every kind. Credit files on individual cardholders, bank customers, borrowers and depositors build up like coral reefs into credit data banks, and credit data banks expand into centralized credit-rating bureaus. Behind all travel and entertainment credit cards and all bank charge cards today are vast stores of computerized credit information. Some of this is in separate data centers, but increasingly, all the data in the separate data centers are becoming available in all others, through ever more sophisticated computerized data retrieval linkages.

In days gone by, a bank or department store credit manager might extend or withhold credit on the basis of subjective factors: he might like your looks, or he might not. But today credit scoring systems are impersonal and objective. Typical systems take note of six basic factors, including:

(1) The income of the applicant, that is, how much money he has available to pay his debts after he has provided necessities for himself and his family.

(2) His job record, particularly his job longevity, which shows his stability and his income level as well.

(3) His credit record, because the manner in which he has paid his debts in the past is a good guide to how he may be expected to pay them in the future.

85

(4) The places where he has lived, his residential stability, may be gauged by whether he is buying his home or renting it, and by the length of time he has lived at the same residence.

(5) If goods and services are being financed, the amount of his own money he is willing to invest in terms of down payment or equity, which is a direct measure of his stake in the goods he is asking the lender to help him acquire.

(6) His "character" is also considered, but not in the sense that he is awarded points for good character. All applicants are expected to be of good character, but "character" is still important in the sense that applicants who are known to be of poor character are usually rejected outright.

Many credit applications do not call for any meaningful exercise of judgment. They are so obviously good, or bad, that they can be approved or rejected without any intervention of human judgment. A computer can be programmed to recognize the above six credit factors and assign values to them. If, for example, on a numerical scale from one to one hundred, experience shows that applications which score 30 points or below can be rejected with little danger that a profitable credit risk has been lost, and that those scoring 75 points or above can be approved with minimal risk of loss, then a computer can process all such applications. Only those which fall somewhere between 30 and 75 then need to be reviewed by the credit manager.

The use of numerical credit scoring systems based on these six factors also makes possible an objective evaluation of credit results. Management can choose a definite number in the scale of credit desirability, such as 30 in the example, below which applications will not be accepted. This largely eliminates ambiguity as to what currently constitutes an acceptable credit risk. Where economic conditions warrant, or where portfolio control is necessary, credit managers can determine the amount to be granted immediately and uniformly by increasing or decreasing the minimum passing score.

Money transfer and credit rating aspects of computerized credit-rating bureaus and linked data banks are but one limited aspect of a social problem that is broader and deeper than the economic structure of the cashless society. That is the nightmarish problem of the increasing loss of personal privacy in modern life. Computer technology thrusts ahead at a faster pace than the laws which are intended to limit the threats it poses. Ralph Nader has warned that corporate and governmental information gathering activities threaten to turn us into a nation of slaves. No discussion of the possibilities of a cashless society can properly ignore this threat.

The Internal Revenue Service has computerized the processing of millions of income tax returns. Although the tax system and the Social Security system are, of course, government systems entirely separate and apart from existing credit-rating systems, existing technology could conceivably integrate them into the information collecting, credit rating and cash transmission system of a cashless society. Every New Yorker knows how much duplication and triplication of effort, how much paper and time he could save if federal, state and city income tax collection systems were combined into one, as some federal and state systems for auditing tax returns have already been integrated. Transmission of tax and Social Security payments and refund checks by electronic means would eliminate billions of checks, envelopes, debits, credits, mailings, stamps and frankings. But doubts about the integrity of the system are a serious obstacle to the possibility of integration of tax and Social Security systems with a general cashless society.

It is widely believed that individual income tax returns are secret, and that their secrecy and privacy is inviolate law, except by order of the President. But for many years the Internal Revenue Service has been selling copies of magnetic tapes containing encoded personal income tax information to state tax departments at $75 a reel to help states catch evaders of state taxes and nonfilers of state income tax returns. There is no guarantee that the information supplied to the states will remain secret. The Internal Revenue Service also sells copies of lists of people who are registrants under various firearms laws.

The most sophisticated, and sinister, computerized records are, of course, those of the Federal Bureau of Investigation's National Crime Detection Center. It provides 40,000 instant automatic teletyped printouts each day on wanted persons and stolen property to all the states and Canada. It also "talks" to 24 other computers operated by state and local police departments in a total of 2,500 police jurisdictions. The Center says its information is all "from the public record" based on local and federal warrants and complaints, and that the sum product is available only to the police. In separate computer records at the Secret Service, there are recorded names of activists, malcontents, persistent seekers of redress and those who would embarrass the President or other government leaders, as well as the names of persons convicted of "threats against the President" and potential assassins.

The Justice Department's Civil Disturbance Group maintains a data bank which produces a weekly printout of national tension points on racial, class and political issues and the individuals and groups involved in them. These data include information on peace rallies, welfare protests and the like. They provide the "data base" against which the computer measures the mood of the nation and the militancy of its citizens. Judgments are made. Subjects are classified as "radical" or "moderate."

The Army's Counter-Intelligence Analysis Division in Alexandria, Virginia, maintains a huge file of microfilmed intelligence reports, clippings and other materials on civilian activity. Its purpose is to help prepare troop deployment estimates for troop commands on alert to respond to possible civil disturbances in 25 American cities. The name of a student who is in a fight in an Alabama high school is recorded in a "spot report" teletyped to Washington and shared by as many as half a dozen government intelligence gathering groups—if the fight was interracial. So is the name of the leader of a Negro protest against welfare regulations in St. Louis. So is the name of a college professor who is unwittingly and indeed innocently arrested for disorderly conduct when police round up a group at a San Francisco peace rally.

There is no law that the computer files from one government agency may not be furnished to other government agencies. There is no law that forbids computers of one agency from talking to those of another—trading and comparing in seconds data that may then be transmitted across the nation. For example, the Secret Service can now ask its computer, and quickly be forewarned that, say, three of one hundred guests invited to a Presidential gathering in the White House Rose Garden are "persons of protective interest." This means that under current Secret Service criteria, they have been said by someone, no matter who, to be the authors of reportedly angry, threatening or "embarrassing" statements about the President or the government. Upon receipt of such notice, the Secret Service may take action ranging from special observation during the dinner, or "proximity to the President," to withdrawal of the invitation itself.

Privacy is one of our most precious human rights, and in today's crowded, prying and disorderly environment, it is one of the hardest to maintain. All of us are leaving longer and longer paper trails behind us: information on birth records, school records, college records, employment records, tax files, Social Security files, police records, gun registrations, auto licenses, hospitals, credit bureaus and the Census Bureau. There is a relentless flow of information about each of us into central files. More and more is recorded in computers, and more and more data banks and retrieval systems are interconnected. What assurance do we have that information from these governmental information gathering systems will not find its way into our personal file at a credit rating bureau as, say, items 7, 8, 9 and 10 on our personal credit rating score?

The association of the all but infinite capabilities of computerized information storage, data retrieval systems and wide telecommunication linkages summons to mind images of an Orwellian police state, in which all personal, idiosyncratic human values and failings have been sacrificed to the "higher good" of the state's system. It is a chilling image. The individual does not know what information about him has been recorded, where it is stored, for how long, whether there are errors in it or who can obtain access to it.

Senator Sam J. Ervin, Jr., Democrat of North Carolina, has said that computerized files already in existence in Washington are leading the country toward a "police state." There is no gainsaying the real and widespread fear that is summed up in Ralph Nader's warning: "Invisible changes are taking place everywhere. We feel them every minute of every day and they are having cataclysmic overtones as to how we operate this society. This is leading to a significant kind of tyranny. The key democratic principle of a man's control over his life is being abused. Unless we do something about it, we're suddenly going to wake up a nation of slaves."

There is a natural human dislike of becoming a statistic in a computer, particularly when the statistic can grow into a lengthy dossier containing more or less intimate details about your person and your daily living habits. When that dossier is secreted within a vast impersonal electronic information system to which any number of unknown people may have access, dislike turns into fear. As our fear of all the unknown snoopers and informers grows, so does our feeling that we must "play it safe," and dare not stick our necks out. Our basic freedoms are guaranteed by the First Amendment, but what good are they if

90

every significant exercise of them is noted down and recorded forever in some computerized credit-rating system, and we find our credit choked off in an increasingly cashless society? Data banks are a subtle kind of blackmail, because their very existence inhibits people from speaking out against them and "blowing the whistle" on the system itself.

These massive computerized and microfilmed files on hundreds of thousands of people for non-economic, non-credit reasons have no obvious or necessary relation to a person's credit worthiness, his right to credit-card credit, his payment of his taxes or his Social Security contributions or his right to Social Security or Medicare payments. But with the possibility of an interconnected grid of government and private data banks, and the seriousness of the threat of a cut-off of credit when an individual lives in a cashless, checkless and moneyless society, the possible misuse of information from these files for political and social purposes becomes a very real danger, no less clear because it is more future than present.

Thoughtful people see the computer and electronic data linkages as facilitating a radical realignment of knowledge, and therefore of power. In itself, this advance in the state of the art is neither good nor bad, sinister nor benign. The computer does not of itself create an invasion of privacy. Snoopers, investigators and all such human agencies are what invade privacy. The threat to privacy posed by surveillance and record keeping has been a fact of life in all countries throughout history. The computer itself does not do the snooping. The facts of life, of your life, of everyone's life, are facts. The observations by other people of your life, and their false statements about you are also facts, but not necessarily the same as your facts. The law has always drawn a sharp distinction between the one and the other. None of this is changed by the existence of the computer or the development of data banks.

The only new element which the computer introduces is fantastic efficiency. Ordinary paper filing systems are self-limiting because of human, space, geographical and indexing limitations on the ability to retrieve information from them. By comparison, computers have an almost unlimited capacity to store and retrieve names and dossiers. The computer can "put it all together"—facts, opinions, malicious statements and all the rest, in an instantaneous printout statement. It is this fantastic efficiency in assembling information under one or another file number, remembering it indefinitely and printing it out in seconds upon demand, that people fear.

Such generalized fear of "Big Brother" in the form of a data bank is perhaps the most serious obstacle that any projection of a cashless society must recognize and deal with. At this point an obvious distinction must be recognized.

Computerized credit rating systems and linked data banks will inevitably serve as the central nervous system of the cashless society. This is, of course, and must remain, a wholly separate and distinct system from governmental data gathering systems which gather noneconomic social and political information about people.

The use of computerized information data banks for purposes not related to the movement toward the cashless society is obviously a formidable threat to every individual's privacy, political freedom and constitutional rights. This threat must be curbed and eliminated by insistence on legal and constitutional safeguards. But above all, the critical distinction should be kept in focus: a credit bureau is not the Federal Bureau of Investigation, and the FBI is not a credit bureau. We must preserve the credit bureau for the cashless society and leave the Federal Bureau of Investigation to the Supreme Court.

In the past there have been few meaningful or consistent rules about who can gain access to an individual's file in a credit-rating bureau. Ralph Nader has pointed out that anyone posing as a prospective employer and willing to pay a fee of $5 or $10 can obtain data on any of 72 million or so Americans whose records are stored in the computerized files of the two largest national credit-rating bureaus—the Retail Credit Company and Credit Data Corporation. The files of these two companies contain information about an individual's job, his associations, marital situation and personal habits, as well as "background" material which may be no more than gossip drawn from neighbors or anyone else who might happen to know one and is willing to talk to the credit investigator.

One attempt to meet this kind of criticism is the new Federal Fair Credit Reporting Act. This law authorizes lawsuits by individuals for damages for misuse of privately held intelligence data and information from credit files. New York and a number of other states have passed other new laws to regulate credit bureaus. Under New York's law, for example, a person who has been refused credit, or a license from a licensing agency, is entitled to disclosure of the name of any credit bureau which has provided a report to the creditor, or the licensing agency. He may then demand disclosure of the report itself, the data behind it and correction of any information in it that is inaccurate. Under the law, credit bureaus may not give reports to anyone but creditors, licensing agencies, law enforcement agencies, persons who are designated by the individual, other credit bureaus and other persons designated in court orders. At six-month intervals, an individual may demand the names and addresses of all those to whom reports about him have been furnished.

It seems only fair that everyone should have the right and be given the practical means to examine what is in a credit bureau's dossier on him and to challenge it if he wishes to do so. He ought to be able to find out who has access to the information and to what outside agencies it may be released. He should also have the right and ability to challenge the release of any private data about him without his consent. The laws should probably make it clearer that personal information is a property right, and penalties like sanctions for tort or conversion should be imposed for improper gathering, storing or releasing of personal information. Safeguards such as these in the credit sphere will preserve the values of the computer credit-rating bureaus and interconnected data banks for us all as we move, as we should, into the cashless society.

There are many ways that safeguards can be designed into computer systems. People allowed to put information into computer systems can be limited to those who are well qualified to do so. Computers can be programmed to check information put into them against a pre-programmed set of values, and reject questionable information. Conceivably, a computer could be taught to recognize hearsay, and reject it. Other ingenious devices could be built into computers to safeguard delivery of information, and keep it secret. A computer could require a password, or limit recovery to narrowly classified types of information, such as bill-paying records, or other information useful solely for credit-rating purposes. It could record each request and the name of the inquirer, so as to pinpoint blame if the person who obtained the information misused it. There are many kinds of technical security systems, very few of which anyone has bothered to put into effect.

Unfortunately, determined men can find ways to circumvent even the best security systems. So more than physical safeguards are required. Computer operating personnel should themselves be screened for trustworthiness. Computer programmers should ask the question more often: "Is this information really necessary? Is it worth the cost of programming it in and printing it out?"

There should also be a time limit, something like a legal "statute of limitations," after which personal data might automatically be erased from computer records, so that a casual indiscretion would not haunt a man for the rest of his life. Drunkards go on the wagon and youthful lechers slow down with the passage of time.

The distinction between use, on the one hand, of computerized credit-rating systems for sound economic reasons in the

94

movement toward the cashless society, and, on the other hand, the use of computerized data systems to exert political pressures on individuals remains basic and real. No conscientious efforts to smooth the way toward a cashless society should try to pretend that it does not exist.

Computerized credit rating systems and linkages between them are spreading and will certainly continue to do so. As time goes on, local bank credit card programs will join national bank credit card networks. More banks will offer charge services to expand their banking services or, as a defensive measure, to guard against losing customers to other banks who do offer these services.

We will see the development of larger credit checking centers to provide credit information for larger regions of the country. No doubt a national electronic network for exchanging information among banks, bank credit card systems, and regional credit checking systems will follow. Cards which are part of American Express Company, Diners' Club and Carte Blanche travel and entertainment credit card systems will eventually be linked to regional and national interchanges, as will the vast oil company, air travel and car rental credit systems.

At present there are so many credit cards of so many different issuers outstanding that no truly comprehensive check for a stolen or canceled card is possible. So another important step is likely to be adoption of a single unique personal identification number and card to replace all the many different credit numbers and cards. Such a card would carry a single identification number for the owner. It might be his Social Security number. It might also carry his signature, photograph, fingerprints, magnetic tape voice print, and be machine-readable. It would of course be far easier than it now is to check such a unique card against a single national list of cards and credit numbers. Since pattern recognition techniques enable computers to recognize certain identifying characteristics of the human voice, it is within reach of present technology to build a machine into which an individual could read his number over the telephone. A computer could interpret the digits and look up a record containing details of that individual's voice characteristics. Just as police use fingerprints to identify a suspect, so the computer could use the details of his voice sounds to determine whether the person speaking is the same one who has that identifying number. With such a voice technique, even the credit card itself could be eliminated.

As technology becomes more efficient, exchanges would develop to provide credit information for all credit granting institutions on local, regional and national levels. A single credit number and credit card acceptable on a national level everywhere for each individual is probably inevitable, although we are still a long way from it today.

Once all regional and national credit rating bureaus and data banks are linked together, there seems to be no technological reason why a single credit card could not be used for all the purposes that all the separate and different credit cards we now have are used for. A Hertz card is honored by Avis and National Auto Rental, and many merchants who honor one bank card honor all, even without the bank's decal on the window.

There are, as usual, legal problems. Large competing private credit card systems and large bank credit card systems are prevented from combining because of possible violations of the antitrust laws.

These stern laws are a sanctified feature of our political economy. Only baseball, the official national pastime, has been exempt. It is not reasonable to expect these laws to be changed any time soon to accommodate credit cards, or smooth the path toward a cashless society. But it is not unlikely that here is an area where a revolution might occur by evolution. If a few cards and then a single card came to be honored by all of the merchants who honored all other cards, it is hard to see how the antitrust laws could prevent all the others from being voluntarily discarded, leaving but one. But such a single universal all-purpose credit card would then be such a powerful monopoly that we could hardly expect it to survive unregulated in private hands. Through legislation the Federal Reserve System or some other national governmental agency might be designated as the issuer, or at least the regulator of the issuer of a single universal credit card. The postal or telephone systems serve as distant analogies. Such a single system might find a way to clear sales slips through the same mechanism it now uses for clearing checks. Once regional and national interchanges of credit data had been created, and a single credit card was honored everywhere, an electronic network could be used to transfer funds between banks, between customers, and between merchants and banks, and checks and bills and drafts could be eliminated.

With the introduction of one credit card, the adoption of a single symbol for each individual for use on all credit communications could be the next step. This would in itself reduce much duplication in credit checking and credit bureau paperwork and files.

Terminal devices in merchant establishments would tie in directly with banks and credit centers. When the network was complete, credit references could be checked electronically in an instant, and transfers of credit balances and debit balances made electronically over a wire the next instant.

In a cashless society, nationally interconnected credit data banks would provide an instantaneous credit check on every individual's economic status each time he made a money commitment. At the same time he would write out fewer bank checks, or none at all.

In a state of cashlessness, an individual's economic status would rarely be in much doubt because his credit would constantly be checked and rechecked. At the same time the quality of his life would be enhanced by eliminating the dull and boring routine of writing out hundreds of checks from the list of his daily chores.

We are gradually becoming used to the new kinds of paper symbols that replace checks and represent only electronic pulses in computerized data linkages. The paperwork that comes out of these transactions records information about the transaction, but unlike a check that is hand signed, torn out, passed, stamped, perforated and canceled as it proceeds from maker to payee, does not represent the transaction itself. The memorandum of these transactions is merely a routine computer printout. It is merely evidentiary, and not in itself a symbol of value.

Electronic data transfers have already been put into pilot operation in some cities. At the Bank of Delaware in Wilmington, shop assistants in selected stores have been equipped with Touch-Tone telephones. Plastic identification cards are issued to selected customers of the stores who also happen to be customers of the bank. When the customer makes a purchase at one of the selected stores, the clerk puts the card into a special slot in the phone and pushes the appropriate buttons. The telephone line transmits data to the bank's computer, whose mechanism reads the customer's number from the card. The clerk at the store keys in the cost of the purchase, and when this information arrives at the bank's computer it adjusts its data files to show the purchase. The purchase price, plus tax, is deducted from the customer's bank account, the payment is added to the store's bank account and the tax is credited to the store's tax account. Neither check nor cash changes hands. Electronic error detection mechanisms are used to insure that transactions are not falsely transmitted and that files are not incorrectly updated. Full evidentiary details of the transaction are automatically printed in bank statements which are sent to the store and to the customer.

When such "pilot" programs take hold everywhere, we will

begin to feel the real impact of a cashless society. You will be able to use your credit card for all but the most minor transactions. When you buy a necktie at Bloomingdale's the sales clerk will insert your money card into a transmitter which connects with the bank. The transmitter will automatically dial your bank account, debit your account for the purchase price and credit the store's account. If the funds in your bank account are insufficient, the computer will check your line of credit, and, if it is adequate, automatically make you a loan. Neither checks nor cash will change hands in the transaction. Money will be nothing more than the electronic transmission of information.

Two weeks after the Cades had heard from Riccar's collection attorneys, and a week after Elizabeth had shown John the FINAL NOTICE letter from the Credit Bureau of Greater New York, a red cashmere sweater caught Elizabeth's fancy during a shopping trip to Lord & Taylor. The sales clerk placed her credit card on the imprinter. Elizabeth watched carefully to make sure that no duplicate sales slips had been placed underneath. The sales clerk's face suddenly darkened. She walked away from the counter and spoke to the floor manager. After a long and mysterious delay, the sales clerk returned and said to Elizabeth, "I'm sorry, ma'am, there will be a slight delay. We've had to refer your charge account to the credit authorizer."

The reader's impatience with these reports of the unfortunate consequences of Elizabeth Cade's acquisition of the Riccar sewing machine has probably reached, or passed, its limit. But the kind of experiences she has been through since she first "won" it are all too familiar to us in non-cashless society. Her experience helps remind you that you are not being asked to opt for a new reality whose advantages are without concomitant problems. Experience suggests that no such reality exists, at least when large questions of politics and economics are passing in review.

6.

Breaking Out
of the Paper Cocoon

Duns, dossiers and data banks undeniably cast a pall over the prospects for the future of the cashless society. But these undoubted dangers have concomitant advantages that are easy to overlook, and yet represent significant humane values all the same. Far from going down for the third time under the weight of an Orwellian police state, without quite realizing it, we may instead be coming up for air.

"He spends his money as if it is going out of style." Styles in money go through cyclical changes much as styles in women's clothes do, but the money time cycle has a longer arch. Gold is rare, infinitely divisible, impervious to rust and lichen, and beautiful enough to inspire the world's greatest poets and the love of its most beautiful women. For at least five thousand years it was the world's preeminent standard of value. But the cycle of this "symbol of preeminence ordained by celestial will" ended on August 15, 1971, when President Nixon announced that the United States would no longer redeem all paper dollars for gold in transactions with national central banks, as it had been required to do by the Bretton Woods agreements of 1944. Now a paper money cycle is ascendant that has practically nothing to do with gold. The dollar and all other money is worth what the issuing state says it is worth. Certainly not more, usually less.

The Canadian dollar bill states that the Bank of Canada "will pay to the bearer on demand" one dollar. The government has nothing to pay with except more dollar bills. There is no gold for this purpose. All U.S. paper money states: "In God We Trust." Cash money which passes from hand to hand, from wallet to cash register to night depository and back again, is nothing more than paper evidence of the holder's supposed ability to pay in similar money.

As time went on, the predominance of paper and cash money as currency reached a crescendo and then in its turn began to fall and has been superseded by the rising cycle of checkbook and credit money. Checks, checking accounts, checkbooks and similar kinds of demand deposit money have been in wide use for only about a century or so, a relatively short span of time in the history of money. For many years, economists did not even count checking accounts and demand deposits as part of the total money supply. Such amounts were regarded as merely substitutes for "real" money, which was, of course, hard cash. The conventional wisdom about money was that the coin and currency in the vaults of the banks stood behind every demand deposit and checking account, and the deposits were nothing more than a bookkeeping entry representing the cash down below. Ordinary coins were merely substitutes for gold coins or bullion, and paper money was merely a substitute for coin.

Just as coins and currency lost their preeminence as the circulating medium about a hundred years ago, demand deposits on which checks are drawn are losing their preeminence today. Ten years and more ago corporate treasurers maintained demand deposits of hundreds of thousands of dollars to meet corporate obligations which were expected to mature within a short time. Today they maintain relatively small demand deposit balances. Instead, they invest the corporate cash in treasury bills, commercial paper, interest-bearing accounts or Euro-dollars.

Just as checks drawn on demand deposits proved to be a more convenient way of dealing with money than passing the gold bullion, or the token coin and currency that represented it, from hand to hand, so credit cards and electronic transfers of credit are coming to seem a more efficient method of providing for money exchanges than checks. So credit, charge cards and check-credit card overdraft credit plans now are taking over in many areas where checking accounts and demand deposits were once unrivalled.

Why should credit card plans and electronic transfers of funds be slowly supplanting the checking account system with which we have become so familiar and which has worked well for the past century? A principal reason is that the capacity of the banking system and the mails to keep up with the sheer volume of paper work the present system requires is breaking down. A recent study by a committee of the American Bankers Association estimated that more than 22 billion checks a year were written at the beginning of the 1970s; and that at the recent rate of increase (about seven percent a year), about 44 billion checks would be written each year by 1980. The cost of paper work created by business in the United States is tens of billions of dollars annually. If this volume also doubles within a decade, the mass of paper will simply choke off existing channels of communication. If there is a similar continuing proliferation of third-class mail superimposed upon bank and business mailings, the physical transfer of paper will simply become an impossibility. To solve the problem, leading bankers and communications experts urge "paperless entries" and electronic transfers of funds.

Credit cards have made it unnecessary to write twenty-five checks when making twenty-five purchases: one check at the end of the month will do for all. But even one check is not necessary, because your bank can make an automatic debit to your account at regular intervals, relieving you of the need to write even that one check. If John Cade's law firm sends his paycheck directly to his bank, and he and Elizabeth make all of their purchases with that bank's credit card, and the bank then settles up all payments at regular intervals by automatically reducing his account by the amount of the charges incurred, his checkbook, like his paper dollar bills, will become totally obsolete.

Once the credit card has replaced the checkbook, the credit card in turn may find itself on the way out. Its logical successor in the ascendancy of the cycle would be nothing more tangible than electronic impulses—information electronically programmed in a computer memory bank.

Think how much a comprehensive system of electronic transfers of funds would mean to John and Elizabeth Cade's daily life. In the old days when he bought that necktie at Bloomingdale's, he signed the sales slip while the clerk verified his credit. At the end of the month he received a bill for the purchase. He sat down at his desk, got out his checkbook, wrote a check, put it in an envelope and mailed it back to Bloomingdale's. Its bill to him and his check in payment of it passed through the mails where it ran the risk of loss or misdirection twice. The credit check at the department store, the mailing of his bill, his envelope and check back to the department store wasted much time and postage.

The simple process of writing and mailing checks consumes a ridiculously large amount of John and Elizabeth Cade's time. If, during the month, in addition to all the regular bills, he has charged purchases at ten restaurants and a dozen stores and rented a car five times, he may find himself writing out forty or more checks at the end of the month. After he has done so, he feels inundated by all that paper work. All that valuable time that could otherwise have been spent in living, has been spent in check writing. He has also spent money that might have been saved to send out payments which occasionally get lost in the mail. John Cade, who records all time he works for his law office clients and bills it at $50 an hour, knows that the six hours each month he spends check writing is a dead loss of $300 to himself, which he has no way of charging to anyone else. But with a bank credit card and an electronic fund transfer authorization, one check at the end of the month, or one simple direction, will pay all these bills, and save all these checks and hours of lost time. Even that single check or payment direction can be eliminated if the bank is authorized in advance to make automatic debits to his account at regular intervals.

There are said to be about 70 million checking accounts in the United States with balances of less than $1000—a combination of two numbers that might lead a commercial banker to mutter under his breath, "what an awful lot of nothing much." But 70 million small checking accounts represent billions of checks and millions of man-hours spent in check writing, envelope stuffing, mailing, letter sorting, letter carrying, statement balancing and minimum balance checking. Millions upon millions of dollars are invested in paper, cardboard, printed forms and postage stamps.

George W. Mitchell, a governor of the Federal Reserve System, and many others have advocated a system that permits direct transfers of funds from savings accounts upon order to the payees of monthly bills—for example, for rent or gas or electricity. This would mean that millions of people could get by without any checking accounts at all. They would no longer have to worry about either maintaining minimum balances, or paying for individual checks. There would be no charge for the service, but the payees would have to maintain accounts of their own with a savings bank. Most commercial banks and savings and loan associations are presently permitted to provide these services for depositors.

This somewhat resembles the giro system used in Britain

and European countries, under which savings are placed in interest-bearing post office accounts, and funds are transferred directly from these accounts to pay regular household bills. No funds are drained away from the bank in "float" while checks are cleared, no outside transfer requirements are imposed and the money position of the banking agency becomes more stable. For the depositor, it is the ultimate in money convenience and the next to last step in the progress toward a cashless existence.

Since the early 1960s, some banks have programmed full details of all accounts in vast random access computer files. Eventually all banks will do this. The next step will be the creation of capability to make direct transfers from one account in one bank to another account in another bank through direct telecommunication linkages. Eventually, the business and financial community will become one vast network of electronic files with data links carrying information between them.

Thomas J. Watson, Jr., then President of International Business Machines Corporation, foresaw the revolution in banking in 1965:

> In banking . . . the advances of yesterday are merely a faint prologue to the marvels of tomorrow. In our lifetime we may see electronic transactions virtually eliminate the need for cash. Giant computers in banks, with massive memories, will contain individual customer accounts. To draw from or add to his balance, the customer in a store, office, or filling station will do two things: insert an identification into the terminal located there; punch out the transaction figures on the terminal's keyboard. Instantaneously, the amount he punches out will move out of his account and enter another.
>
> Consider this same process repeated thousands, hundreds of thousands, millions of times each day; billions upon billions of dollars changing hands without the use of one pen, one piece of paper, one check, or one green dollar bill. Finally, consider the

extension of such a network of terminals and memories—an extension across city and state lines, spanning our whole country.*

As "checkless banking" approaches, banks face new problems. Instantaneous electronic transactions remove the "float," or checks in circulation which have not been presented for payment. In banking today, the "float" may amount to billions of dollars daily and is an important source of funds for bank lending. If, as a result of the credit card and electronic fund transfers, the consumer buys his purchase out of current income instead of saving up for it, the flow of personal savings into financial institutions will be reduced. Banks will have to find new sources of funds to finance their banking business. No one doubts that banks will discover ways to solve these problems and more than make up for any temporary losses they bring with them. From the point of view of society at large, the most serious question is how to avoid ending up with a bank on every side of every economic transaction, behind depositor, credit card, merchant, doctor, lawyer, Indian chief and everybody else.

Beginning in October, 1971, the cashless and checkless society became a reality in Upper Arlington, Ohio, an upper-middle-class suburb of Columbus, when City National Bank and Trust Company and National BankAmericard Inc. sponsored a six-month experiment in the electronic transfer of funds among consumers, merchants and the bank.

Under the plan, when a purchase was made with Bank-Americard at any one of 50 retailers in two shopping centers by any of the 20,000 residents who were BankAmericard holders, the cardholder's account would be debited and the merchant's account would be credited almost instantaneously, so that no paper money or paper checks changed hands. At the same time the bank installed a "total teller," a 24-hour-a-day, 7-

---

* Thomas J. Watson, Jr., "Man and Machines—the Dynamic Alliance," *Proceedings of the ABA National Automation Conference*, 1965.

day-a-week banking machine, at one of the branches. Customers using the machine could perform their own banking services for themselves, depositing, withdrawing and transferring funds.

This is not a question of waiting for evolution to bring about the revolution. Noting that some 62 million checks a day were currently being written in the United States, the Federal Reserve Board announced in June, 1971, that it had adopted policies and programs aimed at speeding transfers of money through electronic recording rather than through checks, "as a matter of urgency." A special committee on improving the payments mechanism estimated that at least half the checks now written could be replaced by a direct computerized system instead.

While it has no direct logical relationship to the subject of the cashless society, the elimination of stock and bond certificates is another technical innovation entirely consistent with instantaneous electronic transfers of funds without checks, with the replacement of cash money by electronic impulses, and with the replacement of bills and checks and other forms of paper with credit cards and electronic credit. Like gold, like paper money, like the personal or corporate check, the certificate of a stock or bond is a tangible article which in itself is the legal symbol of a financial transaction. The technology exists for replacing it with an electronic transfer of information and a printed-out memorandum, and sound reasons exist for doing so. William J. Casey, Chairman of the Securities & Exchange Commission, told a Senate Investigations Subcommittee that the only way to eliminate the securities thefts which have resulted in losses of millions of dollars was to eliminate stock and bond certificates. It was the inability of some famous old Wall Street brokerage houses to keep up with the job of processing millions of paper stock and bond certificates and dividend and interest checks that led to a "paper crunch" in 1969 and 1970, insolvency for some of the firms and financial disaster for many stockbrokers and their customers.

A typical transaction in the public stock markets requires a seller like John Cade, for example, to send the certificate for 100 shares of American Telephone & Telegraph Company stock which he is selling to his broker. His broker must return Cade's certificate, accompanied by his signed stock power or endorsement with signature guaranteed, to the company or its transfer agent for registration of the transfer, issuance of a new certificate, transmittal of the old and new certificates to the registrar, cancellation of the old certificate, delivery of the new certificate to the buyer's broker and from him to the buyer. Checks go from the buyer to his broker, from the buyer's broker to John Cade's broker and from him back to Cade. If a dividend is declared while the certificate is in transit, the check will most likely come to Cade, and must be forwarded by him to the buyer's broker. A survey estimated that in 1968 this tedious process had been repeated 100 million times—give or take a few million—for shares transferred on the New York Stock Exchange alone.

Traditionalists point out that the stock certificate, like the check, has important uses in its own right, and must be preserved: as evidence of ownership of shares or money; as a statement of stockholder rights; as a courier for restrictions on transferability; and as collateral for loans. The law generally protects a person who buys the share certificate directly from a seller without notice by equating the certificate with the share interest that it evidences. But such a legal analysis is based on the way stocks changed hands long ago and far away, not the way most of them flash from hand to hand, firm to firm and bank to bank through stock exchange ticker tapes today. Few transfers today require a legal vehicle. The certificate follows the legal relationship previously established by a telephone call between brokers in the market. The certificate itself no longer creates the legal relationships.

To eliminate all this "massaging of paper," all this routing and processing and registration of the share certificate, there is an overwhelming demand for eliminating the share certificate itself and replacing it with electronic transfer orders. The elements of the necessary electronic system are already in existence, and the pattern will sound familiar to all who have read this far: a computerized market, a computerized stockholder's register, a wire linking the two and a computer printout that is a permanent memorandum of the transaction.

But a great many people, "little guy" and "big brother" as well, fear that a certificateless society would be full of possibilities of loss of securities without any effective recourse. They do not feel secure unless they can pull open a drawer or a safe deposit box, and finger the extravagantly engraved and colored certificates themselves. One plan for eliminating stock and bond certificates would involve use of a customer's credit card to record and verify all aspects of a trade. The customer would receive all of the usual confirmations and advices and, in addition, if he requested it, a separate nonnegotiable confirmation from the company that he owned the shares. Through his credit card, and this compatible computerized system, all relevant taxable details of the sale or purchase might also be transmitted instantaneously to the Internal Revenue Service to help with automatic preparation of income tax returns.

Securities transactions without using certificates would not be a wholly new innovation, nor would it be limited to private transfers of stocks and bonds. The Federal Reserve System already has a bank entry procedure for transferring Treasury securities. This substitutes magnetic records stored on electronic data processing equipment for engraved certificates deposited at Federal Reserve Banks. This procedure now covers approximately $102 billion par amount, or approximately 43 per cent of the outstanding transferable government securities in the United States.

By another "certificateless" arrangement, the Federal Reserve Bank of New York arranges for transfers of government securities by wire among a number of participating banks. Balances of securities and payments for transfers are settled at the end of each day. In 1969, $248 billion of securities were transferred in 353,000 transactions, or a daily average of $993 million.

The cashless society is intended to improve the quality of life. High on the list of the nuisances, annoyances and superfluous appendages are coins, paper currency, checks and stock and bond certificates. No insuperable technological problems stand in the way of eliminating them. A number of existing legal doctrines do. But laws can change with remarkable swiftness when traditional beliefs and practices which give them vitality disappear and new beliefs and usages replace them. A commitment to the cashless society is a commitment not only to the elimination of cash, the elimination of checks and stock and bond certificates, but also to the elimination of a great deal of dead time now lost from the enjoyment of life itself spent in essentially unnecessary and meaningless paper shuffling.

Without our quite being aware of what was happening, as we have built the cash and carry society in which we live to higher and higher levels of economic development, we have been surrounding ourselves with hoardings in the form of useless paper work that shut out light, air and precious time. In a broad sense, cashlessness should mean shucking off this paper cocoon that we have so unwittingly wrapped around such a large part of our lives.

7.

The Lawlessness of Money

Two gunmen posing as detectives drove up to the house of J. E. Morgan, Jr. on Pamela Lane in West Palm Beach one morning in March, 1971. They bound and gagged his wife Fanny and daughter Shari and locked them in a closet. One of them remained to hold Fanny and Shari as hostages while the other drove Mr. Morgan to The Bank of Palm Beach and Trust Company, of which he was President, and robbed its main vault of about $600,000. Residents of the heavily guarded colony of millionaires asked why police had not contained the robbers' escape by raising the four drawbridges across Lake Worth. It had always been assumed that these would secure the colony from lesser breeds without the law, who might one day advance on them from the west—West Palm Beach. But neither armed guards nor raised drawbridges are enough to guarantee personal security for millionaires any more.

The money stolen hardly mattered. It was insured and replaceable. Replaceable or not, the lure of the money constituted a mortal threat to the personal physical safety of Mr. Morgan and his family and a grim warning to all the other residents of the colony that there is no perfectly secure refuge from crimes against the person for money. Homes in New York and Chicago hardly qualified as secure refuges for those who contemplated fleeing the colony by airplanes now subject to hijacking for cash ransoms.

The spread of costly, illegal and more or less addictive drugs from limited use among impoverished underworld classes abroad, to the minority poor in the United States, and thence to wide use among affluent middle and upper classes in Western countries everywhere has brought another dimension to cash money as a lure to lawlessness and a threat to life. Mayor John V. Lindsay of New York has experienced at first hand the lawlessness of cash as a threat to the rule of law in the city. Describing conditions to the 1970 annual meeting of the American Bar Association in St. Louis, where the situation is at least as serious as in New York, he said, "I hear about it from eight million clients."

"A cab driver in the Bronx complains, 'I'm afraid to drive any more. I don't know whether my next customer will tip me or kill me.' "

"A businessman in Queens despairs: 'They steal from my car. They steal from my store. When will it stop?' "

"An old woman in Brooklyn tells me: 'I'm scared to go to the market at night. Does anyone care?' "

"A mother in Harlem wonders: 'How can I raise my son? The junkies are everywhere.' "

"And on Staten Island they say: 'We moved here because it was safe. Will it stay that way?' "

The mayors of St. Louis, Chicago, Cleveland, Boston, Seattle and Los Angeles, of every large gray metropolis, and of small green suburban towns as well, can testify that they hear similar plaints from their citizens every day. One hundred sixty million Americans live in cities, and in one way or another most of us sense the tragic human implications of this new kind of crime for cash. It costs about $40 a day, or about $14,000 a year, to support a heroin habit. That money generally has to be stolen in cash or merchandise which is immediately salable

112

for cash, or earned in cash from prostitution or gambling. Or by selling heroin for cash by persuading new customers to try the drug and become addicted to it. Calls for stopping the flow of heroin into the country are no more than futile political posturing: thousands of dollars' worth of heroin can be brought in in a tobacco pouch; all the heroin used in the United States for a year could be brought in uncut in two trucks. In 1970, 100,000 vessels came into our ports, 345,000 airplanes and 65,-000,000 automobiles crossed our borders bringing in 225,000,-000 people, past a grand total of 1400 customs officials who were doing all the checking at ports of entry that was done.

More crimes for cash and cashable property, often attended by violence, are committed in the United States every year. The rate of increase in robberies, burglaries, larcenies, muggings, yokings and thefts of all kinds is rapidly accelerating. In 1970, for example, there were 297,000 armed robberies, 870,000 auto thefts, 1,500,000 larcenies of cash or property worth $50 or more and 2,000,000 burglaries of homes and business establishments. Eighty-seven percent of all crimes involved direct thefts of property or cash. Eighty-five percent of these crimes were committed on the streets, and in homes and business establishments of the inner cities by youths 24 years old and younger, a major percentage of whom were addicted to heroin. Only about 18 percent of the burglaries, larcenies and auto thefts, and only 27 percent of the armed robberies were cleared on police books as solved. About 80 percent of these cash-related crimes went unsolved.

Bus drivers in New York City, Washington, D.C. and many other cities carry no cash for fear of holdups, and rides are paid for by exact change or tokens dropped in a fare box. Taxi companies have instituted plans for paying taxi fares with exact change, or by credit cards or in scrip usable for limited purposes. Strident political calls for "law and order" have not stopped rates of crime for cash from continuing to rise.

While less than twenty percent of all crimes for cash are

cleared on police records, an even smaller percentage ever reach prosecution in the criminal courts. Yet processing even this residue of the burgeoning number of crimes for cash is thrusting unprecedented burdens on traditional court and penal systems. Under the weight of these numbers the process of justice in the criminal courts of large cities is breaking down. Organized crime is profiting from the situation to its complete satisfaction. Ask any victim of a crime, or any accused defendant.

The criminal courts have been reduced to institutional cripples stumbling along in patterns of an outworn tradition compiling records of incredible inefficiency. Defendants languish in jail, prosecutors and lawyers multiply continuances and demoralized judges work hours that would shame a retired banker. In 1970, of New York's 14,000 jail inmates, 8000 were unconvicted awaiting trial for many months, in some cases up to two years. They were sleeping three in a cell, one on the floor. Their rage that summer sparked a seven-hour riot in an overcrowded city detention center aptly named "the Tombs." Rages and riots gave rise to retaliation by tear gas, broken windows, fires, hostages and disintegration of order in a facility built to restore order. The system has become almost totally unresponsive to the vital needs of the people. If, at the end, this system results in a delayed conviction, the criminal offender usually does his time in a prison that is a school for crime. He is finally released with nothing more than a free bus ride to the slum he came from. It is almost assured that he will return to a life against the law. He has no other life that he can lead.

The presence of vast amounts of anonymous untraceable cash money in the hands of the public has become the bait which lures the poor, the weak and the criminally inclined into addiction and crime. Cash is a danger both in the hands of the innocent first holder and in the hands of the junkie who robs him of it. At the unprecedented rate crime is increasing, cash

114

money is a threat to the orderly processes of law and to the security of the state itself, notwithstanding ever louder political cries for more law and order, more wiretapping, more crackdowns and other stern measures.

As Mayor Lindsay said, "We are living with fear." Rising crime threatens all that we are, and all that we can be. What difference does it make whether we have a recession, or recover prosperity, if the cash which prosperity brings exposes us to crimes for cash that endanger our health and lives? It does no good to end a war in Indo-China if crimes for cash convert the streets of our cities into combat zones.

The lure of money as cash makes every one of us a target for a crime against our own persons. The more affluent the society we live in, the greater is the danger to our lives. Going without cash ourselves does not make us secure. Innocent bystanders, with nothing but credit cards in their pockets, are often victims when shooting starts during holdups, and many passengers on hijacked airplanes are on "Fly Now, Pay Later" plans.

Use of credit and credit cards involves the user and his money in two- and three-party transactions involving a cardholder, a card issuer, a merchant and often a bank. Unlike a cash transaction, the credit transaction is traceable, revocable, cancellable, limitable and recordable through the credit mechanism, all without the necessity of seeking redress in overburdened courts. There is no gainsaying that credit and credit cards lead to abuses and theft, but such uses and abuses involve a different order of danger to person and property than crime against the person inspired by the bait of money as cash. Overpriced champagne purchased for a B-girl at a Baltimore bar does not involve the same order of physical threat to personal safety as armed robbery or airplane hijacking. A general condition of cashlessness in society would open up the possibility of eliminating all violent crimes against the person except crimes of passion by making them unprofitable, as well as illegal.

115

Purposeful crime directed against person and property is the most striking manifestation of the suffering that the lawlessness of money as cash inflicts on society at large. No less real, and on a much wider scale but less striking in its impact on individuals, is the suffering that unpurposeful conduct of usually well-meaning people, businesses and governments as well are able to visit upon society through the agency of cash money. It is the anonymous and freely transferable characteristics of money as cash, coupled with the weight and power of large sums of it, that magnify ordinary human bumbling and bungling into widespread human suffering.

One of the ways in which the rich differ from the rest of us is their serene conviction that their stewardship of large sums of money is their rightful reward for their own efforts and superior virtue, and has nothing to do with such matters as loopholes in the tax laws, early death of parents, strict enforcement of the laws of succession, an oversupply of avarice or a generous helping of good luck. They also believe that whatever suffering their manipulation of money may inflict on others, they themselves will remain insulated from the suffering they cause. The rest of us do not differ with them on this point because in this, their lawyers usually prove them right.

The personal playthings of young Lammot DuPont Copeland, Jr., the great-great-great-grandson of the founder of the DuPont Company, included newspaper companies, a toy manufacturer, a car wash agency, an Arizona cattle ranch and Massey Junior College, an unaccredited school for attractive young ladies whose chief daytime interests included interior decorating and fashion. A thousand or so of these lovely students were kept at Dinkler Plaza Hotel in downtown Atlanta, and transported to and from their classrooms aboard a fleet of double-decker buses imported from London.

Far from being a wastrel squandering inherited wealth on high living and detaining unaccredited fashion models after school, the Harvard-trained son of the chairman of the world's largest chemical manufacturer, estimated to be worth more than $200 million, seemed a rather sobersided young man who viewed many current happenings with alarm. One fund-raising letter sent out by the World Foundation, of which he was chairman, read: "In an era of rampant dishonesty and rising crime, with creeping Socialism attacking our system of free enterprise, we need to uphold the cause of ethical business more than ever before."

Thus, when he filed one of the biggest personal bankruptcies of all time under Chapter XI of the Federal Bankruptcy Act, showing liabilities of more than $62 million, against assets of "only" $26 million, it came as quite a shock to his more than 100 creditors.

One slim, dark-haired fashion student at Massey was quoted by the *Wall Street Journal* as saying, "They'll have to throw us out on the street. We're sticking together until this thing gets resolved somehow."

If a naive young inheritor sticks to Facel Vegas and polo ponies, his opportunities for inflicting widespread suffering on others are limited. But when the dimensions of his fortune and the thrust of serious intentions unaccompanied by business experience or acumen set him wheeling and dealing in the business world, depriving svelte young fashion students of London bus rides in Atlanta is but the least of the havoc his bumbling can spread through the lawlessness of large sums of money.

Rolls-Royce management gambled on its ability to produce an RV-211 engine for the Lockheed Tri-Star 1011 Airbus by purposely agreeing to a contract price that was far lower than General Electric's and Pratt and Whitney's bids without knowing whether they could produce the engines at the lower price or not. When Rolls lost its gamble by being unable to produce the engine at the bid price, more than 20,000 Rolls-Royce employees in Derbyshire, England, were threatened with job losses. The managing directors, whose overreaching had overwhelmed their business judgment, suffered from no such concerns.

When it came out that more than $3 million had vanished from United California Bank of Basel, former chairman Paul Erdman, who at one time had purchased futures contracts for more than half the world's cocoa, was quoted from his dungeon cell as saying, "It was the bank I was thinking of. Oh, I know now I should have called for audit and reported everything. Instead, I thought of protecting the bank. I turned my head when the books were doctored, hoping to gain time to straighten things out somehow."

According to Mr. Erdman, the first reaction of one of the bank's officers was merely, "You win some and you lose some."

It is never easy to enlist wide sympathy for large operators in cash money who deposit it in secret Swiss bank accounts. But does any theory of private enterprise, free market system or any social requirement for the solitariness and anonymity of movements of money as cash require that unlimited opportunity for such activities, and such losses, necessarily be a part of the system?

Disclosure of foreign funds transfers required on U.S. income tax returns for 1970 and later years evoked little popular protest. The presence of the question seems to raise a *prima facie* presumption of illegal activity, or at least suspicion of it, against those who deal in cash money across national borders by requiring disclosure of foreign money transactions, even though such transactions in themselves would not normally affect the computation of an income tax liability in any way.

The most serious of all aspects of the lawlessness of money is its ability to purchase immunity from its critics. This operates on a relatively limited private scale, but on a massive and widespread public scale. Some describe the political system of the United States today as a plutocracy. Nowhere, at any time in history, has so much money been required to attain positions of influence in government, to remain in them or to influence governmental policy. It is all but impossible for a candidate to win major public office without a private fortune or a commitment to interests which control private fortunes. In California, it is now the practice for a few rich men to form a club to sponsor a candidate financially. After Senator Charles Goodell of New York, who is not a millionaire, was defeated in a three-way contest with liberal Richard Ottinger and conservative James Buckley (who are millionaires), he commented ruefully, "If you have had experience running against one millionaire, you should try running against two millionaires, coming at you from both directions."

Television plays an increasingly important part in political campaigns. The electorate has become accustomed to candidates who spend half a million dollars or more to win a seat in the House of Representatives, and five million or more for a seat in the Senate. To win the Presidency, or even the governorship of a state like New York, costs $10 million or more. The laws on reporting political spending are as full of holes as a net for catching whales only, so accurate figures are impossible to gather. But according to the best estimates a record total of $300,000,000 was spent in the 1968 campaigns, approximately 60 cents per vote cast, also a new record. The anonymity and free transferability of money as cash make the best intended legislation designed to inhibit the buying of elections all but unworkable.

Lawlessness of money has inevitably brought debasement and corruption into public life. Most existing laws intended to prevent the politics of plutocracy, loose as they are, are ignored or treated as meaningless. Yet since World War II, public outrage or even mild reproof to the lawlessness of money in politics seems to have faded from year to year, while the prices paid for winning major office have gone up and up. Unless the trend is reversed, the election of candidates will become more a matter of money than of merit, issues or anything else. The greatest strength of the profit-motivated, private enterprise system that the United States is commonly supposed to enjoy today (subject to the various phases of the President's new economic policy) and under which it grew and prospered in freedom for almost two hundred years, has been its innate capacity to grow, change and manage change by evolving new laws and institutions through peaceful, orderly processes of law.

When vast sums of money are spent to win or keep office for representatives of the people, the representatives do not fairly represent the will of the majority of the constituency, only the will of a majority of money, much of which often comes from beyond the borders of the constituency itself. In this way, money as cash stultifies and may ultimately freeze the essential process of peaceful change through responsive reaction of government to the will and reasonable wishes of the majority of the people. In this sense, the gravest threat of all to the survival of our political system is the social and political lawlessness of money as cash.

Social and political reins have been thrown over unbridled laissez-faire in free markets and in the private enterprise economy everywhere in an increasingly crowded world. But money as cash still remains remarkably free, unchecked, unlicensed, unbridled and untamed. In its movements, it is beyond most statutory and judge-made law, as well as most social, political and economic laws. Without an eyewitness to a specific, narrowly defined tortious crime, unlawful use of money as cash remains all but unchecked by law of any kind.

There is no effective control or limit on the amount of money as cash at large in the world. There is no limit to the amount of credit that can be turned into cash. There are but a few broad and clumsy generalized controls on the expansion and contraction of credit, and they apply only within the economic compartments of separate sovereign nations. Cash money derived from credit and debt sloshes anonymously back and forth from person to person, from bank to corporation, from country to country and back again. No comprehensive limits exist upon the amount of cash circulating among the countries of the world. Far from ameliorating the problem, currency restrictions erected on a country by country basis aggravate overall lawlessness. There is no way of limiting, channeling or selecting the use to which money as cash is put, or the person, corporation or government that puts it to use. Once the cash has been created, there is no way to reduce the amount in circulation without bringing about economic hardships unrelated to the benefits the additional money as cash may have produced.

Cash money, divorced from any question of the credit of its owner and without any commodity backing in gold reserve, is printable in any amount, exportable to almost any place on the globe and usually anonymous and freely spendable by its owner. Floods of cash money, particularly dollars, slosh back and forth across the boundaries of sovereign nations without regard to any conscious policy of each nation, social good, political purpose or human wish. It is available in potentially unlimited amounts for any purpose, good, bad or criminal, or for purposeless bungling. It gives large, often non-human agencies, fictitious persons like corporations, banks and governments, almost unlimited power over people's jobs, food, clothing, shelter, livelihood and freedom, without leaving the people thusly affected any legal, political, judicial or other means of protection or redress.

Up to this point, we have described the lawlessness or carelessness of people and organizations who use money as the agency of their activities. Money itself has appeared to be neutral, passive, without responsibility and removed from blame or punishment for these activities themselves. The only part that money has played is that without the availability of money as cash, the suffering and destruction that these activities of people caused would not have been possible.

But what appears to be an intrinsic passivity, what might

be called the morally neutral aspect of money as cash, is an illusion.

In the tragedy of the common described in the introduction, the villagers imposed a $10 fee for permitting cows to graze on the village green. In the self-contained economy of the village, this restricted grazing sufficiently to preserve the common of pasture, at least until the rich New Yorkers came along. To the New Yorkers who grazed cows on the common for the picturesqueness and serenity they contributed to the scene, the $10 fee imposed no inhibitions on grazing, but instead served as a license to use the common for this purpose. Both the villagers who imposed the $10 fee and the rich New Yorkers who happily paid it had the best of intentions. Neither had any malevolent intent. All loved the village and its green. But the use of money, or rather the unregulated, uncoordinated relationship between money as cash and the people and resources involved in the situation, was what in the end destroyed the village green.

People's appetites are fed by money that they obtain by performing services or making or growing things for others, by exploiting natural resources, by theft or other crime, by gambling, luck or inheritance, by receiving Social Security, welfare, insurance payments or charity or by begging. Usually, they think they do not have enough and demand more. National governments and banks, among other institutions, secure and help satisfy these demands for money. There is no evidence that people's appetite for money has yet reached general satiety, although individuals who are satisfied with what they have can be found in all societies. By Western standards, the more such individuals there are, the more backward the civilization seems. Since money ceased to be gold or other commodity money, things of which the finite globe contained only a finite amount, tides of money have been created to satisfy these seemingly inexhaustible appetites.

No human institution has yet been invented that is capable of effectively limiting or controlling the amount of commodity money that can be created to satisfy these inexhaustible appetites. And once cash money has been created, there is no way to cut it back or channel the direction in which it flows. The threat of creating unlimited demands upon the resources of a small finite globe, through printing money in response to the rising tide of human appetites, is no longer a paper tiger. It is a real threat, perhaps all the more so because being essentially a thing of paper, it is easy for people to discount it.

If you inquired among your friends concerning their most pressing personal problems and fears, you would not be likely to hear that the danger of too much money was one that kept them awake nights worrying. Nor would the head of a private business enterprise, bank, insurance company, university, hospital, opera house, charitable foundation, national governmental agency, public or private utility, the governor of a state, mayor of a city or the head of any international agency normally concede that too much money was among his pressing problems, or that uncheckable growth was a danger instead of a desirable goal. Whatever their other differences, all would agree that too much money was no threat to them. To them all, the problem is not uncheckable growth; the real problem is checks on growth. Their response is the same as that of you and your friends: the real threat is not enough money, not too much.

All people and all organizational power centers seek to obtain more money. None considers too much money a threat to himself or his organization. The collective demand for more money shows up in the broad consensus in favor of unlimited growth. There is no constituency in favor of less money for itself. Even advocates of a zero growth rate for the economy at large are busily soliciting large sums of money to advance their cause.

For example, some say the problem is not too much money, but rather the population explosion. Others say it is the unfulfilled demands on finite world resources created by rising levels of expectation of the vast majority of human beings already here. Some say it is rising levels of technology which exploit with ever increasing thoroughness and skill ever greater amounts of finite resources like coal, oil, metals and raw land. Some say it is war, which widely lays waste fertile areas of the world, brings on armament races among nations and exploits resources through manufacture of armaments which fill no genuine human needs. Some say it is the pollution of the earth's water, land and air.

All of these things, separately and together, are, of course, threats to our global future. Each of them has been identified as a threat. There is common agreement on the general idea that these threats must be curbed. Each has its bibliography of doom predictors, its counterbibliography of reassurances that the threat is not quite as serious as the original bibliography has held. Each has its militant non-tax-exempt organizations to rouse the unworried. Each has its non-militant tax-exempt foundations to embalm the problem far from the political arena in multi-volume scissors-and-paste jobs which balance off alarums from the bibliographies with reassurances from the counter-bibliographies, draining both of significant force.

These numbing residues of self-cancelling reports consume a great many trees in paper and shelving. And yet, the targets of attacks contribute profits from extractive activity to help finance the attackers. Standard Oil Company of New Jersey's recent advertising included heartwarming accounts of a happy family that lived next door to a refinery and really hardly noticed it at all. And the photograph on the cover of Standard Oil Company of California's 1971 Annual Report shows a pair of game birds on the wing over blue water in front of a catalytic cracking plant. All the scene lacked was a mess of robins' nests cradled among all the glittering pipes and valves.

Columbus disproved the belief that the world was flat. But the idea that the globe was infinite in size beyond horizons that always receded as one sailed or flew toward them, remained strongly in our collective consciousness until we saw the first moonwalk on television. In that instant, the image of a sphere that looked like a blue-brown tennis ball, alone in a limitless black void, dissolved our old illusion that the earth was all but infinite in size and resources.

No one could fail to see that the globe we had until then thought of as a metaphor for practical infinity was a rather disturbingly small, finite and delicate object in a dangerous, empty and apparently uncaring void. The earth was, of course, larger than the astronauts' spaceship, but in essence ours differed from theirs only in degrees of fragility and scale. And in one other important respect: once they used up their oxygen, water, food and fuel, the astronauts had our earth to come back to; when the rest of us have used up our oxygen, water, food and fuel, our trip is over. There is no earth for us to come back to, and none of these things are on the moon.

Conventional economic wisdom holds that a nation's gross national product must increase continually and multiply the choices open to consumers. As production grows, prosperity grows, population grows and human expectations rise. Natural resources are taken out; open land is subdivided and developed, and clean air and waters are polluted. Everything continually grows. As the "frontier" disappears and populations crowd closer together, areas for the exercise of human political freedom narrow in the interests of social order; the resources available for satisfying rising expectations are consumed, and tides of human expectation overwhelm all resources. Political economists traditionally hold that economic growth is not only a good thing, but the chief objective of all national effort in peacetime.

Late in 1970, the gross national product of the United States reached an annual rate of one trillion dollars. President Nixon dedicated a new "gross national product" clock and proudly noted that the United States had become the first trillion-dollar economy in the world. Administration economists forecast a gross national product of one trillion sixty-five billion for 1971. This rate meant that in that single year the United States would produce more goods and services than it had in the first 85 years of its history from 1789 to around 1875. As economists were proud to point out, the pace of this growth is quickening. Although it took almost 200 years for the United States to arrive at its first trillion-dollar economy, economists estimate that it will take only about ten more years—the decade of the 1970s—for it to reach the second trillion. At this rate, the United States "produces" half as much as all the rest of the world combined. Never has any nation or group of nations operated on such a scale, or at such a quickening pace. No other country in history can match the performance of the United States in gross "growth," as measured by conventional indices.

In his 1971 State of the Union message, President Nixon predicted that in the next ten years the United States would increase its wealth by more than 50 per cent. His budget message called for spending $229.2 billion in the fiscal year beginning July 1, 1971, a budget twice the size of the budget of as recently as six years before. It was purposefully budgeted to fall short of revenues by $11.6 billion and did in fact fall short by nearly $30 billion. In the 1970–1971 fiscal year, a forecast surplus of $1.3 billion had turned out to be a deficit of about $18 billion.

Traditional concepts of governmental budgeting, at least under Republicans, had called for a balanced budget, which suggests to the lay mind an element of equilibrium and a possible checkrein on otherwise unchecked growth. But in 1971, this traditional concept was abandoned in favor of the economists' "full employment budget," which compares government outlays not with estimates of actual revenues from taxes and so forth, but with revenues that theoretically would be collected if the economy were operating at full employment, even though it is not.

With this commitment to the full employment budget, it became obvious that even Republicans had abandoned their traditional commitment to the equilibrium suggested by the balanced budget concept, and had committed themselves to an ever faster rate of economic growth. The political alternative to this was not less growth, or no growth. On the contrary, the Chairman of the Economic Committee of the Democratic Policy Council, Mr. Gardner Ackley, who had served as chairman of the Council of Economic Advisers in Democratic administrations, expressed the official alternative view when he sharply criticized the President for failing to budget a large enough deficit on a "full employment budget" basis to bring about still greater growth. No political economist of prominence in either party was heard to lay a plague on both political houses for their apparent failure to deal seriously with the idea of a budget for zero growth.

With both political factions committed either to large amounts of deficit spending for growth, or else still larger amounts of deficit spending for still greater growth, the ineffectiveness of efforts to manage the economy demonstrated by actual deficits which surpassed budgeted deficits by several multiples of billions evoked little comment, still less criticism and no discernible humility on the part of economic managers.

Stories about the condition of the economy have come to dominate the front pages of serious newspapers by the amount of linage they occupy, if not by the spell they cast upon the attention of the general reader. Economic managers push the prime rate and the rediscount rate up and down; increase and contract the rate of growth of the money supply; accelerate and decelerate tax and tax withholding rates, and depreciation and depletion schedules; enact and cancel investment credits, and encourage and discourage foreign activities with penalties for foreign tax shelters, and extra profits for DISCS. As periodic statistical series are published—rates of gross national product, consumer price index, housing starts, unemployment rates, personal bankruptcies and so forth—learned economic commentaries on the significance of the figures often tend to cancel each other out.

Few things could be more obvious to anyone who plods through all this economic news over an extended period of time than the fact that only the loosest sort of correlation exists between economic policy actions taken, the promised results of those actions and the results of those actions in actuality within finite periods of time. Few things should be of more concern.

Even if, for example, a political consensus existed that a no growth economy were desirable for the United States, nothing in recent economic history suggests that tools of economic management exist which would translate such a policy into actions which would bring about this result within any predictable span of time. The conclusion is unavoidable that no really effective way to control the creation of flood tides of money in the United States economy exists at the present time, even if the will to exercise such control were present, as, of course, it is not.

Assumptions about growth have been fundamental to our idea of human progress: growth in population, production and consumption. But we have learned that the earth is finite and fragile. Believing that the curve of economic growth can go upward forever at an accelerating rate is the current equivalent of believing in a flat earth. The dream of a world existing at the high levels of consumption the United States now enjoys probably can never be fulfilled for the three and three-quarter billion people who are now alive, much less for the six billion or so expected by the year 2000. If all enjoyed the present American standard of living, the earth could probably support only about 500 million people.

The United States economy serves as the prime case history of the consequences of uncheckable growth. More such growth is a threat not only to the United States herself but to all other countries. It serves to remind them that their best defense against United States policy is to follow the policy of trying to stimulate economic growth of their own at a pace which will match or even out-pace that of the United States. The usual, and politically least painful, method of stimulating national growth is to follow the same kind of policies the United States has pursued. One of the most important of these policies is putting large additional amounts of money in circulation through governmental budgetary deficits and other tax and fiscal policies based on creation of ever increasing amounts of fiat money.

While each separate national state may be regarded as occupying a separate compartment on spaceship earth, the compartments are not airtight, water tight or money tight. Far from it. Water, air, money, people and other things flow between, with more or less freedom, both legally and illegally. In the most fundamental respects all the people in one nation state's compartment are dependent upon responsible action by the occupants of the other major compartments for their ultimate survival.

Within short time spans, at least, each national state can create almost as much money and credit for use within its own borders as its government decrees. Policies which call for creation of less money are unpopular, so governments generally create more. Within each national compartment, the national money is accepted because it is accepted. Money from some of the other major compartments is also accepted in other compartments, and represents a call on resources located elsewhere in the spaceship, beyond the issuer's own compartment. Once the money is issued and begins to circulate, there is no practical way to limit the amount of credit that can be based on it, which in turn makes possible the creation of still more money. As it circulates with the freedom and anonymity of cash, it adds one more to the infinite number of demands upon the finite resources of the global spaceship. It continues to be accepted because it is accepted. Eurodollars and other forms of paper money are created by hundreds of agencies in amounts that are all but infinite, while the resources of spaceship earth remain finite. No one knows whether the money claims that people will accept and honor against the resources of the earth now exceed the sum total of resources that exist. Will the money be repudiated before the resources are all gone? Auction prices at the end could reach fantastic levels.

Sometimes, of course, national money is devalued or, what amounts to the same thing, repudiated by exchange controls, taxes or tariffs. Then it is not accepted because it is not accepted. Yet the person who gave value in his labor, property or talent, in exchange for the money, feels as if he has been robbed when he learns that the money he labored for will buy nothing at the auction, and for all practical purposes is worthless. He has been cheated of his effort, labor and talent, with nothing to show for it. His sense of injustice is strong. He is ready to use revolutionary or criminal means to take back what he gave from the person he thinks took it from him. Though repudiation of the money might save the resources of the spaceship from total exhaustion, the mutiny of its crew in anger is also a serious threat to its stability and survival.

In the United States, the traditional reasons for continuing and quickening growth are said to be an expanding labor force, heavy capital investment and a steady rise in the productivity of labor and capital through technology and innovation. This answer seems to satisfy most political economists. Few have remarked that in recent years our expanding labor force has in fact resulted in higher rates of unemployment with many discouraged jobseekers dropping out of the job market, that there has been a decline in capital investment except under governmental stimulus of tax advantages such as investment credits or accelerated depreciation schedules and that the productivity of labor has flattened out and even declined as wage rates have soared. Experts who are content with traditional references to advanced technology, knowhow and advanced forms of industrial organization as explanations for the extraordinary growth in United States gross national product seem to have ignored the real

130

world lately, where the principal impetus to the growth rate seems to be the relatively unchecked creation of a widely acceptable money by governmental action. Advocacy of a zero growth rate for the United States is a position that would probably win fewer votes for candidates, tenured faculty appointments or seats on the Council of Economic Advisers, than a campaign for prevention of cruelty to the diamondback rattlesnake. The doctrine of unlimited growth remains an expedient escape hatch from hard thought about allocation of stringently limited natural resources to satisfy potentially unlimited human wants.

Unlimited floods of paper money as cash buy up scarce medical facilities, scarce land, scarce food, scarce houses and scarce labor. For the mass of mankind, both economic recession and economic inflation reduce living standards, cause unemployment, throw employees in civil-service type jobs off the rungs of their ladders onto unemployment rolls and leave the general run of mankind very little they can do about it on their own. These floods of money are created in unknown, unlimited amounts by lenders, borrowers, banks, national governments, international agencies as loans and special drawing rights, issuers of securities and miners of silver and gold. Enormous sums are churned out by Federal Reserve open-market operations and by the presses of counterfeiters.

The absolute freedom and anonymity of money as cash to pursue earth's finite resources through the doctrine of continuous growth is infinite. No effective form of social control upon these demands of money as cash exists in the political system of any country or international agency.

The economic structures of national states determine how resources, which are finite, are used to supply the needs and wants of their people. These economic structures, at least in the private initiative, free-enterprise economies of Western countries, operate on people, and people operate within these economic structures largely by the use of money. But there is no absolute limitation on the total amount of money which will be accepted because it is accepted. Nor is there any corresponding level of the amount of money which will not be accepted because it is not accepted. Demands and expectations of people are, in the aggregate, unlimited and infinite. By the creation of unlimited amounts of money, and by increasing the velocity with which they use the money, people obviously can create more money and more demands. They place unfulfillable demands on the limited resources of their own compartment of spaceship earth. Reaching out, they place infinite demands on the resources of all the other compartments without concern for leaving a fair share of the resources for all.

Even if the occupants of one compartment should reach a majority consensus that it was wrong for them to use up the limited resources of their own and all other compartments in a generation or two, there would be no way the majority view could be brought to bear on the aggregate amount of cash money freely available alike to majority and minority occupants of the compartment. Nor would the consensus in one compartment necessarily have any effect upon the money aggregates in another compartment, or all other compartments.

Within limited frames of reference of less than global size, within each state compartment from time to time, growth may be desirable, or no growth, shrinkage or a state of equilibrium may be desirable. Too much money, the uncheckable growth of cash money, poses the threat that regardless of which policy may be most desirable for most people, considering the welfare of all compartments, regardless of the fact that the passengers of one compartment may wish to follow a different policy, the nature of money as cash makes it impossible for any to follow the policy that is best for all, except the generally accepted policy of conventional economic wisdom: quickening, uncheckable growth. When this policy is followed by the major economy at the center of the whole system, it is imposed on all the others. The end result of such a policy may be the exhaustion of all earth's resources in a few generations. But conventional wisdom still holds that money and more money for capital investment is a positive good. Even if too much money were recognized to be a threat, no effective means of dealing with the threat on a worldwide basis exists today. As political economists would put it, if they were to admit that there was a threat at all, they would say that there is no macroeconomic answer to the threat.

One way to begin to approach the problem of protecting the earth from unwitting destruction by the unlimited sums of cash that are developing and destroying it, is to replace the cash-and-carry society with new machinery for the rational creation of monetary capital resources on a global basis. This would be the introduction of a cashless society. The structure of a cashless society would place the creation and reduction of monetary aggregates under a system of international control that would increase, reduce, allocate and channel monetary resources on a worldwide basis. The specter of so much power in an international organization, disturbing as it may be, is still less alarming than the threat of uncheckable growth we face now, with no calm voice from Houston on the radio with warnings and contingency plans to tell us when enough is finally enough.

The idea that all money is and must remain money as cash is only an illusion that has a tenacious grip on our collective minds because of our long conditioning by the history of gold, silver and paper currency commodity money. That illusion can be dispelled by an understanding of the reality of money today as essentially credit and debt. The illusion of money as intrinsically cash would not matter so much, if it did not stand in the way of urgently needed social reforms: the elimination of cash from circulation in society.

It is not easy to think of another single measure of social and economic change that holds out so much promise for the safety of our persons, the survival of our cities, the security of the legal order of the state and the preservation of the resources of the finite globe for an unlimited number of generations yet to come.

8.

The Illusion of Money
as Cash

What is meant by the idea that money is cash? And what, then, is meant by the illusion of money as cash? The traditional four-tier definition of money in functional terms holds that it is a medium of exchange, a measure of value, a medium for deferred payments, and a store of value.

As a medium of exchange, it eliminates the need for clumsy barter; as a unit of value, it provides common terms for denominating the value of different things like apples, oranges and innumerable other commodities, services and other things; as a medium for deferred payments, money make it possible for the two sides in a barter transaction to pay each other at different times and places—without it apples which ripen in Oregon in the fall could not be used to purchase Florida oranges in January; as a store of value, money is a commodity like gold, silver or cigarettes, which can be traded or hoarded for future satisfactions.

Sometimes money ceases to have one or another of these characteristics. For example, during the period of price inflation in Germany after World War I, paper marks continued to be handed around, and thus served as the medium of exchange. But at the same time, in many transactions price quotations were made in terms of the dollar, which thus served as the measure of value: the amount of dollars agreed upon for the transaction was related to the quantity of marks which were actually paid by reference to the daily (or hourly!) quotation for the mark in terms of dollars on the foreign exchange market. The mark no longer served as the unit of value, although it remained the medium of exchange. One tier of the four-tier money sandwich had been stripped away.

Generally speaking, as used in any of its four functions, money may take tangible or intangible form. Its tangible form may be a pile of gold or silver coins, a roll of quarters, a stack of poker chips, a package of cigarettes, a $10 Federal Reserve note or a bale of them. It is money we think of as cash, money with a tangible shape, a specific commodity or paper bearing the printed legend of a government. Its intangible form may be an entry posted in an accountant's journal or ledger, a balance in a checkbook, a computer printout of a monthly statement or an impulse remembered by the selenium flake of a transistor's memory; it is credit and debt, expressed in one form or another.

Cash money on the one hand, and credit and debt money on the other, have four other significant characteristics in common: both cash money and credit money are homogeneous, malleable, durable and portable. Homogeneous so that bargains expressed in such money are certain in content; malleable so that a given block or checking account is divisible into equal parts for circulation and making change; durable so that it can function over long periods of time as a store of value and a means of making deferred payments, and portable so that the value of a unit in weight and volume is high and it can be moved from place to place with relative ease. These were once said to be the essential characteristics of coin money. But paper money, and checking account and credit money as well, have these characteristics to a higher degree than coin money.

Both coin and paper money on the one hand, and credit money on the other, are in the nature of a promise by the government issuing it, if it is coin or paper currency, or by the private person or firm which issues a check, that the sum of money stated will be accepted wherever the writ of the issuer's government's courts runs. Price and wage controls drive home the point that the government may see to it that a fixed amount of goods or services shall be surrendered for a fixed sum of the government's money. Coin, paper and credit money all represent an absolute call on another person's assets or services exercisable at any time and place, for any purpose, without any qualification or time limit. The government has thus invested its coin of the realm with attributes of credible authority and power.

All conventional descriptions assume that all tangible forms of money are automatically and properly interchangeable with all intangible forms, and that all intangible forms are freely exchangeable for all tangible forms. All forms that money takes, tangible and intangible, cash commodity money as well as credit and debt money (which may never have existed as a commodity and never will), are collected under the umbrella of the single word money. It would be quite simple, particularly under a system of wage and price controls, for a government to coin or legend cash money and place it in the hands of the public (or for large private financial interests, through a pyramiding of loans) to create more than enough money to purchase all goods and services anywhere offered for sale. This is where the threat of the lawlessness of money arises.

Two further characteristics are assumed to be inherent qualities of all money. First, it is solitary: one man's money is as good as another's. It is as good in the hands of an honest man as it is in the hands of a thief. Second, it is anonymous: it is freely spendable for any purpose at any time or never, and if he is careful about his fingerprints, it carries with it no trace of any previous holder nor any hint of the purpose for which he used it.

These two characteristics are obvious enough when they are ascribed to commodity money like coins of silver and gold.

These characteristics likewise appear to be intrinsic to paper money stamped with the legend of its issuer.

But in terms of volumes, most money today is credit and debt money, not cash and currency money. It rarely if ever changes from its intangible form into its tangible form. By volume, commodity cash money is to credit and debt money as a one-inch blade of ice at the exposed tip of an iceberg is to the volume of all the rest of the iceberg.

Unlike commodity and currency money, credit and debt money is not intrinsically solitary and anonymous. Two and three parties and a separate written record are required every time such money is created or transferred: a depositor, a bank and a check, or a lender, a borrower and a promissory note. The identity and credit rating, or the size of deposit, of the person issuing the check or note is a vital piece of information, not irrelevant as it is when gold, silver or a dollar bill is passed in payment of an obligation.

Two quite different things, money as cash on the one hand, money as credit and debt on the other, are thus subsumed under the single word money, and the word money is conventionally used without discrimination to mean these two quite different things. As a result, by far the most important form of money used in society today, credit and debt money, is automatically assumed to have the same intrinsic attributes of solitariness, anonymity and unrestricted transferability of the vastly less important old-time commodity money. The phrases *cash money* and *money as cash* are used in this chapter and elsewhere in this book to refer to tangible money, which has the inherent characteristics of solitary operation and anonymity, to distinguish it from credit money, which has neither of these characteristics.

Cash money represents a form of absolute freedom and absolute license. Anyone who has a stock of cash money can use it to buy anything he wants or pay for anything he wishes to have done at any time and place in any country he wishes, regardless of whether it is lawful or socially desirable. For such money, there is a price at which almost anything lawful or unlawful can be bought or paid for, or sanction avoided or delayed. A thief can use the cash he steals to pay a lawyer for appealing his conviction. Freedom from reprisal can be purchased by cash bribes. The greater the stock of cash money, the greater the license, the more momentous the potential consequences and the more striking the absence of effective social control over such license. There is no limit to the extent of destruction that a sufficiently large stock of cash money could purchase from a globe whose resources are finite. Sanctions against illegal or antisocial use of cash in a democratic society become less potent as its owner's stock of it increases. It is insistence on assigning all the attributes of cash money to credit and debt money that raises the lawlessness of money to the level of the threat to society that it is.

Most of what passes for money today in our credit card, checking account, and computer-linked economy is no more tangible than an electronic impulse coursing through a wire. What is the cash value of an electronic pulse that activates the printout of a transfer of $1,000,000 of Federal funds across the country? John Cade and most of us still think of all money as cash. We say cash is "real" money. Real money is cash. It is not real money if it is not cash, cash on the barrelhead. Nothing could be further from the truth.

How did the illusion that the only real money is cash money gain such a powerful grip on our minds? If it is true that nearly all of what we really use for money today lacks the two essential characteristics of cash, does it really matter whether we go on thinking of it as cash or not? Is it better, on the whole, that we do?

When we say that we think of "real" money as cash, we think of the coins we use for small change, copper pennies, nickel five-cent pieces and silver-colored dimes, quarters and half-dollars. Silver dollars have disappeared, even in Nevada. U.S. coins in circulation do not add up to very much in total; they are probably less than one-thirteenth of the total supply of cash. The metal in all these coins is worth far less than their face value so they are called "token money." Children think this kind of money is important. Others have less excuse.

Whatever the reasons, of all the beliefs we hold about money in the present age, the belief in all money as cash is probably the one that is most widely held in all forms of consciousness. It is deeply rooted, persistent, tenacious and false. We go on using and thinking about all money today as if it were still essentially the same commodity for barter that it was in the past. Time and change have cut away the truth of the matter from under the belief, but the illusion persists. A look at the way people used and thought about money through past ages shows how different it was from the way we live with money now.

The first primitive money system was, of course, barter. Currency was anything a man could eat, wear, drink, build with, ride or smoke. Cattle were a desirable commodity for trade, and for money, because they supplied everything: meat, milk, hide, bone and transportation. The words "capital," "chattel" and "pecuniary" are all derived from words for cattle.

In 13th century China, under Kublai Khan, the first paper currency was printed on paper made from the bark of trees. Salt was scarce, easy to carry and divide, and valuable as a food preservative and condiment. Wages were paid to Roman soldiers in salt, and African slaves sold for a weight of it. A free man who was the "salt of the earth" might own a slave not "worth his salt." The Roman word was "sal," and what John Cade and the rest of us work for today is a "salary." We are called employees, not soldiers or slaves. Our salary is a debt of our employer and a credit to our bank account; it is not a cash commodity like salt.

Hundreds of different objects have served at one time or another as money, including such things as slaves, gun powder and the jawbones of pigs. The heaviest money ever used was the stone money of Yap consisting of large stones twelve feet across and weighing five tons. The lightest was the feather money of the New Hebrides. Woodpecker scalps, elephant tail bristles, the teeth of porpoises, whales and tigers, tobacco, leather, hides, birds, olive oil, beer and spirits, wampum, beads and shells, huge rocks, chewing gum and cigarette butts have all served as money. In Borneo, during the 19th century, skulls were the monetary standard, and pigs and palm nuts were the medium of exchange. The number of palm nuts and pigs exchanged for any one other thing depended on how it compared in value to a human skull.

Herodotus tells us that King Croesus of Lydia (560–546 B.C.) invented coinage by stamping his royal image on coins of uniform size and value. They were made of gold, silver and electrum, an alloy of gold and silver which was also known as "white gold." Sovereigns of consequence ever since have imprinted their symbols on the coins and paper that passed as their money. Traditional definitions of money begin with "metal, as gold, silver or copper, coined or stamped, and issued as a medium of exchange." All of these things were, and are, of course, cash money.

Through the classical eras and from medieval times to the present, coinages of gold and silver, supplemented at various times and places by coinages of copper, bronze and lead, represented money to most of the world's people. The state or the sovereign, or an agency of the state, would stamp a specified number of ounces of such metal into coin form and impress the seal of the state on the metal to represent weight and authenticity. The issuer often milled the edges of the coins so that the absence of milled edges would warn of light weight, counterfeiting, fraud or debasement.

This kind of money existed for a long stretch of history without arousing any general suspicion that money was not, and need not necessarily be, all cash.

Professors of economics introduce beginning students to the idea of money as credit by means of an old story which tends to reinforce the illusion that the true nature of all money is cash: gold bullion stored in goldsmiths' vaults. According to a sacred parable of the canons of economics, modern banking evolved out of the activities of the guild of London goldsmiths who were experts in assaying, refining and trading gold bullion and coin. Incorporated in 1327 under the mark of the leopard's head, by the end of the 17th century, the guild of goldsmiths had come to dominate the moneylending business in London.

The merchants of the city traditionally deposited their gold bullion in the government's mint for safety, but in 1640 Charles I, unable to persuade Parliament to vote him the money he needed to support his army, seized 200,000 pounds sterling of the merchants' gold bullion from the mint. After this unfortunate experience with governmental "protection" of their cash, the merchants decided not to entrust their gold bullion and coin to the government, but to the goldsmiths, who were after all, private merchants themselves with strongrooms of their own.

The moral of the parable is not supposed to be that students should be suspicious of the government where money matters are concerned; the reference to King Charles I is intended merely to lend a little color and verisimilitude. Of course a surprising number of "C" students of economics whose minds begin to wander after taking the point to be mistrust of government eventually become rather successful capitalists. Their professors who move on to more abstruse points fully trusting the government in economic matters rarely do as well.

The goldsmiths issued "notes accountable," in acknowledgment of the merchants' deposits, each "note accountable" being equivalent to a specific sum of gold bullion. These gradually came to be accepted as money. As time went on, of course, the goldsmiths realized that their vaults were not like a cloakroom whose outstanding "notes accountable" resembled coat checks, because gold bullion was not like a coat; there was no need to return the same bullion deposit to the same merchant who had checked it. Furthermore, unlike theater patrons who checked their cloaks, the merchants never demanded back all of their gold at exactly the same time.

The goldsmiths came to realize that there was nothing to stop them from issuing notes accountable that were not specifically related to any specific gold bullion deposits, but were simply a promise to pay a given sum of bullion, or money, on demand, to the merchant who presented the note accountable. It became clear, and then obvious, that there always was and always would be a substantial balance of gold in the strong room to cover all notes accountable as they were presented. So the goldsmiths found a new way to make money. They used some of the gold entrusted to them for safekeeping to expand the money-lending side of their business. All banking since that time is said to be based on these practices of the London Guild of Goldsmiths.

While one hundred per cent reserves are necessary if the bank is to be liquidated immediately and all depositors paid off in full, one hundred per cent reserves are not at all necessary if the bank is a "going concern." New deposits more than cover all withdrawals. In most banks, only a small amount of ready money, perhaps two per cent or less of total deposits, is normally needed in the form of immediately available cash to pay off depositors upon demand. If a depositor should complain that his banker does not have enough cash on hand to pay him (and other depositors) at the same time, the banker, like one of the goldsmiths, might reply, "Your money is safe. If you don't like my way of doing business, withdraw your funds and deposit them elsewhere."

By using fractional reserves of as little as two per cent to support new loans, the goldsmiths thus were able to create new capital, provide for the expansion of the merchants' business and increase their own profits. In practical effect, the goldsmiths were able to create "additional" money without having additional gold bullion or coins in stock. This is regarded as the basic principle of modern commercial banking, of modern international banking and indeed, of all banking.

As time passed, the issuing of "notes accountable" and other types of promissory and bank notes that passed from hand to hand as money, was taken over from the goldsmiths or their counterparts, as well as from the private bankers, by the national government in Great Britain and in most other countries as well. The credit of the national government was substituted for the credit of individual bankers. But most of the everyday lending and credit functions remained in the hands of the banks, finance and loan companies and other private commercial institutions.

The curious effect of teaching students of economics national reserve banking by the parable of the London goldsmiths is to reinforce the illusion that all money, including paper money and deposit accounts, is cash, and has and must necessarily have all of the characteristics of cash: gold, silver, salt, wampum or palm nuts. The idea that money is credit, not cash, that the notes of the goldsmiths were the thing that had to be trusted, not the gold in their vaults, and that the goldsmiths' notes were more to be trusted than the government's vaults are points that the parable obscures.

The image of the gold bullion being moved from the royal mint to the vaults of the goldsmiths dovetails smoothly into the image of the gold being moved back into the custody of national governments. This in turn dissolves into the image of all national currencies under one system of automatic international control: the classical gold standard.

In theory, the nineteenth century gold standard was an inter-

national system which regulated and controlled all national currencies entirely independently of the control of any single
national government or other human agency. This international
system neatly paralleled the operation of the "invisible hand" of
the free market which Adam Smith had described in *The
Wealth of Nations*. According to Adam Smith, every individual's
free pursuit of his own economic interests would result in promoting the best interests of society at large, provided that
markets were free. The gold standard seemed to be an inevitable
corollary to his view that society at large in its economic organization was built around unfettered flows of cash money from
nation to nation through free trade in free markets.

Extraordinary as it seems today, it was said that under the
classic gold standard there was no central governmental control
or regulation of money. Gold was of right money at a fixed price
for a unit of value. Units of national money were defined in units
of gold, and gold was given a fixed price in national money.
Non-gold national money was readily convertible into gold. The
money of any gold standard country, through melting, redemption, free export and import, free coinage and free purchase of
gold, was readily convertible at a fixed price into the money of
any other country. The price of gold in national money was, in
theory, related to domestic price and interest levels so there was
no incentive to convert non-gold money into gold and sell it for
a profit. Anyone who preferred gold as a commodity to non-gold
money—paper money, check money, bank note money or silver
coin—could convert the paper to gold if he wished. Gold could
readily be obtained for payment in international transactions.
The requirement of convertibility set a limit on the creation of
non-gold money by national governments and banking agencies.
It contributed mightily to everyone's belief that all money had
the same intrinsic value as the gold behind it, wholly independently of what the money might be used for and who owned it.

The automatic operation of the gold standard system could
inflict terrible hardships on a country's economic and political

144

life. If one country, the United States for example, exported a large amount of gold, its supply of money and its price level would automatically go down. This could bring on a "panic" or depression, while theoretically another country, at the same time, would necessarily be enjoying a "boom." The system as a whole thus remained in equilibrium.

Contrary to common belief, the gold standard was not anciently ordained and sanctioned like a rule of private international law, nor did it have a long history in world monetary organization. Its era was short—from about 1816 to 1914—and it rested basically on the ability of The Bank of England to keep sterling convertible into gold, and thus to maintain confidence in the soundness of British currency.

World War I destroyed the system. Looking back on it, John Maynard Keynes wrote in *The Economic Consequences of the Peace:* "Very few of us realize with conviction the intensely unusual, unstable, complicated, unreliable, temporary nature of the economic organization by which Western Europe has lived for the last half century." *

W. M. Scammell wrote that "there can be no doubt that the international gold standard, as it evolved in the 19th century, provided the growing industrial world with the most efficient system of adjustment for balance of payments which it was ever to have, either by accident or by conscious planning." †

The conventional wisdom of economics is that the effective operation of the classic gold standard is a good illustration of the automatic working of an economic institution according to the economic laws laid down by Adam Smith without conscious human intervention. According to the conventional analysis, no such intervention by human wills would have been necessary, desirable, or effective.

---

* J. M. Keynes, *The Economic Consequences of the Peace.* London: Macmillan, 1919.
† W. M. Scammell, "The Working of the Gold Standard," *Yorkshire Bulletin of Economic and Social Research,* May 1965, quoted in Anthony Harrison, *The Framework of Economic Activity,* St. Martin's Press, 1967.

But Elliot Janeway scotched this myth in *The Economics of Crisis,* when he wrote:

> The old gold standard was never self-adjusting; and gold had never, in theory or in practice, embodied any intrinsically immutable value as a benchmark for all other values—the old gold standard was managed, but it was managed by men like Morgan. Above all, it was managed by The Bank of England, then very much a private organization. The Morgans of the world's financial centers achieved what no public agency, national or international, could have achieved at that time: a functioning system of international financial relationships that operate for the public on the basis of private relationships.

Quiet pragmatic intervention and management by powerful human forces like J. P. Morgan and The Bank of England did not fit neatly into Adam Smith's formulations, nor academic economists' equations. So the fact of the matter is all but unanimously ignored, except for occasional exclamations of astonishment at how well the system worked by such perceptive observers as Keynes and Scammell.

The point is raised and emphasized here because the efficient operation of the gold standard under quiet pragmatic intervention and management of powerful human forces in more than one country, with Britain and the United States at the center of the system, serves as a distant precedent for a future system of international management and control of the world's money without gold backing under the cashless society.

The idea of all money as cash, and gold as the commodity basis of all money persisted. At the economic conference at Genoa in 1922, world economic leaders worked out a simulated reconstruction of the old gold standard by creating a system of fixed exchange rates among the major trading countries. National currencies were revalued in terms of gold according to their purchasing power in domestic goods and services. Responsibility for maintaining convertibility of the national money was imposed on national central banks. Countries added gold to their monetary reserves by cutting down on gold coins in circulation. They held other foreign currencies, particularly sterling and dollars, as supplements to gold in order to maintain external money convertibility. All this was popularly believed to be a practical return to the ideal of the pre-war international gold standard. About this time Professor Irving Fisher of Yale was suggesting that the dollar alone be based upon a group of widely used commodities so that its value would remain stable when measured against the cost of living. But the idea of money as gold coin and cash metal was so firmly fixed in everyone's minds that Professor Fisher's sensible proposal was attacked as creating "rubber dollars" and nothing came of it.

The old idea that the economic system in general, and the gold exchange system in particular, worked more or less automatically in normal times lived on and gained new disciples. The example furnished by the parable of the London Guild of Goldsmiths was still regarded as the best working model for national and international money management. It was a positive good for national governments not to meddle with time-honored principles that would in the end work things out for the good of all through fluctuations of the free market. The governments of Stanley Baldwin in Britain and Harding, Coolidge and Hoover in the United States reflected a consensus of the faith in both countries that there was something akin to revealed truth in these notions of money as cash.

But at the end of the decade, in October of 1929, the stock market crash in Wall Street touched off a worldwide depression. Britain abandoned the gold exchange standard in 1931 and adopted stringent restrictions to defend her trading position. The United States abandoned the standard in 1934 and all but a few other countries followed her off. Bank failures, unemployment, widespread misery, distress and starvation caused people in all countries to forget their hostility to governmental meddling in economic matters. The old idea that the national government should keep hands off the economy so that Adam Smith's "invisible hand" could put everything right was forgotten. Suffering populations demanded that national governments expand their roles in economic life, and those that failed to respond were quickly voted out of office, as Herbert Hoover's was in 1932. Each country made domestic economic recovery the primary goal of its economic policy. Economic debate switched from the question of the "cross of gold" to questions of "easy" money versus "tight" money, inflation versus a high rate of employment, higher taxes to slow excessive growth versus lower taxes to stimulate demand and so forth. In the United States, economic debate over public policy remained more or less locked into these artificial polarities until August, 1971, or thereabouts. Shortly after Arthur Burns, Chairman of the Federal Reserve Board, had testified that "the rules of economics are not working in quite the way they used to," President Nixon clamped his "new economic program" on the United States' economy.

The gold standard of the 19th and early 20th centuries, as managed by The Bank of England and J. P. Morgan, performed one of the most important functions that Adam Smith had attributed to the "invisible hand" of the free market. It limited, if loosely, the power of sovereign governments, central banks and private banks to create coin and paper money, bank deposits and credit, to the amount of substitutes that the public would willingly hold in place of gold itself.

Even after the United States went off the gold standard in 1934, the belief persisted that the United States dollar was convertible into gold at thirty-five paper dollars for one ounce of gold metal (except, of course, by private citizens of the United States who were not coin collectors, jewelers or dentists). This belief remained particularly strong in European countries whose currencies were convertible into dollars at relatively fixed rates of exchange. It was not really true that the only reason their money was accepted was "because it was accepted." It was accepted because there was an ultimate commitment by the United States to exchange gold metal for the paper dollars they held, or other currencies convertible into dollars, at fixed rates of exchange.

Through the decade of the 1930s, economic uncertainty abroad and the rise of Hitler in Europe worked together to make the United States the world's haven for money and gold. Few in the United States realized what was happening or had any inkling of the ultimate consequences. By the end of 1939, United States official vaults held more than three-fifths of the world's then existing monetary gold stock.

Jefferson and Jackson's great egalitarian republic which professed to believe that all men had been created equal woke up to find somewhat to her surprise, and for reasons having very little to do with her own efforts, that she had become the leading plutocracy of the world. At the very same time, she had been trying to pull herself out of a domestic depression with very little success. Nor could Hamiltonians claim with much conviction that his policies had finally prevailed. Hard as it may be for Americans to believe, Hitler abroad and depression and deflation at home probably contributed more to creating and preserving the illusion that the dollar was as good as gold than superior Yankee foresight, policy, technology, virtue or the Puritan work ethic.

Before March, 1968, U.S. law had required that coin and paper currency outstanding be backed by a gold reserve of at least 25 per cent. When the law was repealed at the height of the March, 1968, world gold crisis, there was about $40 billion of currency outstanding backed by a gold reserve of about $10 billion. Now, there is no legal limitation of any kind on the gross amount of U.S. dollar currency and coin which may be issued and outstanding.

Since United States citizens cannot convert their paper money into gold, and since credit money, debt money, Eurodollars and personal I.O.U.s outstanding create vast sums of money which are many times the value of the paper currency, such a gold limitation on paper currency outstanding was, in strict reality, all but meaningless. But as a prop to the illusion that all money is cash, it had incalculable importance. The increasing frequency and severity of international monetary crises after March, 1968, through August, 1971, when President Nixon formally repudiated the United States' obligation to redeem paper dollars for gold, and the continuing crises thereafter, have tended to confirm the importance of that belief as a prop to the world money system. Now that there is no prop at all to support the belief in money as cash, now that we are in a more or less permanent world monetary crisis, or dollar crisis, a new prop for belief in the integrity of worldwide money has come to seem more and more necessary, or at least desirable.

Countries other than the United States generally did not maintain any formal limits on the amount of paper money their governments could issue. Until August of 1971, fixed exchange rates between most national currencies and the dollar were maintained by most countries under the supervision of the International Monetary Fund in fulfillment of their obligations under the Bretton Woods agreement of 1944. Since the dollar was freely convertible into gold, and all other currencies were freely convertible into dollars at fixed parities, there seemed to be an ultimate limit, however tenuous, upon the power of all governments to print paper money without limit. This theoretical structure of control was as flimsy a prop as could be imagined to the willing suspension of disbelief in paper money. Nonetheless, it served to preserve the illusion that all the cash was somehow tied to the commodity gold. But after August 15, 1971, not even this prop for such an illusion remains. No formal limit exists which prevents any government from issuing as much paper money as it likes.

Obviously the kind of international structural limitation on the issuance of money, imposed by the necessity of keeping up fixed exchange ratios, did not limit the creation of bank money through loans and demand deposits, nor did it have much practical restraint on the creation of money through government policies, such as changing interest and discount rates, buying and selling government securities, raising and lowering depreciation rates, production and nonproduction subsidies and so on. Nevertheless, as long as popular expectations remain a potent factor governing economic conditions, the public's belief that limitations upon the money supply were somehow imposed by the amount of gold in the vault at Fort Knox and the gold exchange standard, lent a useful color of credibility to the soundness of their money.

Another prop to the idea of money as cash is the belief that coin and paper money is something that only the national government of a country can legally coin or print. The conventional wisdom is that this inspires trust. In the United States, the fact of the matter is, of course, that the government itself does not coin or print money at all; only the Federal Reserve system does, and it is not the government.

The Federal Reserve system, our national central bank, is separate from and independent of the Treasury and the other parts of the Executive branch of the government; it is also separate from and independent of Congress. In a historical context, it made possible the substitution of a single national United States currency—as acceptable in California as in New Jersey—for the patchwork system of local currencies that had circulated before. The system is not directly responsive to the electoral process. But it is composed of men who belong to political parties, follow election returns, owe their appointments to Presidents and part of their funding to Congress, so their independence in form is less significant than their historical sensitivity to shifts in broad political trends. In legal form, the Federal Reserve system consists of twelve Federal Reserve districts which cover the United States, each with its own Federal Reserve bank. The initial capital of these banks is sub-scribed by the commercial bank members of the Federal Reserve system, so each Federal Reserve bank is a corporation owned by its "member banks." All are coordinated by the seven-member board of governors of the system in Washington which is popularly called the Federal Reserve Board. It is hardly an exaggeration to say that the members of this Board, appointed by the President for terms which usually extend well beyond his own, are "the most powerful group of private citizens in America."

The Federal Reserve system requires member banks to keep substantial portions of their assets, such as one-eighth, for example, in non-earning cash deposits with the Federal Reserve bank or in vault cash. This legal reserve ratio imposed by governmental authority is an important means by which the Federal Reserve system controls the amount of new money that commercial banks create by their every-day lending operations. Reserves of the magnitude of twelve percent were not necessary to protect the goldsmiths, nor are they necessary to protect the banks against withdrawals by even their largest depositors. The excess reserve represents the imposition of control by the Federal Reserve Board over the amount of money in circulation.

Probably the most singular thing about our formally independent Federal Reserve system is how little difference there usually is (with a few well-publicized political exceptions) between the way it manages our money and the way national central banks in most other countries, which are unabashedly creatures of the reigning executive governments, manage theirs.

The "private citizens" of the Federal Reserve Board who manage our money today seem no more like the private citizens who comprised the London Guild of Goldsmiths than the Golden Rule resembles the golden calf. All merchants cherish the illusion that their gold is somewhere down in the vaults under control of private citizens and safe from the King, when the fact is they can never withdraw their gold, and it remains in the hands of the agents of the King. All they really have as backing for their money is the assurance of their fellow citizens.

From the guild of London goldsmiths to Pierre Paul

Schweitzer, economists and governmental economic officials and the rest of us as well still think and talk about money as if it were in reality all cash and backed by gold. Our frame of reference is still the parable about King Charles I and the merchants who took their gold away from the government mint and deposited it in the vaults of the goldsmiths. The parable serves a useful purpose as an illustration of how a unit of a banking system can create a large amount of credit and debt on a small base of gold and other cash reserves. But all the other overtones and undertones of the parable—the medium that is the real message—mislead us about the true nature of money.

It perpetuates the false idea that money is a commodity, that it is cash with an intrinsic value all its own, immutable for all times and places, in the hands of anyone. It fosters the deception that in back of all the money outstanding is a vault full of gold; the misconception that a fixed amount of gold in the vault sets an ultimate limit to the aggregate total amount of money that can be created by the goldsmiths and the misplaced trust that the integrity of the goldsmith will limit his issue of notes accountable to a prudently large and safe percentage of the gold behind the money. We are left with the impression that governments are not to be trusted but goldsmiths are, although the truth is that neither can be trusted very far.

The power of money being what it is, there is no alternative to leaving its regulation to governments or agencies of governments. But there is a false implication that disposition and control of money should and can have no significant social consequences.

Nearly everything the parable tells us about money is contrary to the truth about money as it is in the world today.

Well, then, if money is not cash whose most enduring tangible symbol is gold, if it is an illusion to think of money as cash, what is its real nature?

The true nature of money today is as a medium of credit

and debt. Its tangible symbol is weightless, and it proliferates without limit. It is easy to carry and no two samples of it are necessarily alike. It is an inch or two of handwriting, sometimes a humble scrawl, sometimes a proud flourish. One man's signature on a credit card, contract or check may command more intrinsic value than all the gold and silver ever lifted from all of King Solomon's mines. Another's may command none. It is not solitary and anonymous. Two or more people are involved. Of every transaction there is a written record or an electronic impression in the memory of a computer data bank that can potentially relate its consequences and effect to every other transaction. Every such transaction and every feedback effect from it, separately and collectively, may be made subject to the conscious intervention of human intellect. The illusion that all money is cash is one that is as foolish and dangerous as it is unnecessary.

9.

The Reality of Money as Credit and Debt

The tangible symbol of modern money is a handwritten personal signature, without any intrinsic value in itself, not gold or silver. Today, gold and silver are actually worth only the amount that someone will pay for them in credit and debt by signing his name to a check.

Credit is infinitely homogeneous, malleable, durable, and transmissible. But unlike cash it is not anonymous, and its does not partake of absolute freedom and license. As we followed John Cade on his law-abiding daily rounds through the age of credit, we noticed that he had practically no need of cash money, only an occasional token coin. His handwritten signature on checks and credit card vouchers dozens of times a day was as good as gold. Indeed, far better: his signature was more portable, durable, flexible and malleable; and it could not be lost or stolen, although, of course, it might be forged. But if it should be, or if he should make a payment by mistake, there is always the written record to help him prove the forgery or correct the mistake. If his making the payment is questioned, it can be proved. Whether his payment is tax deductible, or not reportable, he has the voucher to prove the fact, or it exists for the government to obtain, depending on which side you are rooting for.

155

The reality of money as credit and debt, and the illusion of money as cash, shows up in money aggregates just as it shows up in the daily rounds of John Cade in a society that is already almost cashless on the surface. On a question of such economic importance—how the money supply should be defined and measured—there is, as is often the case, no general agreement among academic economists. As one prominent economist said a few years ago, "everyone rolls his own definition of money and has his own rules for measurement of the money supply." One measure of money is the amount held by individual spending units for day-to-day transactions. This consists of small coins, paper currency and checking account demand deposits. Economists call this the "narrowly-defined" money supply. For our purposes, it is a generous estimate of the amount of money we regard as cash. At the end of 1970, this stood at a little more than $200 billion. In a population of 200 million this comes out to about $1000 for each man, woman and child.

At the same time, public and private debt stood at about $1,840 billion, consisting of about $483 billion public debt (of federal, state and local governments) and $1357 billion private debt. In 1971, with gross national product at almost $1,050 billion, the total of public and private debt was near the almost unimaginable sum of $2 trillion. For each man, woman and child in a population of 200 million, this came to about $10,000 of debt. Roughly, then, and on average, we are stuck with about ten times more money as credit and debt than we have in money as cash.

This mountain of debt is growing at an increasingly rapid pace. It more than doubled during the 1960s, and more than two-fifths of the increase occurred during the last few years of accelerating inflation. Borrowers anticipated that waiting to spend or invest would be even more costly and that repayment would be made in inflated dollars of less purchasing power. Lenders, on the other hand, demanded premium interest rates to compensate them for this risk.

Individual and non-corporate debt rose about one and one-quarter times in the decade, and accounted for nearly one-third of all borrowings. Non-farm mortgage debt showed the slowest growth, and mortgages on multi-family residential and commercial properties far outgained one-to-four-family housing on a relative basis. Consumer credit rose by 138 percent, while life insurance policyholders' loans nearly tripled. Debt is also rising more rapidly in relation to gross national product. In 1970, debt increased $2.60 for every $1.00 increase in gross national product; during the previous five years, on the average, debt increased only $1.92 for each $1.00 increase in gross national product, and during the first few years of the postwar period, the relative increases almost matched dollar for dollar.

So for every American man, woman and child, the reality is that there is $10 of money as credit and debt outstanding for every dollar of money he has as cash. The inescapable conclusion has to be that on the basis of monetary aggregates, the illusion of money as cash is overwhelmed by the reality of money as credit and debt, ten to one.

In fact, payments and obligations for television sets, automobiles, houses and schools figure in the totals for credit and debt but hardly at all in the totals for cash. They are necessities for which we use credit to pay and rarely if ever use cash.

According to John Stuart Mill, in *Principles of Political Economy*:

> Money, when its use has grown habitual, is the medium through which the incomes of the different members of the community are distributed to them, and the means by which they estimate their possessions. As it is always by means of money that people provide for their different necessities, there grows up in their minds a powerful association leading them to regard money as wealth in a more peculiar sense than any other article; and even those who pass their lives in the production of the most useful objects, acquire the habit of regarding those

objects as chiefly important by their capacity of being exchanged for money.*

The use of credit and debt as money has grown habitual in our society. Credit, not cash, is the medium through which the income of the different members of society is distributed to them, the means by which they estimate their possessions and the means by which they provide for their different necessities. Again, it is in credit, not cash, that they count their wealth.

Therefore, in drawing a blueprint for the cashless society, it is useful to spend some time examining closely how a highly developed credit system works. When your bank lends you money, it creates a credit on its books in your favor and a deposit to your bank account. Two debts come into being at the same time: a debt from you to the bank which you must pay at an agreed future date, and a debt from the bank to you which you can use immediately to make payments to your creditors. Debts to your creditors are payable in money, in coins, bills or checks.

Because all credits created by the banking system are theoretically freely convertible into cash money, the central bank of each country must continue to issue coins and paper currency. Central banks supply local banks with whatever cash money they require. Metallic coins are now all token coins and paper currency represents the typical form of cash. Credit is thus intimately linked with all monetary policy, including all forms of money as cash which itself is based on credit card debt.

Bank credit is only one way money is created. A promissory note is a written promise to pay a specified sum of money to anyone, not limiting the promise to pay to any particular creditor: the promise may simply be to pay the bearer of the note, whoever he might be. The debt may then be assigned from one creditor of the note issuer to another by simple delivery of the note from hand to hand. In a refinement of this procedure, the

---

* John Stuart Mill, *Principles of Political Economy*, 5th edition. London: Parker, Son and Bourn, 1862.

name of the creditor may be specified, but the note may permit alternative payment to anyone else the creditor may designate, or to order. The creditor who is named may then assign the debt to a new creditor, or payee, by writing and signing on the note a direction that it be paid to the new payee. This of course is called endorsing the note, because the direction is customarily written on the back of the note. Through law and custom, if the creditor simply endorses the note by signing it without naming any new creditor or payee, the note is payable to any bearer who happens to possess it. Promissory notes issued by banks payable to bearer on demand have a special significance in the history of money; they are bank notes and have at many historical periods served the same function as cash money.

Historically such credit instruments possess the characteristics of being negotiable. This lends them the same qualities of anonymity and license that are inherent in cash money, but not true credit money. Ordinarily, if I give you a deed to my house and lot, I cannot give you a better title than I own myself. If I buy a watch from a sailor in Times Square, which the sailor has stolen, I may have to give it back to the real owner if he can identify it. If a thief steals my car and sells it to a third person, I can claim the car from the third person. These rules that apply to property generally do not apply to cash money or to many forms of credit embodied in negotiable instruments.

When a thief pays coins which he has stolen to a person who does not know he is a thief, the payee of the money has a perfectly secure title to the coins.

"Negotiable instruments" arise either by statute or by the custom of merchants. The most commonly recognized forms are promissory notes, bills of exchange, bills of lading, bearer bonds, checks endorsed to bearer, bank notes, sometimes even debentures payable to bearer and endorsed stock certificates. If it is in bearer form, it is thus on the same footing as paper money. The common law grants a clear title to any honest recipient who does not know of the theft, and the recipient is not under any obligation to inquire whether the previous holder of the instrument had a clear title. This privilege attaches whether the instrument is payable to bearer or to order; it is divested only by writing the words "not negotiable" upon the note. The effect of negotiability is to make easier the use of credit instruments as substitutes for money and a means of payment.

Negotiable instruments constitute an exception to the general rule that a man cannot pass on a better title than he has himself. Down through the 19th century, when means of communication between individuals and countries were few and slow, and commerce was difficult, the negotiability of negotiable instruments was a distinct benefit. Today, when debt and credit information is transmitted instantaneously from bank to bank and from country to country, the reasons why commercial instruments should be negotiable are much less compelling. The possibility of fraud and theft in the transfer of negotiable instruments, bearer bonds and the like, seems to outweigh by far the advantage to commerce of instruments which are fully negotiable and thus a constant temptation to major fraud, and indeed a perfect vehicle for hiding illicit profits from gambling or drugs or other illegal activity.

It has been estimated that at the beginning of the decade of the 1970s, some 22 billion checks were written in the United States. Obviously, all but a tiny portion of these would be cashed by the payee, and not negotiated from hand to hand. There is no need for them to be. The negotiability of negotiable instruments is an anachronism preserved in law and custom whose benefits inure only to a tiny portion of the business community, and that portion sometimes engaged in questionable activities. As a practical matter, many payees will not accept a promissory note without some knowledge of the credit standing of the drawer of the note, or the endorser of the note.

In effect, a negotiable instrument is cash money. In a cashless society, its creation should be limited to the medium of exchange of the central bank which is legally declared to be legal tender.

The tradition of negotiability has often been carried over into the legal analysis of credit card transactions. As we have seen, in some cases the "holder in due course" doctrine has been held to protect the card issuer from claims by the holder arising out of faulty goods or services supplied by a merchant. In other cases, where the bank that issued the credit card was found to be in a close relationship with the merchant whose credit card vouchers it had discounted, the bank has been denied the protection of this doctrine. The "holder in due course" doctrine is properly under wide attack by consumer protection advocates. It is an anachronism that has no proper place in the legal regime of a cashless society.

In a fully developed cashless society, pieces of paper which themselves embody legal obligations should be eliminated. Electronic means of communication would record all transactions, and a printed out memorandum, not in itself a legal document, would provide a receipt, a memorandum recording the transaction, which would furnish a means of checking the accuracy of the details and a means of correcting any error in it.

While promissory notes are commonly used for borrowing and lending, ordinary checks are the main method of assigning significant sums of bank credit. Drawn on a bank by a customer and payable on demand, not at a distant maturity date, a check is not, in theory, a vehicle for direct borrowing and lending, but only a means of transfer or payment. The bank's customer who has established his credit with the bank draws checks upon it in favor of those to whom he has to make payments. The payees of the checks in all likelihood also have banking accounts and pass on the checks (endorsed, payable to order) to their own banks. Each bank carrying on business at any business center can settle accounts with the others by sending the checks it receives to a central clearing house. Here all the banks' debits and credits are calculated day by day, and the net balances are settled either in money or by check on a central bank. Although the time it takes to transfer check credit and debt balances from bank to bank is short, the volume of checks is so great that the "float" that arises between the time of issuance of a check, and the time it is presented for payment represents a significant proportion of total bank balances.

Payment by check or bank note is still payment in credit, because it is carried out by the transfer of bank credit. Federal Reserve notes, the paper currency of the United States, are really nothing more than bank notes issued by the Federal Reserve system.

In many countries other than the United States, short-term borrowing and lending is effected through the bill of exchange, which is something like a check, but which also involves the extension of credit over a period of time. A promissory note is in effect an "I.O.U." signed by the borrower (the debtor) and delivered to the lender (his creditor). A bill of exchange, on the other hand, is signed by the creditor, not the debtor. It is a written order by the creditor—a tool maker who may be selling tools to a jeweler in exchange for a transfer of a credit by the jeweler to him—to pay the sum due to the bearer of the bill of exchange or to a specified person or order.

There are, of course, many other ways in which credit money is created. Governmental and private agencies of every imaginable kind issue bonds and debentures. Banks lend money; corporations issue bonds and commercial paper, and states, municipalities, turnpikes and seaways issue debt obligations of every imaginable variety.

Most of these transactions are reflected by credit instruments of some kind, but it seems obvious that credit instruments, particularly negotiable credit instruments, are not inherently necessary to the effective functioning of credit markets. Indeed, credits carried on the books of the lender that

162

match debts on the books of the borrower would serve as well, or rather better, since they would not require physical transfer, handling, counting and storage or be subject to loss and theft.

Side by side with credit which is organized through banks, quasi-banking institutions, private corporations and individuals' and government agencies, there continues to survive an older and more elementary form of credit. That is book credit between a buyer and a seller. Dealings between manufacturers, wholesalers and retailers, and credit created in sales to final retail customers in the form of charge accounts, create obligations payable in installments and credit-card credit. In a wide variety of service relationships, credits between the performer of the service and the users of the service, such as the credit in favor of a law firm against the debt of its client, are created without the intervention of any negotiable instrument at all. Speculation in the stock and commodity markets also gives rise to book credits. When a speculator buys a commodity, securities or foreign exchange for delivery at specified future dates, he incurs a debt equal to the price of the commodity for the period of time this takes.

Credit, then, is merely another name for debt. Long-term debts, which play such an important part in the investment markets of the world and in providing capital improvement, are both credit and debt. Governments, municipalities, corporations, international agencies and individuals' contract debts involving the payment of large capital sums at the end of a long period of years, and the payment of interest meanwhile. Such credit and debt may be in the form of bearer bonds which are payable to the bearer or transferable merely by endorsement. These are credit instruments negotiable on the same basis as bills and notes. Interest is paid by means of coupons or warrants which are attached to the bond and are cut off when due and presented for payments, as checks are. Such bonds present all the disadvantages of coin and cash money: they can be stolen, lost, destroyed by fire, require physical counting, physical storage, physical detachment of the coupons and they are eminently useful for criminal purposes because of their easy transferability.

Registered bonds must be recorded and show the name of the creditor on the bond record book of the issuer of the bond. Interest payments are mailed by check to the holder of the bond named on the books. The danger of theft, loss by fire or other physical destruction is greatly reduced, but it remains possible for one who fraudulently obtains physical possession of a registered bond to obtain transfer of the record ownership to his own name on the books of the company. The existence of the certificate itself creates the opportunity for loss and fraud, as well as the other complications inherent in the obligation being represented by a physical document.

What if the debtor does not pay? The wide use of credit and debt requires effective practical and legal remedies to provide security against the debtor's default, whether as a result of fraud, mismanagement or other fault of his own, or through loss for reasons beyond his control: the farmer who raises 40 acres of cherry trees and then finds there is no market for his crop. If possible, the lender takes physical possession of an asset as security for the debt, with a margin for the risk of depreciation and cost of collection.

Sometimes notes or bank advances are secured by a lien on goods in a warehouse or even in course of production, such as growing crops; sometimes by bonds, stocks or other negotiable instruments which may be deposited with the lender bank or transferred to it.

If all borrowers were of unimpeachable credit, or if the credit of a particular borrower could be established easily by the lender's making an inquiry into the retrieval memory of a computer data bank, such complexities as the use of bills of lading or physical transfer of documents for security purposes could be eliminated. Bonds or debentures of a corporation are secured by the assets of the company, or a mortgage on land or buildings. Creditors of a government usually have to depend on the good faith of the government, but sometimes they reinforce their security by obtaining a commitment of revenues from some particular government project or property, such as a toll road or a housing development.

The depositors of a bank are usually content to leave their deposits entirely unsecured, except to the extent of the guarantee of the Federal Deposit Insurance Corporation, relying on the general soundness and credit of the bank. Banks often grant loans or advances or overdrafts without security to customers who have large deposits, or good credit ratings.

Shares of stock in corporations whose shares are listed in the stock market look like debt instruments but are not. They do have some of the characteristics of money or credit instruments: value on any given day is fixed and they are liquid because the markets in them are extensive. They are often used as collateral security for loans. The problem of theft, loss, destruction and replacement of stock certificates is similar to the case of registered bonds. Numerous other forms of financial obligations also resemble to a greater or lesser degree registered bonds and stock certificates: voting trust certificates, certificates of beneficial interest in trusts, interests in oil ventures, theatrical production syndicates and even partnership interests. The securities laws define an extremely broad range of such financial instruments as "securities." The word "securities" does not mean that any such instruments necessarily represent a secure investment, or, indeed, are in any way secured by collateral.

No market for capital assets could exist without large credit institutions. Successful functioning of the market requires a concentration of liquid resources in the hands of dealers, and turnover in the market must be large in comparison with the greatest single transaction it is called upon to carry through.

165

For example, if there are a hundred dealers in a market with available liquid resources averaging one hundred thousand dollars each, then without large credit facilities the market could buy and hold two million dollars worth of the goods dealt in and no more. Once this limit was reached, the buying and selling would come to a dead stop. But if, on the other hand, the dealers could borrow nine thousand dollars each on the security of ten thousand dollars worth of goods or securities, the limit would be raised tenfold to 100 million dollars worth. If the dealers, in addition to the capital that they place directly in the market, also have other investments, they may increase their dealings still further by pledging these investments.

In the case of financial markets where dealings are carried on in stocks and bonds, debentures, foreign exchange, insurance or tangible commodities, dealers must be prepared to buy and sell very large units. Effective credit markets of this kind exist only at a very limited number of great centers throughout the world. New York, London and, to a lesser extent, Paris, Zurich, Frankfurt and Tokyo, come to mind. With electronic communication and computers, it would be possible to establish effective markets of this kind at many such centers and to link all such credit centers with a few central credit systems, or a single worldwide one. Without such credit systems and facilities, there could be no markets in the strict sense at all. Every transaction would be the subject of intricate, noncompetitive bargaining. It is only by the existence of well-organized financial markets that enterprise on a great scale is possible. Large credit institutions are the indispensable cornerstones of the whole system. If all large credit institutions were linked together in a computerized network, the effect on an individual doing business with any one of the institutions which were members of the network would seem little different than at present. In routine transactions, from an individual's point of view, it would not be surprising if the efficiencies of such large scale were offset by the inefficiencies of such large scale.

The Reality of Money as Credit and Debt

Credit is essential to economic development in the modern world. A community without the practice of borrowing and lending would limit the scope of every trader's operations by his need to provide cash for all purposes. He would have to conduct his business so that the maximum need of working capital would not exhaust his resources. The result would be that when the need of working capital was at the minimum, he would be encumbered with a large balance of idle money. But if he tied up too much of his capital in permanent investment in his business, he would miss trading opportunities for want of ready cash, or become involved in bankruptcy through unforeseen losses. Every trader's position would be a compromise between these two disadvantages if large credit institutions were not available. All capital invested would be irretrievably sunk in the enterprise. The amount of liquid resources available to cooperate in any important new development would be extremely limited.

Before our semi-cashless society arrived, it was already true that credit supplied the world with its principal medium of payment. Credit secured untold economies in the use of precious metals, for coins, and saved the costs which would be involved in mining, refining, handling, counting, stamping and keeping specie money safe. With credit, and without cashlike negotiable instruments, bonds, stock certificates and the like, the dangers of counterfeiting, theft and fraud are reduced. So is the possibility of loss through inadvertent destruction of the physical evidence of value.

More important still is the vital advantage that elasticity lends to the monetary system. Elasticity may, of course, cause problems as well as bring benefits. One of the seemingly inevitable features of the business cycle is a concurrent credit cycle which according to the conventional wisdom of economics brings on recurrent depressions in trade. Alternation of credit expansion and contraction manifests itself first by periods of rising, and then of falling, prices.

But it must not be assumed that an alternation of prosperity and depression would not exist in a community without large credit institutions which was on a purely cash money or specie system. On the contrary, elasticity conferred on the monetary system through universal use of credit and elimination of cash money offers the best hope of avoiding monetary fluctuations and smoothing the peaks and valleys of these cycles by the effective regulation and control of money as credit. The possibility that this can be done remains more a hope or a goal than a reality, despite the bold claims made by economists and central bankers for the miraculous things that can be accomplished by their "fine tuning." Nonetheless, it remains the best hope that society has.

Many of the difficulties we have with money today arise because we continue to cherish the illusion of money as cash, when it is completely unnecessary for us to do so. Cash money may not be accepted for many reasons. Gold, which is cash money in most of the world, has not been accepted as money in the United States since 1934 because it is illegal for citizens to own it. In August of 1971, the United States repudiated its obligation to redeem paper dollars offered by foreign central banks for gold at $35 an ounce.

A checking account deposit is money, and there is a good reason why your check is accepted, or is not accepted. A check on a demand deposit (included in the narrow definition of cash money supply) is accepted because the person accepting it knows the person who drew it, and knows that his credit standing is good. If a check you draw is refused, it may be because the drawee does not know you, knows that you do not have enough in your bank balance to cover it or suspects that your signature is forged. Beginning with 1970 income tax returns, taxpayers must disclose whether or not they have a foreign bank account or have made a transfer to a foreign country, even though this has no consequence one way or another as far as their tax liability is concerned. The presumption grows that transfers of cash money originate in illegal activity. The presumption grows that cash is not accepted because it is not accepted.

While the campus communes occasionally blow up conveniently located branch offices of banks, to illustrate their contemptuous attitude toward money, American Express Company, the Diners' Club and the head offices of the largest banks go on issuing credit cards which they tell us are in effect "the new money" which ushers in the cashless society. The conflict between the gurus and the bankers, two traditionally counterpoised centers of countervailing power, as symbolized by the bombings of the bank branches, is hardly as remarkable as the general agreement that "the new money" will usher in a world without money as cash.

According to Mill, quoting from Montesquieu:

> It is said that there are African tribes in which this somewhat artificial contrivance actually prevails. They calculate the value of things in a sort of money of account, called macutes. They say one thing is worth ten macutes, another fifteen, another twenty. There is no real thing called a macute: it is a conventional unit, for the more convenient comparison of things with one another.

This is the one definition of money that is meaningful. It is not cash. It is not gold. It is a unit of account. And that is all.

One of the principal criticisms to be made of academic economists is their gay nonchalance about money. While throwing off comments about "narrowly defined money," "high powered money," "broadly defined money," "Eurodollars" and "liquidity ratios," they are surprisingly inarticulate about such prosaic but nevertheless significant aspects of money as those we have been grappling with in this and the preceding chapter: few express much concern about every American man, woman and child's burden of $10,000 of debt to $1000 of cash, for example.

In *Principles of Political Economy*, Mill set the insouciant tone which the profession has generally maintained to this day when he wrote: "There cannot, in short, be intrinsically a more insignificant thing, in the economy of society, than money; except in the contrivance for sparing time and labour."

It is true, of course, that Adam Smith's economic revolution of 1776 changed the basic concept of the wealth of nations from the possession of gold to the power of a nation to produce real goods and services. Adam Smith's revolution ushered in a deeper understanding of the role of the market and individual self-interest as a means of increasing national affluence. Somehow, Irving Fisher's idea of linking the basis of money to a commodity index was not effectively pursued.

In the early 1800s, the economic revolution initiated by the work of David Ricardo turned economists' attention away from the nature of money itself, and the growth of national wealth, to questions of the distribution of income among social classes. In a sense, the Marxist revolution was one outgrowth of Ricardo's revolution.

In the 1870s there was a marginalist revolution in economics which gave economists a new technology for breaking complex economic problems into small component parts. This change in emphasis tended to convert economists themselves from philosophers to technicians, although the social philosophy which was so much a part of the work of Adam Smith and David Ricardo remained implicit in many later economists' works. But despite the focus on economic technology, the nature of money itself remained pretty much where it had always been: the illusion of the cash on deposit with the goldsmiths.

John Maynard Keynes, in the 1930s, focused on the problems of unemployment. Classical economics had all but ignored this social problem and had assumed that full employment was the natural state of a free economy. But Keynes showed that this was not necessarily the case. To solve the problem, he proposed a policy of raising government spending despite deficits in government budgets. But Keynes' analysis, which focused on the question of unemployment and social dislocations, failed to solve the problem of inflation. The Keynesians defended their master's doctrines by asserting that it was not their fiscal theories which had failed, but the politicians, who had spent too much and taxed too little.

Professor Milton Friedman and his followers of the "monetarist" school reacted strongly to Keynes' emphasis on unemployment by putting forward the thesis that moderate and steady growth in the money supply would solve both the problems of inflation and unemployment, and that the money supply was far more important than fiscal policy—tax and budget changes—as a determinant of the level of economic activity and of prices. The monetarist doctrines were, in essence, an updating of the old quantity theory of money, which reaches back to a time even before Adam Smith. Their moment of ascendancy came with the escalation of the Vietnam war in 1965, and the failure of the Keynesian economists to control the inflation that it brought with it.

The monetarists took charge of national policy when the Nixon administration came to power in 1968, and the opportunity they had in the following years to test out their theories did not prove their validity. If anything, the exercise demonstrated that monetarist theory was no more able than Keynesian theory to accomplish all that had been claimed for it. Unemployment and inflation rates jogged as high as, and higher than, ever. The experiment ended as an acknowledged failure with introduction of the President's "new economic policy" in August, 1971.

Now that both fiscal and monetarist economic methodologies have been thoroughly tested in application and found wanting, an entirely new approach to national economic gover-

nance is needed. Such an approach would avoid such rigid polarities as the supposed correlation between rates of inflation
and rates of unemployment. It would focus instead on the
fundamental nature of money itself and the central role it
should play in society.

Once the illusion of money as cash has been dispelled, it is
no longer a paradox to say that money will play a central role
in society most effectively if the society is a cashless society.
When the solitary, anonymous and arbitrary characteristics of
money as cash have been replaced by the multiparty characteristics of money as credit and debt under the effective control of
human intelligence, the chance is real that economic prescrip-
tions to cure economic and social ills can be carried out and can
overcome the countervailing "feedback" forces that would have
frustrated them in a cash and carry economy.

In a cashless society, changes up and down in rates of interest, in expansion and contraction of the money supply, increases and decreases in tax and withholding rates, rates of
tariff, depreciation schedules, investment credits and government spending might have a chance of working, since both the
policy measures themselves, and the reaction to the policy by
the people affected by it, would all be part of the same single
unified system. A money system which would effectively carry
out the conclusions reached by the rational application of human intelligence would of necessity be a cashless money system.

10.

Reconciliation to
a New Resource

The movement from a cash and carry to a cashless society would mean yielding the anonymity and freedom, intrinsic to the idea of all money as cash, to the easily checkable, multi-party revocable license inherent in the theory of all money as credit and debt. All such credit and debt money would have to clear through a computerized data bank at a large central banking institution. There is no gainsaying that in a cashless society, this central clearing institution would add a new dimension to the power that governments already wield over their people's lives in all contemporary political states.

When we see the power of government over our lives reaching out in this new direction, most of us are alarmed at what we see. If more governmental aggrandizement is what the cashless society is all about, does it not entail a sacrifice of too much of what is left of our precious personal freedom? Is not this simply too high a price to pay for a cashless society? It is not enough to respond that in a democracy where the people control the government, central economic control should give people still greater control over their own lives. Our unease is not dispelled.

It is time to take a closer look at these familiar fears, compare them with the realities of late 20th century national life, and determine to what extent these attitudes have a meaning-ful relationship to those realities. If there is little or no rational relationship, arguments based on them should not be taken as useful criticisms of the ideal of a cashless society.

It seems unarguable that the powers of all governments over the lives and economic welfare of their people are growing as populations grow, and so is the dependence of people every-where upon their governments' exercise of these powers. The ultimate consequences of this convergence seem to many to be government as the Stalin-like Big Brother described in George Orwell's *1984*. We recoil in horror from his extrapolation of the world of 1945 to our very near future:

> The hallway smelt of boiled cabbage and old rag mats. . . . On each landing, opposite the lift shaft, the poster with the enormous face gazed from the wall. . . . BIG BROTHER IS WATCHING YOU, the caption beneath it ran. . . . Winston Smith moved over to the window: a smallish, frail figure, the meagerness of his body merely emphasized by the blue overalls which were the uniform of the Party. From where Winston stood it was just possible to read, picked out on its white face in elegant lettering, the three slogans of the Party:
>
> WAR IS PEACE
> FREEDOM IS SLAVERY
> IGNORANCE IS STRENGTH

We often feel, as Winston Smith does, that we have been transformed into cogs in a vast governmental machine we do not understand. Professor Charles A. Reich in *The Greening of America* argues that this is a more or less realistic portrayal of conditions in the contemporary United States:

> The American Corporate State today can be thought of as a single vast corporation, with every person as an involuntary member and employee. It consists primarily of large industrial organizations, plus nonprofit institutions such as foundations and

the educational system, all related to the whole as divisions to a business corporation. Government is only a part of the state, but government coordinates it and provides a variety of needed services. The corporate state is a complete reversal of the American ideal and plan.

If, as Professor Reich asserts, the American corporate state as it exists today is "a complete reversal" of the American ideal and plan, what is the true American ideal and plan that has been turned around?

Thoreau's observations based on economic arrangements at Walden probably still provide us with the most widely accepted and cherished image of what American economic life would be if only the American corporate state had not preempted it:

> If one would live simply and eat only the crops which he raised, and raise no more than he ate, and not exchange it for an insufficient quantity of more luxurious and expensive things, he would need to cultivate only a few rods of grounds, and it would be cheaper to spade up that than to use oxen to plow it, and to select a fresh spot from time to time, than to manure the old, and he could do all his necessary farm work as it were with his left hand at odd hours in the summer; and thus he would not be tied to an ox, or horse, or cow, or pig, as at present. I desire to speak impartially on this point, and as one not interested in the success or failure of the present economical and social arrangements. I was more independent than any farmer in Concord, for I was not anchored to a house or a farm, but could follow the bent of my genius, which is a very crooked one, every moment. Besides being better off than they already, if my house had been burned or my crops had failed, I should have been nearly as well off as before.
>
> I am wont to think that men are not so much the keepers of herds as herds are the keepers of men, the former are so much the freer.

What, really, would it be like if everyone simply followed his "crooked genius," moved outside the structure of the American corporate state, and tried to live off the land like Thoreau? According to a March 1971 article in *The Farm Index*:

> If all the land used for farming in the United States were divided equally among U.S. families, your family's share would be about 27½ acres.

✼ ✼ ✼ ✼

> About 22 of your 27½ acres would be actually in your farm. A little less than 9 acres of your farm would be cropland, nearly 10 would be pasture, grassland or range. You also would have about 1½ acres of woodland which you use for grazing and 1½ acres in farmstead, roads, and nonfarm uses.
>
> ... The rest of it was in fallow, held out of production under government programs, or idle for one reason or another. You had nearly 3½ acres in grains, over half of which were corn and wheat. You had over an acre in hay, and a soybean field of eight-tenths of an acre. Your other crops were in garden-sized plots.
>
> Your herds and flocks present some puzzling biological problems. You had only one-fourth of a dairy cow but she managed to produce 2.287 pounds of milk in the year. The beef cattle herd of 1.8 head dropped three-fourths of a calf, while your lone hog has had a litter of 2 pigs. Only four-tenths of a sheep roamed your pasture.
>
> You had 6.4 hens during 1970. They had 113 dozen eggs. You also produced 58 broilers, but only 2¼ turkeys.

✼ ✼ ✼ ✼

> Your 27½ acres grossed $1,068 in 1969. Production expenses took $752 of that, leaving you a net income of only $316.

Obviously, to realize even $316 net income from your family's own family farm, you would probably have had to work harder, and with many more and different skills, than you ever have before. Even so, much of your $316 net income would be money from government subsidies. It is not necessary to enumerate other benefits beside subsidies derived from governmental and industrial organizations to demonstrate the absurdity of attempting a Reichian reversal of the contemporary reality of the American corporate state.

At Chamber of Commerce luncheons principal speakers discussing American economic life usually eschew such Reichian phrases as "American corporate state" with all its Orwellian overtones. Their rhetoric respectfully describes the political, social and economic system under which we live in the United States as a private enterprise, profit motivated and free market system. President Nixon's New Economic Policy of 1971 brought some changes in the usual script, at least during the 90-day "freeze," but these were more like footnotes than fundamental revisions of the accepted form.

This made all the more remarkable a speech delivered to The Greater Los Angeles Chamber of Commerce 1970–1971 Business Outlook Convention by A. W. Clausen, President of The Bank of America, the world's largest nongovernmental money institution and issuer of BankAmericard, the most widely used bank credit card. The prominent banker's remarks gain force from his uncharacteristic acknowledgment that they may have a heretical ring.

> It may sound heretical to some in this room to say that business enterprise is not an absolute necessity to human culture. . . . Ancient Egypt functioned more than 3000 years without anything resembling what we today understand by the term "corporate enterprise," or even "money." Within our span of years, we have witnessed the rise of the Soviet socialist empire. It survives without anything you or I would call a private corporation and little that approaches our own monetary mechanism. It survives and is far stronger than anyone might have expected from watching its turbulent beginnings in 1917. . . . It is easy to mislead ourselves into thinking that there is something preordained about our profit-motivated, free market, private enterprise system—that is, as they used to say of gold, universal and immutable.

177

Mr. Clausen's almost obligatory phrases for what we believe we have in the United States—"our profit-motivated, free market, private enterprise system"—subtly flatter us that we are engaged in struggles for survival of the fittest under the law of the jungle. We are loath to dismiss such heroic self-images from the dead level of our lives, and cling to them the more tenaciously because they are so far from humdrum reality. Detroit sells to the same consumer psychology when it calls its bourgeois Pontiacs, Dodges and Plymouths by names like Tempest, Duster, Barracuda and Fury.

But the obligatory phrases are not what make Mr. Clausen's speech so remarkable. The remarkable part is that the head of the world's largest private banking institution so readily acknowledges that civilized societies can function perfectly well over long spans of time not only without private corporate enterprise, but even without money. In our own time, as he pointed out, our archrival, the Soviet socialist empire, functions and is surprisingly strong without anything resembling our own monetary mechanism. We mislead ourselves if we think that these features of our system, private corporate enterprise and a highly developed monetary mechanism, are things preordained, universal and immutable. Mr. Clausen's allusion to gold quietly reminds us that over and over again, year after year, governmental officials insisted that the place of gold in the world money system was "immutable." We all know what has happened to gold: its place has proved to be mutable.

Once the bank president has conceded that a cash and carry society is not preordained and immutable, and refused to rule out the possibility that a society without money would work satisfactorily in the modern world, it becomes important to take a closer look at the details of how people in a Western nation really live. Perhaps life in a cashless society would not be so different, frightening and Orwellian after all.

Before we can compare and contrast what would be different in a cashless society from the way we live now, it is necessary to reach some reasonable consensus about the way we really do live now. Are we, for example, locked into a lifelong competitive struggle with one another, as the hallowed rubric about the profit-motivated, free market, private enterprise system holds, or are we locked into something altogether different?

In addition to being the world's largest private bank and credit card issuer, The Bank of America is one of the world's largest bureaucratic organizations. Most of its 100,000 or so employees, from tellers, cashiers and stock transfer agents all the way up to Mr. Clausen, its president, live out their working lives untouched by the unpleasant consequences of anything resembling a "dog eat dog," profit-motivated, free market, private enterprise system. Depending on their skills, throughout their working lives they move slowly up through layers of organization with fixed incremental pay increases at all levels, until it is time to retire. If they leave, or are discharged, which is rare, they usually find a job at another bank—Union Bank, for example—at roughly the same salary level. None of this seems to impinge upon their illusion that they work in a "dog eat dog," rough and tough, free market, private enterprise system. This memorable fiction remains an article of unshakable faith precisely because it is so far removed from the reality of their everyday lives.

A truer image of the economic and social context that Mr. Clausen and the other employees of his bank, most of the rest of us in our own jobs in the work force of the United States and, to a greater or lesser extent, most people in the more developed countries of the world inhabit, is that of a large civil service organization. The conditions of labor and life of the typical employee of the bank are not very different from the conditions he would find if he worked for a large governmental bureau. The bank's personnel policies are not so different from those of a reasonably well-run governmental agency that they could not adequately be described as civil service policies, and the bank itself as a civil service organization.

Private enterprise was so named because once, in an earlier era of small firms and broad free markets, the firm was subordinate to the market, and those in command of the firm gained their authority from ownership of private property. But this source of legitimacy of authority plays a much reduced role in contemporary economic organizations.

Professor John Kenneth Galbraith has observed, in *The New Industrial State*, that:

> It is part of the vanity of modern man that he can decide the character of his economic system. His area of decision is, in fact, exceedingly small. He could, conceivably, decide whether or not he wishes to have a high level of industrialization. Thereafter, the imperatives of organization, technology and planning operate similarly, and we have seen through a broadly similar result, on all societies. Given the decision to have modern industry, much of what happens is inevitable and the same.
>
> Jobs and occupations in the society are rigidly defined and controlled, and arranged in a hierarchy of rewards, status, and authority. An individual can move from one division to another, but he gains little freedom thereby. For in each position he is subject to conditions imposed upon it; individuals have no protected area—of liberty, privacy, or individual sovereignty beyond the reach of the state. The state is subject neither to democratic controls, constitutional limits, or legal regulation. Instead, the organizations of the corporate state are motivated primarily by the demands of technology and of their own internal structure. . . . In the corporate state, most of the "public" functions of government are actually performed by the "private" sector of the economy. And most "government" services are performed for the "private" sector.

It is necessary to admit the reality that there are no organizational—or anarchical—escape routes from the reach of the modern corporate state or modern corporate government. From the point of view of the individual, both together make up the civil service state, and the practical differences in a job with the one or the other are less significant than the similarities.

"Individuals have no protected area—of liberty, privacy, or individual sovereignty, beyond the reach of the state." The thesis here is that the monolithic corporate state that Professors Galbraith and Reich have described will not "wither away," but will remain the economic structure within which all of us must live our lives. But it is an important corollary of this thesis that life in the American civil service state need not be an Orwellian nightmare. With proper understanding of what we gain from it, as well as what we owe it, the cashless society in a civil service state need be neither an Orwellian nightmare nor a Thoreauvian daydream, but a rather simple adjustment to the imperatives of contemporary industrial organization.

Professor Reich suggests that there is another way to escape the presumed evils of the American corporate state. He says it will be ended when all the young, blue-jeaned, fringed and hairy members of Consciousness III teach all other members of society their liberating life style and end "the domination of self by false goals and false consciousness." In *The Greening of America* he concluded: "When self is recovered, the power of the corporate state will be ended, as miraculously as a kiss breaks a witch's evil enchantment."

Nothing *The Greening of America* tells us about the simple, affable, naive, inarticulate and singularly unskilled young people of Consciousness III suggests that they could survive in the woods at Walden, or on their own 27½ acre farms for more than a short time. Nor does the economic history of the past 200 years offer much encouragement for the thesis that "the power of the corporate state will be ended" by a change in consciousness "when self is recovered." If IBM, General Motors and the Pentagon were to vanish "as miraculously as a kiss breaks a witch's evil enchantment," that would be a miracle indeed. But a change of consciousness that surrendered the illusion of going back to Walden, or a 27½ acre farm, and accepted the idea that reasonable employment at The Bank of America or another arm of the civil service state is "where it's at," would be a useful prelude to acceptance of a cashless society as a desirable aspect of contemporary reality. A shift in consciousness that would accept and not reject the more or less permanent reality of the civil service state, and the cashless society as a valuable new feature of it entirely consistent with the reality of its structure, would not require anything as miraculous as a kiss that breaks a witch's evil enchantment. Nor would it require as great a strain on the imagination, or the Department of Justice, as the breakup of IBM.

Does anything in the economic structure of the civil service state preclude the introduction of a cashless society to it? Could the existing economic structure be successfully adapted to accommodate a cashless society? The various groups of people who make up a national society may be classified in many different ways. In *The Greening of America,* Professor Reich classified them by levels of consciousness. His descriptions of Consciousness I, II and III led to fascinating psychological insights, but left the economics of their situation pretty much where he found them: to wit, in Professor Galbraith's *New Industrial State* country, which Professor Reich renamed the American superstate.

To analyze the process of shifting from a cash and carry society to a cashless society, it is useful to reclassify the members of society according to their economic roles. The conditions of employment of the work force at The Bank of America seem typical of many other kinds of employment in contemporary industrial societies. Employment which has all of the same civil service characteristics is so widespread and typical, in fact, that the salient characteristics of such employment suggest by synecdoche calling the society as a whole a civil service state.

Not everyone, by any means, is employed in jobs in large organizations with civil service characteristics. If those with civil service kinds of jobs may be identified as the largest single group and called civilians, at least three others may also be identified as having significantly different economic roles. They may be called, respectively, holders, voluntares and dependents. The question to be examined here is whether retention of money as cash in the economic structure of society is necessary or desirable for any of these groups, or whether introduction of a cashless society would not perhaps benefit the conditions of life of all. Who, indeed, needs money as cash in the civil service state?

Traditionally, the civil service is the body of people who are employed in the lower and middle ranges of government service. They perform innumerable jobs of a rather routine nature whose duties are more or less clearly defined. Holders of such jobs obtain them by passing civil service examinations whose subject matter changes little from year to year and is highly predictable. A few obtain appointments to "exempt" positions, usually in the upper ranks of the structure, without passing a qualifying examination. Once employed, the civil servant's tenure is reasonably secure. Within the system, there is little reward for extra effort or ingenuity, but there are also few sanctions to punish mediocre work, paper shuffling or incompetence.

A John Cade who worked for The Bank of America, or a large organization in Britain, France, West Germany or, indeed, in Russia, probably would find the basic conditions of his employment fundamentally similar. He would become secure in his job and adapt his mode of life to his salary. His performance would be rated periodically by his superiors. It would usually not be difficult for him to avoid unfavorable ratings, or comments or remarks against his progress in the organization, by maintaining a low profile and keeping his nose clean. It would be important for him to have a clean collar and a neat suit. Firings would usually occur for reasons having nothing to do with the quality of his work—drunkenness, disorderly behavior, incompatibility with a boss—and usually only to serve as a warning to keep other members of the structure in line. Pay increases would come slowly, but vacations and sick leaves would be generously provided, and at retirement there would be an adequate pension.

Civil servants traditionally observe the social proprieties, are decently polite, not rude. The adjective "civil" pertains to citizens, to the state or to relations between citizen and citizen, or citizen and state, as regulated by law. Service denotes performance of labor for the benefit of another, and performance of official duties for a sovereign or a state. It denotes conduct contributing to the advantage of another or others. The service sector of our economy now is larger than the industrial, farming or mining sectors, and continues to expand by comparison with them. Although some people in all societies would consider a civil service job stultifying, the majority of people in most modern societies would give their eyeteeth to have one.

As far as the civilian is concerned, civil service jobs have similar general characteristics whether they are with the government or with a large bureaucratic organization like The Bank of America in the "private sector" of the economy. Jobs that, from the individual's point of view, have functional characteristics similar to government civil service jobs exist by the millions in banks, business corporations, insurance companies, universities, publishing houses, railroads, airlines and everywhere else in the "private sector," as well as at all levels of government, welfare departments, poverty programs, postal services, Social Security and Veterans Administration offices, county courthouses, state capitols, the Pentagon and countless other areas of the "public sector."

As large organizations, both public and private, grow in size, civil service jobs proliferate at a still greater rate, in accordance with Parkinson's Law, to fill the available time and space. In accordance with the Peter Principle, people within the system are promoted to the level of their incompetence. No single word or phrase can adequately sum up the innumerable kinds of individual employment in a society as heterogeneous as that of the United States. But even most people who work in blue collars, no collars or overalls, may fairly be said to work in jobs that are economically similar to civil service jobs.

It has been estimated that 2,000 of the largest American corporations account for 80% of our gross national product. They employ more than 16 million people. Federal, state and local governments and public agencies employ another 16 million or more. To these 32 million may be added the large numbers of employees of educational institutions, hospitals, military organizations and large accounting and law firms. Although many of the corporate employees are traditionally thought of as blue collar industrial workers, their wage levels compare favorably with traditional white collar scales, and are no barrier to the workers' obtaining mortgage loans, credit cards or consumer credit. Workers in construction and allied trades, carpenters, electricians, plumbers, painters and the like, particularly if unionized, aspire to civil-service-like job regularity and enjoy civil-service-level wage scales, or better. Even many farmers have given up the rugged independence of their traditional way of life for the regular corporate pay check of a large-scale farming organization. Given reasonable definitional flexibility, it is probably fair to say that over half the working people in the United States are in the civil service class.

Although he regards himself as a member of an elite profession, even John Cade, as an associate lawyer employed at a fixed salary by a large law firm, is really a civilian in the civil service state. Like all other employees of the civil service state, he is eligible for credit of all kinds, including credit card credit.

Grouped in this way according to their ability to qualify for credit, wage- and salary-earning civilians constitute by far the largest of our four economic categories of people who live in a modern national state. The Federal and state governments, large corporations and foundations and other large organizations, taken together, form a unitary, monolithic economic establishment which it seems useful to call by the shorthand name of the civil service state, taking its name from and giving its name to the civilians who serve in its ranks at all levels throughout their working lives. John Cade's ancestor Jack promised: "There shall be no money." Earlier chapters have demonstrated how a credit-worthy member of society like John Cade has very little use for cash in his daily life and, indeed, is far better off, and safer, without it.

Acceptance of the reality of the structure of the civil service state does not mean that the civilian must be an "organization man," with all of the dismal qualities that that overused phrase ordinarily connotes. Far from being a helpless cog in a vast machine, frozen into a narrow unchanging niche in a rabbit warren of bureaucracy, he would be free to advance or withdraw as his talents, or lack of them, demand of him. He would have to face up once and for all to the fact that there is such a thing as the slavery of freedom.

Most people would still want to perform work or some other form of useful service to society in exchange for economic and social rewards which exceed the minimum levels. Most people perform such work now, some for the satisfaction of the work itself, some for the economic rewards and most—indeed almost all—for a complex combination of both sets of reasons. The civil service character of employment in industrial society today, as well as the leveling of income scales and the leveling out of the differences between the lowest and the highest, was illustrated in Sweden early in 1970. Fifty thousand judges, lawyers, doctors, engineers, railwaymen, teachers and white-collar workers, many of whom earned $10,000 and more, staged a series of strikes which were called everything from "luxury strikes" to "the college graduate walkout." Although their pay was about twice the average wage of a Swedish worker, they nevertheless were dissatisfied because, for example, university

186

workers' "real income" after rising taxes and prices, declined from $750 a month in January, 1968, to $613 a month in January, 1971. In the same period, a female industrial worker's real monthly income rose from $260 to $270. There had been a 7 per cent net decrease in buying power for state employees, while in the same period there had been a 7 per cent increase in buying power for industrial workers.

The implications for all advanced societies are plain. It is the relation of skills and possession of skills to available jobs that command salaries. If the trend in Sweden continues, a plumber's salary will be as great as a judge's, a carpenter's as great as a college professor's. Nor does this shock us in the United States, because our wage scales are moving in the same direction.

In the civil service state, it is what a person is, what he can do and what his skills are, not his education, social status, family connections or capital assets that determine how he lives. In an important sense, this might be described as the demonetization of man. There is a passage in *Future Shock* that describes the new civilian:

> We find the emergence of a new kind of organization man—
> a man who, despite his many affiliations, remains basically un-
> committed to any organization. He is willing to employ his skills
> and creative energies to solve problems with equipment pro-
> vided by the organization, and within temporary groups estab-
> lished by it. But he does so only so long as the problems interest
> *him*. He is committed to his own career, his own self-fulfillment.*

Over his working career, the advance of technology and the process of change would require the civilian to maintain his education, learn new skills and perhaps learn entirely new disciplines and strange jobs. The organization for which he works may change its own structure in response to the onslaught of

---

* Alvin Toffler, *Future Shock*. New York: Random House, 1970, p. 134.

change. Whether he chooses, or is able, to hold a job within the changing structure of the civil service state, his freedom from anxiety about satisfying his basic needs for food, clothing, shelter and receiving the general respect of society, would leave him no excuse for failing to move toward realizing his fullest social potential. He would be able to shake free of the cocoon in which society's and his own image of himself as an economic man has shrouded him, and spread his social wings.

A second economic category of people in the civil service state, small in number indeed beside the civilians, is the holders. These are the present owners of substantial amounts of wealth, in the form of land, stocks, bonds, works of art and other forms of wealth of high money value. They might also be called inheritors, feoffees, donees, owners or, indeed, capitalists. In communist and strictly socialist societies, such people are theoretically nonexistent. They are somewhat anachronistic in capitalist societies too. Estate, gift and income taxes take their toll. At current U.S. estate tax rates, a single holder who dies with a taxable estate of $1,000,000 may pass less than $700,000 of it through his estate to the next generation. State governments take some of what is left. No constitutional amendment would be required to reduce the sum a holder could pass to the next generation, after taxes, to nothing or practically nothing. A "reform" or "adjustment" of death tax rates and exemptions would do the job.

Through investment, the holder's capital finds its way into large corporate enterprises, where it sometimes exerts control, or at least insures secure employment of the holder, if he chooses to seek it. These enterprises in turn provide much of the capital necessary to carry on much of the world's work. But individual stockholders and landowners still remain the ultimate owners of the large private corporations, banks and insurance companies. So ownership of most enterprises in the private sector must ultimately be traced back to individual holders with significant capital investments, and to individual civilians and voluntares who are clambering into the holder class.

With the constant increase of taxation and the increasing rate of inflation, the assets of private holders relatively are not increasing, but the large fortunes which holders have been able to build up through this process of accumulation, as well as what they inherited from earlier generations, have left a permanent legacy of great inequality of property in Western society today. One finds it easy to make money if one has some, and next to impossible if one has none.

The holders retain an important place in United States society. John Maynard Keynes' description of capitalists, who "were allowed to call the best part of the cake theirs on the tacit underlying condition that they consumed very little of it," applied to the old style holder-enterpreneur managing a business that he had built up through use of his own resources of capital and energy. There are still a few of them, but in the main, industry and trade are now dominated by managerial capitalism, that is, by companies which are nominally owned by a shifting population of shareholders, but are actually run by a salaried staff of civilians. The holder's rights as the owner of shares of such a company usually concern him only in cases of extreme emergency. The return on his shares is what really concerns him. Since this is merely an alternative to the interest he might earn on a loan, or the rent he might receive as a holder of real estate, his role in business is largely passive, like that of a rentier.

The distinction between civilians and holders is easy to see in the majority of cases, but drawing or defining the line makes for schematic neatness. So a holder may be said to be one whose income from his investments is sufficient to permit him to live without the necessity of having to hold a job in the civil service state in order to avoid falling into the fourth class, that of the dependents. Many holders carry little or no cash in their pockets. Cash and money as cash is a greater threat to them than to any other class, and a cashless society would be a greater boon.

A third and still smaller class, and yet one for whose benefit it might be said that all others ultimately exist, might be called the "managerial elite," but that would be too narrow a phrase. This category would take in the "professional specialists" who seem to derive their rewards from inward standards of excellence, from their professional attainments and from the intrinsic satisfaction of their tasks. It embraces men and women with exceptional skills and abilities, unusual drive and unusual talent. But these exceptional men and women are not found only, or even most often, in business and government. These people are also the professional musicians of talent, the symphony orchestra conductors, the first-violinists, the singers of operatic quality, the composers, playwrights, artists, poets, prize-winning novelists, the Nobel laureate candidates in science and the economists who construct recognizable images of reality. Their inner qualities are such that they do not depend on performing within a structured civil service system. They are able to create systems of their own. They are men and women who have universal skillfulness, the energy to put it to use and the daring not to be afraid to do so. Some of them have genius. All societies need them, and in most societies they can instantly be identified, even though they may choose to hold civil service jobs, or are fortunate enough to be holders. If their appearance in a particular country at a particular time were fostered by the size of a country's economy, or its affluence, or even the easy accessibility of higher education, the United States should have produced many more of them than have appeared in the present generation.

These exceptional men and women have no more need for cash money than ordinary civilians; they are better equipped to look after themselves in all circumstances. For shorthand pur-

190

poses, they are here called voluntares. The word reminds us of volunteers who enter into, or offer themselves for, difficult or worthwhile service of their own free will, and have the talent to excel in whatever they volunteer to do. Incidentally, it also reminds us of the philosophical doctrines of Fichte and Schopenhauer that conceive will to be the dominant factor in experience, and in the constitution of the world.

These three classes, then—the civilians who are the vast majority of the working members of the civil service state, the holders of capital, smaller in number, free to join the civilians at work or not, as they choose, and the voluntares, the talented managers, the skillful politicians at the top managerial levels of the state, and the artists, writers, composers, musicians, scientists, scholars, golf champions and chess masters—are three of four distinct groupings of the citizens of the civil service state by economic position. There is, of course, much overlapping and movement from one group to another. John Cade might continue to hold his salaried job in his law firm as a civilian, but if he wrote a best-selling novel on the side, which also received critical acclaim he might, as a novelist, qualify for membership in the small circle of the voluntares. At the same time, his royalties, and sale of the motion picture rights, might also qualify him for the happy ranks of holders.

The principal thing that these three classes have in common is that, by and large, their members need have no fundamental economic problems. All civilians receive enough to live on from jobs they hold in large organizations; holders have no economic worries by definition, and voluntares seem always somehow to be able to survive all economic vicissitudes.

Like John Cade, all of them can qualify for extensive amounts of credit: credit cards, bank loans, mortgages, checking accounts and consumer credit. None has any real need for cash money. All, indeed, are better off and safer without it. For many of them, the cashless society has already arrived as a matter of natural evolution. They take its existence for granted. They have no reason to resist it. It is what they already have.

But there is, of course, the remaining class. The fourth class is the revolutionary threat to the security, property and lives of all the other three. This class may be called the dependents.

They are all of the poor, the unemployed, the old, the young at school and college, in communes, on remittances from home, all thieves and prostitutes and pimps, all who cannot qualify as civilians, holders or voluntares. They are the chief victims of inflation and also of war, drought, disease, floods and governmental bureaucracies. Stereotyped concepts of them are useless. By no means all of them are lazy, incompetent, dishonest, slovenly dressed, insecure, in poor health or unhappy with their status as dependents. A common characteristic is that necessity forces them to carry on their economic lives in cash because few of them qualify for bank credit or credit card credit in a society that is otherwise evolving into cashlessness. Such checks as they receive from the government, or from home, they immediately cash. From that point on, they deal entirely in cash or goods. The name for them as a class is dependents because, in one way or another, they are largely dependent for their economic existence on the energy, talent and capital of the three cashless classes. Civilians who retire and become dependents on Social Security payments are not really an exception because with continuing inflation, higher Social Security eligibility levels, higher withholding percentages and higher payment levels, their current Social Security payments depend more on the contributions being made currently by civilians and voluntares now working than on their own past contributions.

It is necessary to dwell on the number of the dependents, and the sense of outrage that this status provokes in many of them, to realize that sweeping changes are in order, not only in the interest of relieving their condition, but also in the interest of protecting the society that the civilians, holders and voluntares enjoy from the possibility of destruction at their hands.

At the beginning of the decade of the 1970s, 24.3 million people in the United States, more than one out of ten people, were living below the poverty line. This line is drawn by Social Security Administration income definitions that vary with the size of the family, sex of its head and whether the family lives on a farm. For example, the poverty line for a non-farm family of four headed by a husband was $3745 annual income. For farmers, the line was $3197. Negroes and other minorities accounted for 31 percent of the total living below the poverty line, although they made up only about 12 percent of the total population. In Sweden, where the standard of living is unequaled in any country except the United States, over 200,000 people were living in poverty. In Britain, unemployment had reached 691,000 people, and the number of working poor had doubled over the previous four years.

In 1960, there were fewer than seven million people on welfare, but at the beginning of the 1970s there were more than 12.5 million. In New York City alone, one of every seven residents—1,165,000 people—were on welfare. As the 1970s began, the number on the welfare rolls was growing by 15,000 to 18,000 each month.

Welfare has become the largest single budgetary expense in New York City and a great many other localities as well. The workings of welfare are weird: it offers the equivalent of a tax-free income estimated as high as $5624 to a family of four which may (or may not) actually have been deserted by its father; it holds out a bonus for additional illegitimate children; a recipient can double his monthly payment by claiming to have lost a check, and in New York it has even included a weekend at the Waldorf-Astoria Hotel as poverty-level housing. In other parts of the country, welfare is an outrage because it may guarantee nothing more than grinding poverty and an income of less than $1600 for a family of four people.

A London social worker, Pauline Ross, was quoted in *The New York Times* as saying, "Poverty perpetuates itself, it can't help it. Boys tend to drop out of school early, at 15 or 16, to work in a shop. People marry at a young age and have children immediately. The cycle doesn't change." And after 25 years of observing poverty in many forms and many countries, Oscar Lewis, in his introduction to *La Vida*, wrote that poverty and its associated traits was a culture or, more accurately, a sub-culture with its own structure and rationale as a way of life handed down from generation to generation along family lines.

The welfare system based on handouts of small sums of cash is an outrage from the human point of view, and a failure from the public point of view. Increasingly, it is a threat to order in the civil service state. This was forcefully illustrated at the beginning of 1971, when Mayor Lindsay arranged for the City of New York to sue the federal and state governments to strike down the laws that mandate welfare costs to New York City which it cannot raise the money to pay. At about the same time, Governor Ronald Reagan of California vetoed a $1.8 million Federal grant for the California rural legal assistance organization, an anti-poverty group. Clearly the cash and cash-less status of the dependents in the civil service state is a threat to all civilians, holders and voluntares, as well as to the security and safety of the civil service state itself.

To relieve the sorry plight of dependents in modern society, governments, legislatures, economic agencies and economists carry on constant tinkering with general economic forces in society. These general economic forces, and all the tinkerings, affect civilians, holders and voluntares, as well as dependents. Increasing or decreasing the money supply, raising depreciation rates, lowering income taxes, raising interest rates and installing wage, price and credit controls are all tried, largely in the name of improving the lot of dependents. Many of these measures have a disastrous impact on members of the other three

194

classes, but unfortunately provide no compensating relief to the dependents. The real problem of the dependents is that of not having enough money, and no credit. Like none of the other three classes, they have no choice but to subsist on the vagaries of the ebbs and flows, handouts and, if necessary, thefts, of money as cash.

Welfare payments, food stamps, social security for the elderly and other forms of governmental economic assistance to dependents are acknowledged to be obligations that all modern states must fulfill. But present-day systems of providing assistance of one kind or another to dependents is a patchwork of overlapping and conflicting laws that often work at cross-purposes. They hardly provide social security at all.

A rational social security system would include two basic features—an assured minimum annual income for all, and access to a higher minimum annual income for a transition period in the case of a civilian, voluntare or holder with a high level of spending commitments who suddenly fell into the dependent class. All of these social obligations of society at large should be paid in the form of credit, not cash, so that the invidious distinction between dependents as people who were not credit worthy, and the other classes, would end.

The basic right of everyone, man, woman and child, not just dependents, but also all civilians, holders and voluntares, to a minimum annual income is slowly coming to be recognized and acknowledged, just as Edward Bellamy foresaw that it would in *Looking Backward*. It would be paid in the form of a credit, not cash, and would be at the same rate for all. If it were available to everyone, whether or not he had a job or income-producing assets, it would at once place dependents on an equal footing with all other members of society and remove the stigma of dependency that is inherent in all existing welfare and minimum income programs and proposals.

To place all recipients on an equal footing, to make sure

that the minimum annual income would be used within appropriate time frames for appropriate purposes, to minimize cheating, to make such cheating as occurs traceable through written documentation and to avoid the dislocations caused by cash, such a guaranteed basic annual income might be drawn one-twelfth each month on an all-purpose credit card direct from the Social Security Administration, or other agency, and would not be affected by the recipients' other income. The annual level of such a credit could be raised or lowered depending on available governmental tax revenues, other governmental commitments, levels of fiscal and monetary aggregates and other social purposes to be accomplished by the revenue gathering and disbursing system. Each person could be allocated the same minimum annual amount, whether he was employed or not, or had other income or not. For example, a current year's level might be $1500 for each adult, $600 for each child under seven and $1000 for each child over that age. Like present Social Security and other types of assistance payments, the basic annual income would be tax free.

In the early 1970s, rising unemployment, a business recession and rising prices dropped many civilians into the dependent class for the first time in their lives. Recessions, changes in technology, bad health, bad luck, corporate takeovers, stock market reverses, accidents and many other things could cause a civilian, voluntare or holder to lose his high income or income-producing assets. Yet such a person often has had spending commitments that did not immediately disappear with his lost income: mortgage payments, rental payments, private schooling for children and a host of other commitments characteristic of the standard of living of people who are not dependents. A comprehensive social security program would provide such a person with a maintenance of income level for a reasonable time in an amount related to the amount of income which he had lost. This would cushion the sudden economic shock of the loss of a high-paying job. The maintenance of income level would gradually be reduced as commitments representing the higher standard of living could be liquidated.

Such a system of minimum guaranteed annual incomes for all, and temporary maintenance of annual incomes in certain cases, would, of course, place a heavy burden on federal, state and local tax-gathering systems. Although the basic federal system of taxing "net income," with its growing number and kinds of exemptions, exclusions, deductions and credits, is becoming more and more like a leaky sieve, the Social Security tax involves no such exemptions, exclusions, deductions and credits. And Social Security tax rates, which apply to nearly all earned income, continue to creep upward. There is very little political resistance to this continuous upward crawl, since every increase is accompanied by an increase in benefits to a large bloc of voters. A substantial increase in the Social Security tax, to pay for the substantial increase in Social Security benefits represented by the basic annual income and maintenance of annual income proposals, would appeal to another large bloc of voters, so it would be a practical political possibility. All collections of tax and distributions of benefits could be handled without cash through a nationwide system of cashless credit.

Dependents would lose their dependent status since they would qualify for governmental credit like civilians, voluntares and holders, although all four classes would, in a broad sense, become to a greater extent dependents of the civil service state. None of the classes in it would then have any cash money or any need for money as cash, except token money for small transactions. This is the kind of revolution that would produce lasting change: a revolution through evolution. The power of the corporate state would not be miraculously ended, but its people would come to understand that it, as with any civil service organization, makes demands but also provides security. In a cashless society, that security would extend not just to

197

civilian, holder and voluntare members, but evenhandedly to them and all dependents as well.

The sum of such evolutionary increments might add up to revolutionary change in the structure of society and the function of money within it. Demonetization means to deprive a coin or paper money of standard value as money. This is what a cashless society might do for the people who were its members. No longer would they or their efforts of necessity be rated in money terms. Everyone would be regarded as being equally entitled to support, without regard to what he did, did not do or did not attempt to do. The demonetization of money, by replacing the illusion that it is cash with understanding that it is credit and debt, might include as a valuable by-product the demonetization of men and women.

Dr. Abraham Maslow holds that as soon as their basic needs for food, clothing and shelter are satisfied, human beings begin to drive toward "self-actualization." *

According to Dr. Maslow's thesis, the "self-actualizing" syndrome provides a basis for a theory of psychology oriented toward man's highest potentialities and values. Because the cashless society removes economic shackles which so largely prevent self-actualization, and makes it possible for the process to begin, the cashless society might make possible and ultimately lead toward the real demonetization of social man.

A demonetized person is one who could become exceptionally healthy psychologically. He could move as far in a positive direction from the so-called "normal" personality as the neurotic or psychotic person moves in a negative direction. Once demonetized, there would be no limit to the desirable, or at least currently popular, human qualities he could display. While not all of these qualities would have appealed to the highest

---

* Abraham Maslow, *Toward a Psychology of Being*, 2nd ed. New York: Van Nostrand Reinhold, 1968; and *Motivation and Reality*, 2nd ed. New York: Harper & Row, 1970.

thinking of all ages—not Pericles' nor Pope's, nor Augustus' nor, indeed, Bellamy's—they provide a useful catalogue of the benefits of demonetization for people in our own. He would be free from fears and inhibitions that cause others to distort and cover up a reality which they find too threatening for direct encounter. He would tend to accept himself, others and nature. He would have enough self-esteem and confidence to have no need of criticizing others. He would be aware of the faults of others, but also of their possibilities and their humanness.

With such a demonetization of man, the broad classifications of people within the civil service state as civilians, holders, voluntares and dependents might slowly fade away. Most would remain civilians who perform some useful service, but all would be dependent on the state, and all would have the chance to become demonetized people. While it is difficult to predict the final outcome, this might finally result in all of them joining a one-class society that would consist entirely of voluntares.

11.

An Economy of Cashless Equilibrium

No real revolution occurs except by evolution. In matters of social and economic organization, giant strides occur only by increments of inches. Here and there in earlier chapters, note has been taken of symptoms of a cashless society. We have seen the proliferation of innumerable kinds and numbers of credit cards. We looked toward the consolidation of the many into one, or a few, a single credit number for each individual and nationwide linkages of many forms of credit in individual local ledger accounts for each member in good standing of the civil service state. This, in turn, would make possible the elimination of checks and checking accounts, promissory notes and the holder in due course doctrine, and all kinds of pieces of paper that are like currency in themselves and represent money-equivalents and substitutes for money as cash.

It has become easier to see that the real nature of money is not as gold, but as credit and debt, merely information about individual people that can be programmed into a computer system. We have begun to suspect that money is not necessarily what the government says it is. Nor a value that "In God We Trust." Some do not, and find a BankAmericard sufficiently trustworthy for all practical purposes.

We have identified the lawlessness of money as an active agent that escapes blame for many social, economic and political ills whose origins are not usually associated with too much money, but rather too little. Once we recognize cash money as an agent provocateur, it occurs that we may not be helpless in the face of such threats as that of uncheckable growth. Once we lose our awe of money as a thing of gold divinely constituted, a "symbol of preeminence ordained by celestial will," the conclusion follows quickly that if we can govern its lawlessness, it is time we made a start on doing so. Such a large but nonviolent and nonpolitical revolution in society, politics and economics by evolution is a prospect opened by the idea of a cashless society.

The steps so far described in the direction toward it are in the nature of mere technical developments and improved computer technology and capabilities, or else relatively moderate extensions of presently existing and proposed welfare, Medicare, Medicaid, Social Security and revenue-sharing measures. Each of these steps in itself seems but incremental and evolutionary in nature. It is the thesis of this study that all these steps may bring us past the point where what may be described without hyperbole as a nonviolent revolution in economics, politics and the general form of organization of society will have occurred.

Sir Roy Harrod once observed that gold is "the sheet anchor of liberty." By removing the gold characteristics of our money, will we be turning ourselves into slaves of something else? What are the social and political implications of these separate steps toward a cashless society, taken together? Will we be walking unwittingly into a whole new set of social, political and economic traps for ourselves that will leave us less free than before we took the first step?

Choice souls of philosophic and generalizing set of mind have grappled with this sort of question since long before Plato without reaching any consensus of right answers. Nor has the generality of mankind carrying out its daily chores seemed to suffer much from the shade of such incertitude, nor insisted that it be dispelled, nor will any catholicon be offered here. Nonetheless, for what it may be worth, some observations of a general nature about the prospects that a cashless society would hold out for the generality of mankind who have read this far may be in order.

It seems likely that the chief obstacle to reaching what may be a more satisfactory form of social and political order is a failure to understand, and as a result to make appropriate responses to, the lawlessness of money as it exists throughout society today, particularly Western-style free enterprise society. By the same "token," one effective means of attaining such a form of social and political order would be through understanding and making full use of the techniques for controlling money which the cashless society offers to us.

What might such a form of social and economic order be like? It would develop out of recognition of the reality of the civil service state. The characterization of the economic system that would prevail when the civil service state had acknowledged and made the most of these possibilities would be an economy of cashless equilibrium.

In an economy of equilibrium, an individual member of society might note with favor at least four significant differences from the way economic life is organized now. First would be the differential access to credit which each member would have with his all-purpose individual local ledger account. As credit cards were issued by many different issuers, the scope and amount of credit available to each individual would broaden, the time permitted for payment would lengthen, the number of sellers of goods and services who were willing to extend credit would increase, and many credit card issuers would make available loans of cash as part of their services. Satisfactory repayment experience might in time demonstrate that each individual could successfully carry a far greater load of debt

202

than banks and consumer credit companies were ever willing to lend before the age of cashlessness. If everyone had an all-purpose local ledger account, there would be no contraction in the amount of credit the credit worthy were allowed to carry, and far less uncertainty and confusion about just what that amount would or should be at any particular time than is presently the case.

But such newfound credit would be available only to the "credit worthy." Those who did not already have credits in local ledgers, or good credit standing from past repayment experience, or held low-paying jobs, or whose job record was spotty, might find it harder than ever to obtain extensive credit, beyond the minimum allocation. We sometimes speak of the split in society between "haves" and "have nots": a new kind of division which we have already seen today between the credit worthy and the non-credit worthy would open up along more or less the same seam. But since even the non-credit worthy would still have their guaranteed annual credits, none would be in want. The achievement of credit worthy status would depend on the individual's efforts to attain and preserve it. So it could not very well be charged that in a cashless society all economic incentives for an individual to better his status would be absent.

Second, the all-purpose local credit ledger would create a new and all but completely efficient way of linking supply and demand in the economy. The linkage of individual credit ledgers with computerized management systems would make available to managements minutely detailed information as to the wants and dislikes of the public. Even now a rudimentary example of such a system is found in the direct linkage of certain chain stores to the factories that supply them. Each time a store sells an article, the purchase is recorded and the information is sent to the factory manager, who is able to replenish the store's stocks, or if sales are slow, discontinue the line, on the basis of all related information compiled in the factory's records. Not only that, the factory manager can also direct production on the factory floor with far greater efficiency and responsiveness to what we the public really want and when. The communications link between the point of consumer purchase and the place of manufacture and supply through local ledgers would give all of us greater influence on what is produced and offered for sale. At the same time, it would force the manufacturer to be more responsive to our desires. In a sense, the individual would vote his preferences many times a day, and those votes would be tabulated, recorded and acted upon for his benefit with a responsiveness that does not exist today.

There is a further point here: money was once the common denominator for all commercial transactions. Sales results in terms of money summed up consumer trends, and management based its decisions on results summed up in money terms. But money terms are, in reality, only one way of reflecting consumer wishes. Money is only the lowest common denominator, so to speak, when it comes to measuring results. Electronic communication links switching information concerning charges at the point of purchase would make it possible for management to break data down into many significant particulars besides money—colors, sizes, shapes and seasons—that are presently hidden by the need to translate all commercial data into money terms for management analysis.

The third extraordinary feature of the local credit ledger would be the opportunity that it would create for government, and the threat it might pose to the individual, of complete control of the individual's personal like through potential total control of his economic life. An issuer of a credit card can cut off its holder's credit, or reduce his credit limits, through design or through error. With a single local credit ledger and transfer system, no anonymous cash transactions outside the system would be possible, and control by the credit supervising authority, whether it be bank or government, would be total.

The fourth revolutionary feature would be the machinery

that the individual's local credit ledger and its national inter-connections would place at the disposal of government economic managers for manipulating everyone in society for political and social purposes determined by the government and carried out by the managers. Increasing or reducing credits either directly, or through raising or lowering income, and income, gift and death taxes, would place in the government's hands one of the most powerful kinds of sanction possible in a society which is cashless.

But it is worth reminding ourselves that the process need not be an authoritarian one. The ability of the system to feed back individual responses to governmental action by means of a process similar to consumers registering their product preferences—the second feature described above—suggests that, at least in a democracy like ours, governmental economic management would necessarily have to become more consensual and less authoritarian.

The possibility that communications in both directions would cause the government's economic managers to exercise their increasingly vast powers with wisdom and restraint is by no means a complete answer to the possibility of despotic authoritarian control that would be inherent in the interconnection of local credit ledgers in an ultimate form of a cashless society. The earlier discussion of the pursuit of cashless happiness in a civil service state acknowledged that a rather unpalatable fact of modern life is that demands of technology, capital requirements of modern business structures, pressures of exploding populations and rising standards of living and human expectations are forcing the United States, as well as all other modern nations—whether democratic, socialist, communist, fascist, monarchist or whatever in political structure—into centralized forms that tend to resemble each other in more and more aspects of economic organization. Even so, they continue to differ significantly from one another in political and social aspects. Compare the United States or France with Russia:

most Western countries recognize that all citizens are entitled to political protections of the same sort guaranteed by our Bill of Rights and Constitution. These political rights are unrecognized by governments of communist, socialist and fascist countries that are in some cases less, in some cases more, economically monolithic than ours.

One might suggest that on a subliminal level which serves as a true index of human feeling, such as fashion in dress, the youth culture of America has understood the distinction here noted. On the level of talk, a more superficial level of consciousness than dress, the young speak of rebellion and revolution against what they see as the monolithic corporate state. Yet they have adopted as their characteristic style of dress, indeed their uniform, the drab blue denim overalls that are the mandated garb of Orwell's police state of 1984. In talk, they oppose the corporate state but at deeper levels of consciousness they demonstrate their desire to join it by adopting its prescribed uniform.

While the young may be in vocal rebellion against what they see as political repression or unwise policy of the political civil service state, they seem to reveal their true desire to live in an economic civil service state where all would be taken care of by a guaranteed annual income, and none would be required to perform work useful to the state from economic necessity. Incidentally, their adoption of the uniform Big Brother prescribed has been a boon to free enterprising manufacturers like Unitogs and the Levi Strauss Company. Big sales of blue denim pretensions to poverty to well-to-do middle-class youth turned those companies into two of 1970's hottest new issues in the stock market.

Centralization of economic power in national governments, whether they be communist, socialist or democratic in political form, and convergence in form of their economic structures, does not necessarily mean that people under every such government are doomed to live under political repression.

No think-tank test more complicated than a comparison of political and economic structures of major countries around the globe is necessary to show that different countries with similar degrees of economic concentration, centralization and convergence present remarkable divergencies in the degree of political freedom that their citizens enjoy. The contrast between political life in the United States and the U.S.S.R. need not be belabored. The point is that political freedom is neither a necessary product nor victim of the advanced state of a nation's economic convergence. Accordingly, frank recognition of such convergence is no barrier to offering the suggestion that for the United States, at least, a cashless society could bring with it an era of political freedom more extensive, humane and responsive to the needs and desires of all its people than any nation has experienced in history.

In 1970, a beautiful young woman named Suzy Averill helped start a weekly newspaper called *The Weekender* in Traverse City, Michigan. According to a story in *Time* magazine, after *The Weekender* had exposed a scandal in the local state mental hospital, the hospital superintendent reputedly got in touch with businessmen who had been advertising in the struggling new paper and they withdrew their advertising. So *The Weekender* went broke and died, but not before publishing Suzy's "Thoughts on a Snowbound Day," under an epigraph from Mark Twain. As well as anything else, these thoughts express many people's general uneasy feeling about life in a cash and carry economy like ours which has reached an advanced stage of convergence:

> Vast material prosperity always brings in its train conditions which debase the morals and enervate the manhood of a nation —then the country's liberties come into the market and are bought, sold, squandered, thrown away, and a popular ideal is carried to the throne upon the shields and shoulders of worshipping people and planted there in permanency. . . . It is curious

207

— curious that physical courage should be so common in the world, and moral courage so rare.

—Mark Twain: *Mark Twain In Eruption*

"Snowbound on a cold blustery day inside your rented quonset hut, you can't help but start thinking. And sooner or later you arrive at the thought of how much better everything would be if you just were rich. Oh, maybe not rich, even, just debtless. Rich enough, anyway, not to have to worry about how you're going to pay for the things you already have, let alone the things you want.

". . . the white collar, middle-class worker is the man in chains in the twentieth century. He's far enough from the bottom to think he can get to the top, and far enough from the top to never get there. He will struggle his entire lifetime to reach an unattainable state of wealth, until his frustration, hopelessness and indebtedness to his creditors brings him to the point of a 'Marxist' revolution. . . .

"Now that I am a part of this middle class—I am even more convinced that I was right about the middle class. Now that I, too, feel the pangs of how to meet the bills, how to have some sort of leisure that I can afford, I see more than ever that it will be the middle-class worker who will have to say, 'Look, I don't want this any more. I don't want to have to work to live. . . . I'd rather live to work and be happy at my work . . . and be paid a fair and decent wage for it.'

"We are forced to work for the money, not for our own satisfaction and sense of accomplishment. . . .

"When you can't see any farther than the dollar that's going to buy medicine for your sick kid, where are you? . . . You're forced to stop questioning your worth in society, your family and job and keep working for the dollar which enables you to maintain status quo. And what you are contributing becomes less important than what you're earning.

"Drop out? How? Not all of us are ready to give up, necessarily. And where would you go? . . . The money is the problem, not the answer, for so many Americans.

"So they dream . . . on a snowy day as I do . . . of riches and comforts, perhaps not beyond their means, but only enough to let them breathe for awhile. And hope to win the Reader's Digest Sweepstakes, or the McCall's prizes . . . as they drive to work in their yet-unpaid-for car." *

Suzy Averill and her generation accept the monolithic civil service state with remarkably little lamentation over the implied end of the free market, individual initiative, private enterprise system. All she asks from the civil service state is basic economic security and an opportunity to perform psychologically satisfying work.

This is the same note Edward Bellamy sounded when he described what had happened in the United States between 1887 and the year 2000 when it had reached his cashless form of society:

> While as yet commerce and industry were conducted by innumerable petty concerns with small capital, instead of a small number of great concerns with vast capital, the individual workman was relatively important and independent in his relations to the employer. When a little capital or a new idea was enough to start a man in business for himself, workingmen were constantly becoming employers and there was no hard and fast line between the two classes. But when the era of small concerns and small capital was succeeded by that of the great aggregations of capital, all this was changed. . . .
>
> The movement toward the conduct of business by larger and larger aggregations of capital, the tendency toward monopoly, which had been so desperately and vainly resisted, was recognized at last, in its true significance as a process which only needed to complete its logical evolution to open a golden future to humanity.

---

* *The Weekender,* January 28, February 4, 1971.

Early in the last century the evolution was completed by the final consolidation of the entire capital of the nation.*

A key to Bellamy's golden future was the fact that people not only lived better materially, but that they became different psychologically, and rather easily recognizable as Dr. Maslow's self-actualizing citizens of the civil service state. In the citizens of 2000 A.D., there was no hunger for money and the things that only money could buy. There was no individual antagonism, but what Bellamy described as a sense of solidarity and love. This included, among other things, translating the Golden Rule into practical day-to-day economic relations, complete equality between the sexes, and no need for deceit and manipulation.

The technical discipline of economics concerns itself with two levels of theory. First, the total economy—general relationships between production, consumption, saving and population —and the ways that these can be manipulated to achieve economic growth. This is called macroeconomics. Second, the technical discipline concerns itself with detailed relationships between the prices of various goods and services, the relative wages and salaries paid for these things, the determinants of rates of interest and levels of production. This detailed and quantified study of limited parts of the economy is called microeconomics.

Both macroeconomics and microeconomics focus on economic activities within one or another of the more highly developed countries, treating each country as a separate compartment. Generally, only highly developed countries keep meaningful economic statistics, and statistics compiled in one country rarely match those from another: for example, methods of reporting national rates of unemployment produce different numbers from country to country that cannot properly be compared with one another. This kind of thing is mentioned in

* Edward Bellamy, *Looking Backward: 2000-1887*. Boston: Houghton Mifflin, 1926.

210

passing only to alert the uninitiated to the fact that economic statistics often mean a good deal less than they seem to.

When making judgments in matters of economic policy it is necessary first to distinguish between the technical aspects on the one hand, and the political and social aspects on the other. Professional economists are usually capable of speaking with authority on the technical aspects of economic problems: the technical possibilities, probabilities and effects of particular courses of action. They make particularly effective use of statistical series and econometric models, for example, showing annual gross national product and level of consumer debt, to describe aspects of "economic reality" in tables of numbers and wavy lines on graphs. As historical records such tables are of great interest; as the basis for forming judgments about future economic, social and political realities, they may prove a great deal less than they pretend.

Because of their imposing statistical and mathematical apparatus, these technical analyses of the real world are quite persuasive to the uninitiated, and practically impossible to argue with, yet they are based on certain simple assumptions about the real world that Suzy Averill and Edward Bellamy would instantly brand as contrary to their experience of it. But a closer look at some of these assumptions shows that they may not be the formidable obstacles to the cashless society that at first blush they seem to be.

The assumption that all human beings are "economic men" ruled primarily by economic motivations, as distinguished from social, political, religious, mystic or sexual motivations, or just plain laziness, is, of course, gainsaid by the works of uncounted philosophers, dramatists, novelists, poets, composers, historians and what-not from long before Plato to long after Freud. Some men and women, to a greater or lesser degree, are moved by economic forces—more perhaps today in highly developed countries than in societies of the past. But efforts to reconstruct models of society at large based on the premise that all men are economic men can hardly fail to strike noneconomists as foolish. A cashless society of the kind suggested here might well correspond much more closely to the reality of the whole dazzling range of noneconomic human motivation.

Hardly anybody claims any more that all businesses in a national economy are small, and that no firm has power to distort or control the market in which it operates for its own advantage. It is obvious that the firms that do most of the business in the most important markets in the economy are large in size and relatively few in number. Both individually and by collective action which government usually cannot effectively prevent, they have significant power to control the markets in which they operate, and the government agencies established to regulate them, for their own advantage, without regard to the general interest of the public. A cashless society would face up to this fact and acknowledge the need for controls in the general interest of all its members.

The assumption that there is no governmental intervention in a market economy, and that the government does not use its power to raise or lower the prices of goods and services, or distort wages, salaries or farm commodity prices in free markets seems just as old hat. The reality is, of course, that the government intervenes in markets in innumerable ways. Direct government purchases, wage and price controls, farm price support programs, tariffs, taxes and Lockheed-type loan guarantees need only be mentioned to illustrate the quaintness of such an assumption. A cashless society need have no obligation to pretend to live by it.

That wages should be based on productivity, and that workers will follow available employment and not distort prices by combining, would come as news to George Meany and Leonard Woodcock, who are not inconsiderable forces on behalf of union members organized behind them. The impact of cost push inflation impresses the unorganized with the strength of these forces.

212

The conventional wisdom of economics is that all firms and workers seek and obtain prompt, correct and complete information about the condition of the market so they can switch their products, services and manufactures into lines which are in greatest demand so as to maximize their profits and respond to the needs of their customers, in accordance with Adam Smith's doctrine of how the "invisible hand" of individual self-interest operates collectively for the general benefit of society at large. Yet it is readily apparent that as a result of governmental controls, advertising, the inability of factories and individuals to move from place to place or skill to skill with any real degree of flexibility, simple inefficiency and the lack of accurate information about the condition of the market, switches in economic pursuits are all but impossible as a practical matter. A cashless society would seem to have little interest in perpetuating such a myth.

It is implicit in most assumptions of technical economics that there will be no fundamental changes in national conditions over time—neither political, technological, social, religious, nor psychological. Yet alternation of liberal and conservative Presidents, Congresses and Supreme Courts, trips to the moon, hippie communes, Jesus freaks, mind-altering drugs and books like *Future Shock* are evidence that fundamental changes are occurring all the time at an accelerated pace.

Like the simplistic idea of "economic man," the assumption that the wants of all people are unlimited, while it may be true of a limited number of people at limited times and places, as a general proposition is simply nonsense. Bellies are finite, and an individual's wakeful hours are limited in number. Much of what we most want and consume is not a service or a manufacture which is bought and sold in the marketplace; the part that is may be small and constant.

It is said that work is effectively performed only if it is structured into specialized jobs, and money incentives are patterned in such a way as to force people to hold jobs. And yet the sloppy performance of highly paid workers on the most efficiently structured automobile assembly lines in the world, and the brilliant performance of a first novelist whose years of writing usually do not earn enough royalties to cover his publisher's advance, verify the truth of an opposite reality. In a civil service state, a secure although modest level of income would be important to all civilians, but a higher level of money income might make relatively little difference to many of them, as long as they were secure in the knowledge that what they had would not be taken away.

In calculations of gross national product, and other important economic statistical series, the costs of economic growth in terms of extraction from and exploitation and degradation of the environment are generally ignored, notwithstanding that before the present century is over, generations now alive will dig up, burn out, use up and wear out a significant portion of the earth's total resources of soil, petroleum, minerals, water and timber that nature took millennia to create. The economic costs of consumption and degradation of the limited resources of the globe have become too high to ignore. Are we free from all obligations to account to future generations for the use we have made of what the past has left to us?

Of all the canons of economics, the one that is probably closest to an article of unquestioned faith is the tenet that in normal times jobs must be found for all who desire them, and that all who desire jobs must be able to find them. This belief brooks no cavil that "normal times" hardly ever occur, or that a jobseeker ought to be qualified for the job he seeks, or that many seek jobs for which they are not qualified, merely because they naturally like the idea of high pay or short hours. Yet the more common sense one tries to bring to bear on this belief, the more ridiculous it seems. One corollary of it is that the public must be prepared to purchase all products of extraction and manufacture, and all services that are offered. Otherwise, of course, there will be a shortage of jobs, and some people will be making things, and offering services, which no one else wants. Yet the reality seems to be that neither the number of desirable jobs nor the public's wants are unlimited. The quantity of love beads, hand-tooled leather goods, stained-glass peace symbols and fringed things offered for sale to the public along the roadsides nowadays appears to overwhelm any conceivable levels of public demand. A cashless society would be a first step toward a means of rationalizing the prevailing confusion among useless manufactures for profit, the pursuit of pleasant hobbies and passing the qualifications for optional merit badges mandated by The Boy Scouts of America.

Finally, the competitive model of society leaves no way for people to maintain a decent standard of living without holding a job. Governments are hectored to find ways to insure that every family unit has at least one jobholder in it. As a result, jobs are created to perform unneeded work; jobholders who are not competent to perform the jobs they hold are promoted to make room for other jobholders, or they contribute to papershuffling and inefficiency, or simply produce defective products or perform inefficient services. All this exacts a cost in terms of waste and entirely unnecessary consumption and spoilage of natural resources. A fully established cashless society would acknowledge frankly that no amount of retraining or makework jobs would be likely to enable the precise number of people who are without jobs to perform effectively the exact number of jobs that were available and useful. Acknowledging the existence of this problem, a cashless society would eliminate makework jobs, and not place civilians in jobs they were incompetent to perform. It would thus be able to increase the aggregate total of efficiently manufactured and priced products and services, as well as the time for hobbies and other noneconomic activities available to all.

The conventional teaching of economics is that man's nature is essentially economic, not social. In a market economy, labor as well as land are regarded as commodities, just as money is. Both are treated as if they had been produced for sale. Both the private enterprise, profit motivated, free market, capitalist society of the United States, and the publicly owned, state-controlled socialist societies under Marxism tend to convergence on the view that human nature is essentially economic. Many authorities more up to date than Aristotle support their side of the argument.

Like a great many other debatable insights, the contrary idea that man is essentially a social being, not an economic being, is attributed to Aristotle. That is, man's interest in goods, possessions and money is primarily a means for making himself secure in his social status with his family, friends, acquaintances and enemies. His money insures the respect and, if possible, the goodwill of society at large. In this view, money is a means to an end but not an end in itself.

The four categories of civilians, holders, voluntares and dependents into which the preceding chapter divided the classes of people in the civil service state for purposes of analyzing the impact of a cashless society upon their lives remains bleakly economic. Removing the stigma of dependency on cash from dependents, and from the other three classes the dangers inherent in lawless and uncheckable growth of money as cash by giving dependents the same access to credit as the other three classes, would place all four classes on the same money footing, but still deal with them as economic men. So would awarding everyone in all four categories the same minimum annual income, and the same maintenance of income guarantee funded by higher Social Security taxes.

But the ideal of a cashless society may be seen as a supportive structure for introducing social and political policies that gain wide popular support into society at large with greater effectiveness and within shorter time frames than is possible where money remains money as cash. In this light, it may be seen as a means for putting the myth of economic man at last to rest. Its existence might help do away with pervasive human fears of loss of basic economic support, or with fears of sudden insolvency through loss of a high-paying job. It holds out promise of relief from the physical dangers and social stigma of being required to use cash for all transactions, since all economic transactions would be carried out by use of credit and credit cards. It might make it unnecessary for a man to hold a specific job within the structure of the civil service state, and remove the social stigma of not having a job, or of losing a job. It would make it easier to face up to the hard fact that there are probably not enough jobs of the kind everyone wants for everyone who wants a job.

If the dozen or so assumptions of academic economics challenged in the preceding paragraphs should continue to serve unchallenged as the guidelines of national economic policy, it seems inevitable that governments, business firms, labor unions, all civilians, holders, voluntares and dependents will continue to be forced to pursue policies which press always toward the maximum rate of economic growth in all sectors of the economy of every country. All are "locked in" to an unlimited growth policy, because the always increasing, indeed unlimited desires of economic man, and his insistence on a job which he desires to perform, regardless of his competence to do so, admits of no alternatives, given unquestioned adherence to the conventional theology of economics.

In his essay "The Theory of Countervailing Power," Professor John Kenneth Galbraith explained that private economic power is held in check by the countervailing power of those who are subject to it. The first begets the second. The long trend toward concentration of industrial enterprise in the hands of a relatively few firms has brought into existence not only strong sellers, but also strong buyers. The two develop together, not in precise step but in such a manner that there can be no doubt that the power of the one grows in response to the power of the other, and counterweights it.

Accepting the validity of this ingenious defense of existing arrangements for certain periods of our history does not concede it to be a checkmate to the economy of a cashless society. Relatively few of us are members of strong pressure groups, or benefit from the efforts of one struggling with another. When, after a strike that brings hardships to many nonparticipants, steel workers receive a wage increase with a new contract, the steel companies immediately raise steel prices, and sooner or later most other prices in the economy also rise. Fifty years ago, Kin Hubbard had Abe Martin say: "If capital and labor ever do git together, it'll be Good Night for the rest of us." For all practical purposes, as far as most of us are concerned today, they have and it is. No countervailing power to match theirs exists anywhere in society except in governmental economic managers.

The elimination of all forms of money as cash and substitution for it of electronically transferable credit would erect a technological structure with a capability for economic management subject to human intervention which could be dedicated to the service of social ends. The risks of mismanagement of a frankly managed economy are great. But in the face of the lawlessness of money and the threat of uncheckable growth, the risk of having no management capability of this kind at all appears to be a far more serious risk. If this proposition stands, the cash and carry political economy of the present should give way to a future cashless economy of equilibrium.

Each of the dozen above mentioned beliefs of academic economics about the nature of our economic system is challenged above by what is perhaps too confidently called common sense, and by the counter-possibilities for dealing with the same area of economic life in a safer, and more efficient and lawful way through a cashless society.

Each of the dozen challenges to the conventional wisdom thus serves as a plank in a platform for an economy of cashless equilibrium. But what is meant by an economy of cashless equilibrium? The utopian society Edward Bellamy described has often been criticized on the ground that in its state of perfect equilibrium, there was no need or possibility for further development. This is really a criticism only insofar as one agrees with the premise that all men are "economic men," operating under the conventional expansive rules of economics. In Bellamy's society of 2000 A.D., there was no lack of development of trades, science and talent for literature, music and the other graceful arts. The manners of the people themselves seemed gentler and more cultivated toward one another than ours do. Many people today, not just property owners and bird watchers, would agree that the most hideous word in the English language was the word *development*. In the sense that gross national product is not continually growing, the time may be approaching when the ideal society is static on a nationwide basis. But if one does not accept the idea that all men are essentially economic men, to say that a society is in a state of equilibrium may be the highest kind of praise for it.

The thesis here is that in an advanced form of cashless society, the possibility would be present for the economy of a nation and of the world taken as a single economic unit to suffer no growth in overall economic aggregates from year to year. The growth that most nations have experienced in the past has brought the globe and its populations somewhere near the point where there is no assurance that its resources are adequate to support all members of generations now living at the level of economic development to which the conventional wisdom of economics forces them to aspire, to say nothing of future generations. Indeed, it seems quite possible that some generation in the near future will find itself left without the resources it needs to maintain material standards of living as high as the levels we now enjoy.

The proposition suggested here is that, taking into account all the national economies of the world on an aggregate basis, a mechanism should exist which would place the possibility of arresting further economic growth under the rational control of human agencies, and remove it from the control of the irrational forces of money as cash as it is now. This is not to say that there should not be rapid growth from time to time in one or another particular country, especially if it is an "undeveloped" country. But such rapid growth in one country would have to be offset by slower growth or by a retraction of growth in another country or a future year.

The alternative is not growth versus decline. Glib use of the word "decline" as the alternative to growth hides from us the reality that a retraction of growth is often better for people than growth. Cancer serves as an illustration of this, and so do housing developments at the margins of woodlands and marshlands.

Nor would the economy of equilibrium be an economy that was necessarily stationary, although the economy of the stationary state is another name for it. A stationary state suggests a stasis in all sectors; an economy of equilibrium would be full of movement in all sectors, but the movement of each part would be intelligently related to that of all others, a little like the elliptical metal planes, fins and vanes of a huge Alexander Calder mobile, turning and springing up and falling to rest in a gentle breeze, in motion everywhere, stationary nowhere, except at the still point of fulcrum or suspension.

A cashless society in the place of the lawlessness of money in our cash and carry society would provide a medium through which human intelligence could begin to construct social and economic forms that would lead to social states of kaleidoscopic equilibrium suggestive of that which is observed in the ever-changing, never the same, aspects of Calder mobiles. This concept is the economy of cashless equilibrium. With astonishing prescience, John Stuart Mill was concerned with the same idea, but named it for its fulcrum instead of its fins. In *Of the Stationary State*, he writes:

... Towards what ultimate point is society tending by its industrial progress? When the progress ceases, in what condition are we to expect that it will leave mankind?

It must always have been seen, more or less distinctly, by political economists, that the increase of wealth is not boundless: that at the end of what they term the progressive state lies the stationary state, that all progress in wealth is but a postponement of this, and that each step in advance is an approach to it.

This impossibility of ultimately avoiding the stationary state —this irresistible necessity that the stream of human industry should finally spread itself out into an apparently stagnant sea— must have been, to the political economists of the last two generations, an unpleasing and discouraging prospect; for the tone and tendency of their speculations goes completely to identify all that is economically desirable with the progressive state, and with that alone.

I cannot, therefore, regard the stationary state of capital and wealth with the unaffected aversion so generally manifested towards it by political economists of the old school. I am inclined to believe that it would be, on the whole, a very considerable improvement on our present condition. I confess I am not charmed with the ideal of life held out by those who think that the normal state of human beings is that of struggling to get on; that the trampling, crushing, elbowing, and treading on each other's heels, which form the existing type of social life, are the most desirable lot of humankind, or anything but the disagreeable symptoms of one of the phases of industrial progress.

The density of population necessary to enable mankind to obtain, in the greatest degree, all the advantages both of cooperation and of social intercourse, has, in all the most populous countries, been attained. A population may be too crowded, though all be amply supplied with food and raiment. It is not good for man to be kept perforce at all times in the presence of his species. A world from which solitude is extirpated, is a very poor ideal. Solitude, in the sense of being often alone, is essential to any depth of meditation or of character; and solitude in the presence of natural beauty and grandeur, is the cradle of thoughts and aspirations which are not only good for the individual, but which society could ill do without. Nor is there much satisfaction in contemplating the world with nothing left to the spontaneous activity of nature; with every rood of land brought into cultivation, which is capable of growing food for human beings; every flowery waste or natural pasture ploughed up, all quadrupeds or birds which are not domesticated for man's use exterminated as his rivals for food, every hedgerow or superfluous tree rooted out, and scarcely a place left where a wild shrub or flower could grow without being eradicated as a weed in the name of improved agriculture. If the earth must lose that great portion of its pleasantness which it owes to things that the unlimited increase of wealth and population would extirpate from it, for the mere purpose of enabling it to support a larger, but not a better or a happier population, I sincerely hope, for the sake of posterity, that they will be content to be stationary, long before necessity compels them to it.

The placing of controls over the lawlessness of money itself, of checking uncheckable growth through the elimination of money as cash, of comprehensive controls over credit through computer capabilities created by modern technology subject to "the deliberate guidance of judicious foresight" was not foreseen by Mill. But the local credit ledger with nationwide electronic interconnections for each individual opens up this possibility for the civil service state.

Having shackled the lawlessness of money and put a checkrein on the threat of uncheckable growth, and in possession of powerful electronic machinery of a kind undreamt of by Mill or Edward Bellamy for regulating the economy, "under the deliberate guidance of judicious foresight," the cashless society could be a means of improving and elevating the universal lot of those who are now living, and preserving the limited resources of the finite globe for as many future generations of our offspring as we would then no longer need to try to number.

12.

The Cashless
Society

The economic history of the United States has seen many changes that at first seemed radical and revolutionary, but as time passed came to be understood as products of historical necessity. The cashless society seems to be coming upon us in very much the traditional way.

After Andrew Jackson had prevented the renewal of the charter of the Second Bank of the United States in 1836, throughout most of the rest of the nineteenth century the money system of the country was a checkerboard of currency chaos. At one time or another, 1600 or more banks issued 10,000 or so different kinds of bank notes. These notes were the principal medium circulating as money because checkable demand deposits were then still largely unknown. Notes of a bank located in one state were usually unacceptable in other states, or if they were accepted at all, only at deep discounts of 10 or 15% or more. Nobody planned the "system" that way, nor was it a system at all. But this nonsystem grew and served the economic needs of the nation during one of its greatest periods of growth. In time, a more centralized system of monetary control replaced it.

Under the Federal Reserve Act of 1913, based on the National Banking Act of 1863, the Federal Reserve system was established to unify and centralize money and credit in the national economy. In the national economy, the Federal Reserve notes it issued replaced bank notes of the state and local banks as money. As the years passed, in function if not in name, the Federal Reserve system took on the powers, duties, obligations and mystique of a national central bank for the United States.

If it had been called the Third Bank of the United States, the central bank's name would have certified to the truth of the fact that not even intense political opposition like that which had put out of existence the First and Second Banks of the United States could prevent the imperatives of history from working toward a stronger and more effective institutional central banking structure as years passed. Calling it the Third Bank of the United States would not have obscured its pre-eminence over all of the First National Banks in the country put together.

In this historical context, aspects of a cashless society that would require a national reserve system to maintain nationwide data linkages of each individual's and organization's ledger account with every other, and a nationwide balance of individual credits and debts in lieu of money as cash, appear to be no more than a further movement in the same direction that history has been moving the money system of the United States for 200 years.

In typically free economic societies like those of the United States and Britain, national central banks like the Federal Reserve system and The Bank of England are expected to take some responsibility for such broad social objectives as general welfare and growth, full employment and economic stability within the country. Although innumerable other agencies also carry on activities designed to affect one or another of these aspects of economic welfare, national central banks play the most conspicuous role. They fulfill their responsibilities essentially by regulating various national monetary aggregates as aggregates of cash. In theory, at least, central banks do not "print money."

By adjusting bank discount or rediscount rates upward or downward, by raising and lowering national banks' ratios of liquid reserves to deposit liabilities, by selling and buying government securities to and from the banking system, thus raising and lowering interest rates and by permitting officials to make "jawboning" statements about economic matters, central banks increase or decrease the amount of money available to the banks and businesses and private citizens and government of the country, and seek to influence public opinion on economic matters. Such central banking activities are far removed in scope and complexity from the methods the goldsmiths' guild of London followed when they raised or lowered the percentage of gold bullion they held in their vaults as backing for "notes accountable," but the historic model for the basic structure of modern national central banking remains easily discernible.

The economy of the United States in the late twentieth century no longer lends itself to reproduction in terms of such a simple model. With a 1972 gross national product of about $1,150 billion, and $2 trillion predicted for the mid-1970s, it is a national economy that is almost unimaginably huge in size. Banking organizations subject to the reach of the Federal Reserve system's direct regulation of monetary aggregates are responsible for large volumes of money and credit, but non-bank agencies outside the reach of Federal Reserve regulation, entirely beyond the effective reach of central bank monetary control, create additional vast volumes of money and credit. Such non-central bank agencies include government agencies and quasi-government agencies like the Federal National Mortgage Association, corporate securities issuers, issuers of commercial paper, commercial credit, private lending operations and the like. Outstanding balances on credit card transactions form a significant part of this vast but uncontrollable volume of credit and money. All of these sources of money as cash contribute greatly to a trend opposite to the direction of a cashless society.

Major governmental and international policies, such as the financing of wars, foreign aid, subsidies to farmers, import and export duties and tariffs, tax shelters and loopholes for innumerable activities deemed worthy of special favor, or favored by the electoral constituency of the political party in power, are carried on for many reasons not primarily economic. Such policies run counter to all central bank efforts to pursue general welfare, growth, and economic stability.

So do worldwide economic events which are beyond the control of any one government: balance of payments deficits and surpluses; devaluations and revaluations of national currencies; rises and declines in rates of inflation and labor productivity from country to country; political revolutions which raise costs of scarce natural resources like petroleum and copper; currency exchange policies followed by multi-national corporations; international flows of Eurodollars and other forms of credit and money used as a medium of international exchange, and so on.

All of these economic tides are beyond the effective reach of any system of national control by the Federal Reserve system, any other national central bank, the International Monetary Fund or any other human institution.

Control of national economies falls less and less within the effective control of national central banks and lodges elsewhere, or nowhere. The power and ability of the Federal Reserve System in the United States, and of other national central banks, to exercise firm, timely and effective controls whose end results are reasonably predictable over national economies has grown attenuated to the point of invisibility.

The Federal Reserve system's "tight money" policy of 1969 failed to make more than a temporary "dent" in the rate of

United States inflation, and may have helped cause the subsequent acceleration of the rate. United States banks got around the "tight money" policy by simply borrowing funds at higher interest rates in the unregulated Eurodollar market. The Federal Reserve system's early 1971 policy of expanding the money supply at extremely high annual rates of 10 and 11 per cent for the purpose of restoring growth and prosperity in time for the 1972 national elections lagged disappointingly in accomplishing either objective. In recent years, the all but futile efforts of the central bank money managers to manipulate the economy are no longer spoken of as "fine tuning," except by way of derision. In the summer of 1971, no less an authority than Arthur Burns, the Chairman of the Federal Reserve Board, told a Senate Committee that "the laws of economics are not working quite the way they used to."

The Republican President's new economic policy of August 15, 1971, froze prices and wages, promised to cut government spending and taxes, proposed investment credit tax incentives for business, a ten percent tax on imports and unilaterally repudiated the United States' treaty-imposed obligation to exchange gold for dollars at $35 an ounce. Few other economic options were left to the President. His new economic policy certified in the most dramatic way possible the truth of Dr. Burns' rueful observation.

Professional economists were all but unanimous in their early praise for these Draconian measures, which most of the Democrats among them had been urging all along. Few among them criticized scrapping the free market, the Bretton Woods system, the theoretical convertibility of the dollar or the faith that Adam Smith's invisible hand operating through private enterprise in a free market would regulate the economy for the general good more effectively than any authoritarian central control such as the new economic policy imposed.

Few spoke out in defense of existing or traditional arrangements. Far from being too long a step in the direction of central governmental control of the national economy, it seemed that a cashless society would be the next logical step. Or if the new economic policy should fail to work in its subsequent phases, its authors may even reach the point of demanding a cashless society as a last resort.

Piecemeal, limited and of dwindling effectiveness to accomplish their purposes within their own countries, national central banks like the Federal Reserve system are paragons of power and efficiency by contrast with the complete chaos that reigns on the international monetary scene. No international agency, nor any national central bank, has any significant power to control international monetary tides and currents. The International Monetary Fund goes through the motions of carrying out the Bretton Woods agreement without being able to exercise any real influence or power. The position of national central banks in the international arena is roughly comparable to the position of separate state banking regulatory systems in the United States after the demise of the Second Bank of the United States and before the National Banking Act. The result in the growing United States was a continent-wide checkerboard of currency chaos. The separate national central banks in each separate country today find themselves in a far more chaotic situation.

Paradoxically, however, the world economic scene has been working with cashlessness as a normal part of its day-to-day business for years. Under the gold standard and the gold exchange standard, gold was seldom shipped from country to country to balance transactions. The promise of shipment, or "gold tomorrow," was all that was necessary. Under 1967 amendments to the Articles of Agreement of the International Monetary Fund, $10 billion worth of Special Drawing Rights, or "paper gold," was created to be activated over a three-year period beginning in 1970. The total would represent about one-fourth of the value of the Western world's supply of monetary gold.

When the peculiar institution of "special drawing rights," or SDRs, or "paper gold," was created, the United States argued that SDRs were really newly created money, while France argued that they were merely additional credit. Othmar Emminger, the Vice Chairman of the West German Bundesbank, joked that they were really zebras: "One can say that they are a black animal with white stripes and another can say that they are a white animal with black stripes." No truce in the conflict between the illusion of money as cash and the reality of money as credit and debt was yet at hand.

In essence, SDRs are a pool of monetary reserves in the International Monetary Fund that become available to participating member governments as decided by the Fund, but they are not like ordinary drawing rights in the Fund which are like loans, or credits, and must be repaid, because they do not represent a "quid pro quo" for an existing deposit. They are new reserve assets created by fiat of the Fund by vote of its members and they have a continuing international life of their own. They have a unit value expressed in terms of gold, but they are not represented by any metal, coin, or paper currency; they are merely a book entry, an entry in the international reserve system's central data bank. Technically, the new asset was established by electronically computing and transferring each participant's allocation onto a computer magnetic tape, since all accounting for SDRs is done by means of a computer. The principal feature of the system is that it was designed to compute and record in detail all movements of SDRs either from one participant to another or from a participant to the General Account of the Fund, or to any other authorized holders (although at present there are no other authorized holders).

Special drawing rights in the International Monetary Fund are a striking example of a kind of reserve asset which exists nowhere except in a computer's memory. They are a prototype of a kind of credit that might provide a medium of exchange and a substitute for all other kinds of money in a cashless society. Unfortunately, in the chaotic state of the world monetary system precipitated by the introduction of the new economic policy, the effective growth and use of special drawing rights will be delayed until such time as broad new changes in worldwide monetary arrangements can be agreed upon by the leading nations. Nevertheless, the example of special drawing rights in the International Monetary Fund and the experience in computer technology gained through handling them there will serve as a valuable model to build on when cashless societies are introduced into national economies.

The voting rights of the countries of the European Economic Community, voting as a bloc, are such that no additional special drawing rights can be created without their approval. So in this respect the European community, not the United States, holds this key to the door of a worldwide cashless society, if it is to be based on credits derived from special drawing rights.

If special drawing rights, the new kind of cashless worldwide money weaned through years of planning and negotiation under the aegis of the International Monetary Fund, may be compared to a hothouse plant, then Eurodollars, another important kind of cashless worldwide money, may be called a rank weed. Eurodollars start out simply as United States dollars deposited with banks outside the United States, but instead of being converted into the local currency of the country where the bank is—British pounds or French francs, for example—they continue to be denominated in dollars. Once the foreign bank has acquired the dollar deposit, it may lend it directly to another customer still denominated in dollars, or it may convert it into another currency for lending to a local customer. Or, indeed, as often happens when the deposit is with a foreign branch of a United States bank, it may send the deposit back to the head office of the bank in the United States. Creating Eurodollar deposits was, in effect, a way almost any person or corporation could create money that in the beginning, at least, was not subject to effective controls by any national central bank or international agency. No one knows the total of Eurodollars outstanding, but estimates at the beginning of the 1970s ranged up to $50 billion and more. For a time, in the late 1960s and early 1970s, Eurodollars became for many practical purposes a worldwide international money. They represented a long step forward in international economic integration.

As it turned out, their principal flaw was that they were interchangeable with domestic United States dollars used in the United States' domestic economy. When the United States' domestic economy became unstable in the late 1960s as a result of high rates of inflation, a recession and vast unfunded military expenditures for the Vietnam war, confidence in Eurodollars abroad began to erode as foreign confidence in United States domestic dollars and policies at home eroded. Notwithstanding powerful arguments and tough talk by United States economic officials to their European counterparts in the months following announcement of the new economic policy, it seems unlikely that the Common Market countries will vote to unlock more SDRs until they receive believable assurances, or believable evidence, that Eurodollars are effectively locked up.

Even before adoption of the United States' new economic policy, central banking authorities of most advanced Western countries had unilaterally imposed one or another form of exchange controls and direct interference with the course of world monetary movements, primarily to curtail the disruptive movements of Eurodollars. For example, France split her foreign exchange market into a commercial sector to handle trade and commerce, and a financial sector for capital movements. The central bank supported the "commercial" franc at a level near its IMF parity, but let the "capital" franc "float"; Japan, for another example, has a network of controls and guidelines that limit domestic banks' holding of United States dollars. In spite of these officially isolationist tendencies that have developed, the major economies of the world are becoming more intimately stitched together by the activities of multinational corporations, international banking and financing groups, increasing travel and tourism and broader international aid and inter-governmental cultural exchange programs. As a result, the efforts of separate central banks in each separate country to maintain its country's economic position by "across the board" regulation of monetary aggregates has become less and less effective.

In a 1971 report, the International Monetary Fund roused itself from its customary cultivation of a low profile and called for a system of selectivity in international capital flows. It recommended that separate countries be prepared to head off or moderate occasional large capital movements and thereby ease excessive pressures on exchange rates. The Fund's report identified a number of "simple and flexible" tools that could quickly be brought to bear during periods of unusual currency activity. These tools include regulation of the net cash positions of central banks, of banks' reserve requirements and regulations against foreign borrowings or lending by large domestic enterprises. Such measures are now being widely used by a great many countries. Whether these measures represent progress or retrogression in the international economic sphere may depend upon whether your point of view is that of the United States, which tends to oppose such controls, or that of most other Western countries, which increasingly tend to resent the hegemony of the dollar and accompanying United States influence in their own national economies.

There can be no doubt that the world lacks and seriously needs a strong international central bank which could do for the national central banks of each separate country, and the separate currencies used by each separate country, what the Federal Reserve system did in the United States for the separate state banking systems, and the separate locally issued bank note currencies that it largely superseded. Unfortunately, the

International Monetary Fund, as it operated from the time of the 1944 Bretton Woods agreements until the international money crises of 1971, failed to fulfill this international central banking function, and fell far short of furthering the noble purposes envisioned for it by the Atlantic Charter of 1941: "to strive to promote mutually advantageous economic relations" between the nations, and to further "the enjoyment by all peoples of access on equal terms to the markets and to the raw materials which are needed for their economic prosperity."

Under the powers assigned to the IMF by its Articles, it could have done, or attempted, a great deal more than it did. The absence of effective striving by the Fund in the international arena, apart from its more or less bureaucratic administration of the system of fixed exchange rates, has forced the separate national central banks to struggle as best they could with the mounting problems that beset them on the international scene, with indifferent results. With the onset of the long-drawn-out international money crisis that began in May 1971, the system of fixed exchange rates between currencies weakened. When the system broke down completely the following August, the separate nations were left well short of where the separate states of the Union had stood after the end of the Second Bank of the United States in 1836 and before the National Banking Act of 1863. All countries collectively were threatened with a breakdown of world trade, a return to protectionism, the erection of world trade barriers and a worldwide depression. Special drawing rights remained in limbo, at least until the crisis could be resolved. Eurodollars were suspect, while Eurobond and Eurodollar financing dwindled.

The seemingly irresistible progress of the international monetary system toward a cashless society came to a halt, temporarily at least, at a time when the inability of each separate national central bank to deal unilaterally with its own country's economic problems was never more apparent. The need for a strengthened international reserve system was never greater.

Under an effective international reserve system, a single international money as a unit of account for all credit and debt transactions would move a few steps closer to reality: Like special drawing rights which have no tangible symbol in the form of cash, such a universal medium of exchange would be most useful, if cashless in form.

Early in 1972, the amount of United States paper money and coin in circulation stood at a record high of nearly $61 billion. This was about $292 for each man, woman and child in the nation, compared with only $182 per capita in 1960. Individuals seem to hold the great bulk of this cash. Currency holdings by businesses, mostly as till money, account for only about 20 per cent of total cash outstanding. Contrary to a famous statement of the late Willie Sutton's, banks are not where the money is either. Their working cash balances range between $7 and $8 billion. These figures may suggest that we are moving away from a cashless society, not toward it.

Such large aggregate holdings of cash are not useful for most law-abiding citizens, but they are the essential medium for operations of organized crime, political racketeering, corporate adventurism, large-scale tax evasion and, of course, counterfeiting. They are also a factor in inflation, international currency imbalances and international monetary crises.

The time to do something effective about all this lawless cash is at hand. We have begun to see that credit cards are more than merely superficial symptoms of the times. Before such hopeful economic structures as we have crumble under the cash pressures upon them, it may be useful to screen a scenario to show how a truly cashless society could come about.

As the first step, all existing credit card systems would be linked, the many duplicating credit ledgers consolidated, the overlaps eliminated and a single credit ledger established for each individual and organization. A single all-purpose credit card and number would be issued to everyone to replace all existing credit cards. An all-purpose credit card would also be issued to everyone who had a Social Security or employee identification number, even if he had never before used a credit card. Minimum and maximum credit limits would be established for each individual ledger.

A date would be announced after which the old paper dollar and coin currency would no longer be accepted or honored as valid. All holders would be given a prior period of grace to turn in their paper currency at banks for further credit-card credits recorded in their favor. All transactions after the announced date would be by credit card. All paper currency outstanding after the end of the period of grace would be void.

A limited number of new token coins would be issued for circulation as tokens for convenience in small transactions, vending machines, paying tolls and similar purposes. The bank deposits established through redemption of the paper currency would strengthen the liquidity of the banking system immeasurably. Over time, in carefully planned steps, all paper which serves as money, or represents in itself, within its four corners, an instrument of value, would be eliminated from circulation. Federal Reserve Notes, Treasury bills, bearer bonds, registered bonds, negotiable certificates of deposit, bankers' acceptances, commercial paper and all forms of U.S. Government agency securities would be deposited in a central depository. Ordinary checks would be eliminated as well. Savings bank passbooks that ordinarily would be presented every time a withdrawal or deposit were to be made would also be surrendered. At later stages along the way to a completely cashless society, other types of documents that represent contingent credit and debt obligations would also be surrendered for credits: installment sale contracts, mortgages, land contracts and consumer credit contracts.

For each such money item surrendered, the central credit bank would issue a computer-printed memorandum to the depositor reflecting the fact that he had deposited a certain sum of money, or a bank balance, or a Treasury bill with a 90-day maturity date, and a cost of, say $97.00. This computer print-out memorandum would not be negotiable in any way, but would merely serve in the way that a bank advice or broker's confirmation slip serves as a written record of the transaction. A similar computer process is now used by airlines. The passenger who has previously reserved his ticket comes to the counter to pick it up, the clerk behind the counter presses the appropriate buttons and all the particulars of the flight, including flight number and times and dates of arrival and departure, are printed out exactly as they appear in the airline's records.

All the money, Treasury bills, bonds and other money assets that the individual turned in to his local bank would be entered on his local ledger account at that bank. Each citizen's salary would, of course, be credited to his local ledger account. If he received welfare, guaranteed minimum income or Social Security payments, these also would be credited to his local ledger account. Bills rendered to him by creditors, if approved by him, or if approved for payment automatically by him in advance of their being rendered, would also be charged to his local ledger account.

A man need no longer display his wealth for society to accept the fact that he has it. The entries in his local ledger would show in an instant how credit worthy he was. Money is information, not cash, and in the cashless society only two kinds of information would be required in each credit transaction: a record of the transaction and proof that the payer has sufficient credit, or credit worthiness, to fulfill his commitment in the transaction. If the idea of a guaranteed minimum annual income supplied by the government to every member of society had been accepted when the time came to eliminate money as cash, a credit would be made to each individual's account at the beginning of the year. If he had a record of using his credit prudently, an individual might be allowed to draw against it throughout the year without restriction. But if he developed a history of overdrawing early in the year, thus leaving himself with no credits for the latter part of the year, for example, he would be allowed to draw only a pro-rata portion of the year's total credit each week or month.

In a cashless society, all members' holdings would be entered on the books of the card issuer, or the central bank, and no cash money would circulate anonymously. The central bank would have open to it the possibility of adjusting monetary aggregates by extending or contracting credits on a comprehensive, selective and precise basis. As a method of control this procedure would be more responsive to policy objectives than the present method of attempting to influence economic trends by adjusting monetary aggregates through general regulations which apply to money across the board.

If all consumers saved most of their earnings instead of spending them, the resulting downturn in economic activity might work to the detriment of all. If the national central bank had the power to impose a policy which over time would cause a contraction in totals of unused credits in favor of citizens, it would have the effect of forcing or at least stimulating the citizen to spend his savings before the central bank reduced his credit balance. This obviously would have a stimulative effect on consumer spending in the economy at large.

On the other hand, during a period when the economy was slack, the central bank could increase the amount of the guaranteed minimum annual credit of cititzens who had no excess cash reserves. Selective application of both policies—to reduce excess credit balances and to increase guaranteed minimum individual credits—would result in a still more effective method of maintaining control over the national economy.

Broadly speaking, national central banks have large powers to increase money aggregates in the economy, but no effective powers to decrease them. As noted above, many other agencies and national policies work to increase national monetary aggregates but are presently beyond the reach of effective central bank control. Forcing interest rates higher, and forcing the banking system to absorb more government debt through open market operations, often prove to be counter-productive. The hard fact is that central banks lack effective tools for limiting the expansion, and forcing the reduction, of monetary aggregates in the national economy.

The possibility of limiting, restricting or reducing the credits available to citizens by the elimination of money in the traditional sense, and the use of individual credit controlled through central banks would be the most precise and effective way imaginable of regulating economic activity in a single society. It obviously would be more comprehensive, and yet capable of more timely and precise adjustment and adaptation and selective application than present central bank efforts to regulate economic activity by adjusting broad monetary aggregates. Such central bank control of individual credit would open up many possibilities for rationalizing other aspects of economic life as well.

Inflation at the recent high rates is stealing from the poor to help the rich. In the name of preserving the private enterprise, free market system, President Nixon's new economic policy introduced a comprehensive program of controls over wages, prices, money and other aspects of economic life whose end is nowhere in sight. By comparison, a cashless society as here suggested would be a no more drastic departure from the economic features of society we have known in the past. Yet it would be a far more efficient and economical way of making possible the accomplishment of the same objectives.

Chief criticisms of all such sweeping programs are: that they "do not work"; that they are simply too big and complex; and that it is impossible to control all wages and prices because too many millions, indeed billions, of transactions are involved. But if every individual and corporate money transaction were recorded on an individual local ledger with a memorandum to support it, the records necessary for enforcement of such a program would be readily available, and a surveillance system adapted to computer operation could be introduced that would be far more effective and less costly in a cashless society than it can possibly be in a cash and carry economy flooded with cash.

Given the premise that individuals spend their funds so as to maximize satisfaction, individual expenditures for goods and services provide a more efficient indication of consumer preferences than do priorities established by legislative action or administrative fiat. At present, government subsidies and controls force patterns of consumption on citizens that conform more closely to the taste of the authorities than those of the individual. For example, in public housing, despite the sizable subsidies provided to occupants who have incomes low enough to qualify, a large proportion of public-housing units are often vacant, or quickly vandalized by the occupants, and the operation of public housing is often in a state of insolvency. A cashless society would not eliminate individual choice, but by recording all individual choices, would make it possible for economic managers to be more responsive to the desires of all because managers' decisions would be based on more complete and accurate information concerning peoples' desires as expressed by them through the choices they made in the marketplace. In a cashless society, information about planning errors of the authorities would be fed back quickly to them, the errors could be corrected and future errors of the same kind punished or avoided.

In a cashless society, the area of tax administration and collection offers other dramatic possibilities for saving labor and paper shuffling, not to mention eliminating innumerable traumatic confrontations with oneself, and with revenue agents as well. If all of every citizen's credit and debt transactions each year were recorded in his local ledger account, the Internal Revenue Service might some day be able to record his gross income, subtract his deductions and exemptions, apply the appropriate rate schedule to the result and tell him the amount of tax he owed for the year. Pressing a button on an appropriately programmed computer might be all that was necessary. His local ledger account could then be debited with the amount due on April 15, and the Service would mail him the usual advice of the transaction. If he disagreed with the Service's computation of his tax, he would have the usual right to appeal its computation within a specified number of days.

Introduction of a cashless society offers other prospects for improving the processes of law enforcement. Since no one would carry any cash, there would be none to serve as a temptation to burglary, robbery and hijacking. Since all money transactions would be recorded in a local ledger linked to a central ledger, the possibility would exist of having evidence available to prove any illegal money transaction. Since ordinary civilians would carry no cash, use of substitutes for cash in payments to prostitutes, to beggars, to airline hijackers, for bribes, to purchase illegal drugs and to carry on other unlawful transactions would make payments traceable, rescindable and preventable. After the commission of a crime had been proven in the ordinary legal manner, a punishment by fine could readily be levied against the convict's ledger account. Monetary sanctions levied against the accounts of those who overdrew their credits in their ledger accounts would discourage overdrafts and encourage regularity in use of such accounts.

But the cashless society is not just the society we have with the cash removed from circulation. It is not merely the issuance to each individual of a single national credit card bearing his signature, his photograph, his fingerprints and his voice recognition computer print. It is not simply the linkage of all local banks and credit-rating institutions to each other and to a single central computerized information interchange under the supervision of the Federal Reserve System, or some newly established central credit data bank. It is more than just a national society in which checks, promissory notes, bills of exchange, bearer and registered bonds have been removed from circulation. It is a society where the lawlessness of money as cash has been placed under a system of record-keeping and -tracing which makes available all details of all money transactions. It is a way to place the proliferation of the aggregate totals of money and the demands it makes on the scarce resources of the earth under rational control. It is more than a way to change present-day society to curb and prevent economic excesses that threaten it. The cashless society opens the way toward a more rational general society.

There are probably not three more shopworn words in current English usage than "New American Revolution." President Nixon, the Black Panthers, the FBI, *Women's Wear Daily* and *Harper's Bazaar* all find them in vogue. Partisans of current self-styled "revolutions" bring fierce verbal overkill to their clamor against political governments in all countries for their failure to bring instant political solutions to such problems as, for example, poverty in the midst of abundance, city ghettoes whose rents support luxurious affluence in surrounding suburbs, the destruction of nature through poisoning of water, air and earth, the position of women, inattention to youth, irrelevance of academic curriculums, the lack of vitamins in breakfast foods, the absence of whole wheat grain from bread, etc. It is as if the clamorous partisans' ignorance of history denied them the knowledge that change was inevitable. It is as if none had ever heard of Heraclitus.

The primary meaning of "revolution" is a progressive motion of a body round a center or axis, such that any line of the body remains throughout parallel to its initial position, to which it returns on completing the circuit. The clamorous partisans use the word in its secondary signification to denote "a total or radical change, as a *revolution* in thoughts," or "a fundamental change in political organization, or in a government or constitution; the overthrow or renunciation of one government or ruler, and the substitution of another by the governed; as the American Revolution. . . ."

Political governments rest upon economic foundations. To a considerable extent, the clamorous partisans who assail political regimes in the name of violent revolution also owe their strength to their own economic security in society. By itself, a cashless society would not necessarily solve any of society's political problems. Without a cashless society, however, the lawlessness of money and the threat of uncheckable growth driven by too much money render most political efforts to meet the problems raised by these challenges ineffective, or counterproductive.

The temptation is strong to claim that the cashless society is a new American Revolution, not in the trivialized secondary sense, but in the primary sense of the word. No political government need be overthrown. It would be a nonviolent, nonradical, yet progressive motion in the economic mode of society through the use of credit cards and other methods of credit verification around a center or axis consisting of computerized data banks linked together. Since this primary denotation of the word "revolution" is too easily confused with its shopworn secondary meaning, a better way to characterize the cashless society is as a new American evolution.

Its introduction would be part of an evolutionary process that would not cause any notable changes in any of the higher realms of political and economic theory. But it would, nevertheless, be the economic axis around which the societal nebula would revolve.

No revolutionary status is claimed for the cashless society because in the primary sense of the word it is already with us. Money may be said to be following a progressive motion around the economic center of society in the direction whence it began in Egypt, where a high degree of civilization existed for more than a thousand years without the use of any tangible physical object that we would identify as money. In this context, a cashless society would provide a sound economic underpinning for all the self-styled political revolutions that are in contest with established values in present-day society, pretty much as Heraclitus foresaw they always would be.

It is often claimed that all men are created equal, but we know that they are not born equal in physical strength, intelligence, determination, drive or familial environment, and that they will never attain true equality in any of these senses. We do acknowledge that they are "endowed by their Creator with certain unalienable rights," and that as time passes governments discover one after another additional "unalienable rights" by which they are and may be made more nearly equal to one another in society. Only the day before yesterday, it seems, the discovery was made that all men and women are entitled to minimum basic support from the state, blacks to equality with whites and women to equality with men.

At about the same time these new inalienable economic and political rights were being discovered, the advance of technology was creating wholly new capabilities whereby the work of a comparatively few members of the total population was able to fulfill the basic needs of all members of society for food, clothing and shelter. What could be a more natural course of evolution than that, out of these new economic patterns of existence, new inalienable rights should arise to claim recognition?

This new and different economic context of life requires reexamination of the beliefs and customs of the past that grew out of the soil of the earlier context: the Puritan ethic of the redeeming value of work; the necessity for a human being to establish his right to all consumer goods because of his own productivity; the acceptance by society of the fact that some fraction of the population must be unemployed and go hungry, and the neglect of externalities in the market such as the cost of industrial pollution and the depletion of irreplaceable natural resources.

Many habits of economic thought that have served well for the last hundred years are less meaningful in the new context. The old system of isolated economic units—individuals, families, banks, states, national governments—with unfettered power to create money or money equivalents, in one way or another, no longer produces economically predictable or socially desirable results. The marketplace and the competitive price system, with anonymous and solitary money as cash as its lifeblood, are no longer adequate as the playing field of our economic lives. Countervailing power, which serves to maintain strong positions for members of the countervailing power centers but grinds down those who are not within the power centers, is not an adequate substitute.

One new requirement for our new economic situation is that the scope of our accounting system must be enlarged to encompass a whole earth system. It ought to have the capability of informing us that we are, for example, consuming too much capital that belongs to future generations without setting aside adequate reserves for depletion. Such a whole earth accounting system should be able to tell us how close to the brink of bankruptcy we are. Without making intelligent use of the technological possibilities now available to us through the computer's capacity to replace the lawlessness of money as cash, such a rational whole earth accounting system would be impossible and indeed inconceivable. Failure to make use of the newly available technology would be inexcusable in light of man's historic success in meeting past threats by his unique ability to invent, adapt and change.

The name, *cashless society*, would not mean a repudiation of monetary capital created in the past. On the contrary, a cashless society would recognize society's debt to its past by accepting monetary capital from the past at a stable face value as the sum of the past human effort that it represents. It would make possible a new economic ordering of society in which the present generation humbly acknowledged its accountability to both past and future generations for what it has inherited from the one and ought to leave to the other.

Little social or economic injustice can be perceived in an accounting system under which economic resources inherited from earlier generations, and economic resources owed to future generations, could be segregated from values created in the present generation by the individual efforts of individual members of it. It is possible to admit that inalienable economic rights to resources inherited from earlier generations, and economic opportunities in the present generation, may yet be discovered. Likewise, future generations may have inalienable economic rights in economic resources on which the present generation should be forbidden to trespass. It is enough to suggest that a cashless society offers the most promising starting point for the invention of an accounting system that would have the capability of permitting intelligent resolution of these issues.

It is perhaps more than enough to claim for such a system the capacity to make possible an approach to a society of equilibrium, or what John Stuart Mill called the stationary state. At any rate, the objective is plain. The stationary state may be the ultimate form of progress. To paraphrase the passage from Mill quoted at the end of the preceding chapter, the increase of mankind under the deliberate guidance of judicious foresight can make the conquests wrested from nature by the intellect and energy of scientific discoveries the common property of the species, and the means of improving and elevating the universal lot.

Bibliography

Of hundreds of books, pamphlets and articles about cash, credit, credit cards, stock certificates, money, political economy, the natural environment and other matters related to the cashless society, the following are some of the most useful, listed alphabetically by name of author or authorial organization.

"A.B.A. Will Issue Route Numbers to Bank Card Units," *American Banker,* June 28, 1967, p. 1.

Abouchar, Robert J. and Magnis, Nicholas E. "Bank Credit Cards—Implications for the Future," *Bankers Monthly* (London), Jan. 15, 1967.

American Bankers Association, *Credit Card and Revolving Credit Survey.* New York: Instalment Credit Committee, American Bankers Association, 1967.

Anderson, Dr. Clay J. "The Quest for Stability." *The Business Review,* February–May 1950. Reprinted by Department of Public Information, Federal Reserve Bank of Philadelphia, Philadelphia, Pa.

"Association for the National Interchange of Bank Credit Cards Under Discussion," *American Banker,* Aug. 18, 1966.

"Bank Credit Card Service Organization and the Bank Service Corporation Act," *Federal Reserve Bulletin,* November 1967, pp. 1912-13.

Bank Credit Cards—Bases for Evaluation. Conference at Loyola University, Chicago, Illinois, Mar. 29, 1967.

Barringer, E. L. and Martin, Gerold T. "You Have a Choice to Make in . . . the Checkless Society," *Hardware Age,* March 15, 1967.

Bazelon, David T. *The Paper Economy,* New York: Vintage Books, 1963.

Bellamy, Edward. *Looking Backward: 2000–1887,* New York: The New American Library, Signet Classic, 1960.

Bibliography

Berger, Marshall C. "The Stolen Credit Card—Who Pays?" *Stores*, November 1967, pp. 41-42.

Blumberg, Phillip I. "Introduction to the Politicalization of the Corporation." *The Record of the Association of the Bar of the City of New York*, Vol. 26, No. 5. May 1971, p. 369.

Board of Governors, Federal Reserve System. *Annual Reports 1968, 1969, 1970, 1971*, Washington, D. C.

Board of Governors, Federal Reserve System. *Bank Credit-Card and Check-Credit Plans*, Washington, D. C. 1968, p. 102.

Board of Governors, Federal Reserve System. *The Federal Reserve System: Purposes and Functions*, Washington, D. C., Federal Reserve System, 1963.

Board of Governors, Federal Reserve System. *Survey of Financial Characteristics of Consumers*, Washington, D. C. 1966, p. 166.

Board of Governors, Federal Reserve System. *Selective Credit Control*, Washington, D. C. 1969. p. 9.

Board of Governors, Federal Reserve System. *The Legitimacy of Central Banks*, Washington, D. C. 1969, p. 16.

Brandell, R. E. and Leonard, C. A. "Bank Charge Cards: New Cash or New Credit," *Michigan Law Review*, Vol. 69, May 1971, p. 1033.

Breth, Robert D. "How to Make Credit Cards Profitable," *Banking*, February 1968, pp. 51-53.

Brimmer, Andrew F. "Bank Credit Cards and Check-Credit Plans: Developments and Implications." Speech delivered on Aug. 3, 1967, in San Francisco, California.

"By Credit Card (Carte Blanche)," *Economist*, Oct. 21, 1967, p. 322.

Cavers, David F. "Low Visibility Environmental Law." *Harvard Law School Bulletin*, Vol. 22, No. 2, December 1970, pp. 25 et seq.

"Charge Now, Pay Never," *Sales Management*, Oct. 15, 1967, pp. 49-50.

Coha, Stephen P. "Credit Card Frauds," *Bankers Monthly* (London), June 15, 1967.

Cole, Robert. "Financing Retail Credit Sales Through Charge Account Bank Plans," *Business Management Survey No. 5*. University of Illinois, Bureau of Business Management, 1955.

Consumer Credit in the 70s: An Overview. Symposium, *The Business Lawyer*, Vol. 26, Jan. 1971, p. 753.

"The Credit Cards," *Finance*, January 1968, pp. 8-11.

"Credit Card Banking—Is It for Us?" *Bankers Research*, Apr. 25, 1967, pp. 1-3.

"Credit Cards: (1) The case for the credit card; (2) A reader's guide; (3) Are credit cards inflationary?" *The Bankers*, July 1966, pp. 444-54.

"Credit Cards: How Many—and Whose?" *Business Week*, July 9, 1966, pp. 137-38.

Davenport, William B. "Bank Credit Cards and the Law." *The Bankers Magazine*, Vol. 152, No. 1, Winter 1969.

Davenport, William B. "Bank Credit Cards and the Uniform Commercial Code." *Valparaiso University Law Rev.*, Vol. 1, p. 218, Spring 1967, reprinted in 85 Banking Law Journal 941.

Davey, Gerald I., "Automating the Credit Inquiry Process," *Proceedings, the American Bankers Association National Automation Conference.* New York: American Bankers Association, 1967, pp. 63-66.

The Diebold Group, Inc. *Summary Report of a Survey on the Impact of Electronics on Money and Credit.* New York: The Diebold Group, Inc., 1967.

"Enlarging the Charge Card; Bank of America's Nation-wide Credit-Card Plan Is One More Sign of Banking's Ardent Pursuit of This Business," *Business Week*, May 28, 1966, p. 42.

"Europe's Reluctant Move Toward Credit Cards," *Banking*, February 1968, pp. 45-46.

"Fourth District Developments in Bank Credit Cards and Check-Credit Plans," *Economic Review*, Federal Reserve Bank of Cleveland, April 1967, pp. 27-35.

"Furness Asks for Curb on Unsought Bank Credit Cards," *Advertising Age*, Nov. 13, 1967, p. 1.

Galbraith, John Kenneth. *American Capitalism: The Concept of Countervailing Power*, Boston: Houghton Mifflin Co., 1952. Reprint: Sentry Edition, 1956.

Galbraith, John Kenneth. *The Affluent Society*, Boston: Houghton Mifflin Co., 1958. Reprint: The New American Library, Mentor Books, New York, 1958.

Galbraith, John Kenneth. *The New Industrial State*, Boston: Houghton Mifflin Co., 1967. Reprint: The New American Library, Signet Books, New York, 1968.

Greene, Wade and Golden, Soma. "The Luddites Were Not All Wrong: Ezra J. Mishan." *The New York Times Magazine*, November 21, 1971, pp. 40 et seq.

Greenspan, Louis. "The Bank/Retailer Interface," in *Proceedings, The American Bankers Association National Automation Conference,* New York: American Bankers Association, 1967, pp. 58-63.

Hambelton, James R. Series of seven articles pertaining to bank credit cards; *American Banker*, July 20, 1966–July 31, 1966.

Harrod, Roy. *Money*, London: Macmillan & Co. Ltd., 1969; New York: St. Martin's Press, 1969.

Hartquist, David A. and King, John E. "Citizen Remedies—A Report From Capitol Hill," *Harvard Law School Bulletin*, Vol. 22, No. 2, December 1970, pp. 20-24.

Hazelton, Lared E. "From Credit Card to Instant Banking," *Finance*, January 1968, pp. 16-17.

Bibliography

Head, Robert V. "The Checkless Society," *Datamation*, March 1966, p. 22.

Hendrickson, Robert A. *The Future of Money*, Englewood Cliffs, N. J.: Prentice-Hall, Inc., 1970; London: MacGibbon & Kee, 1970.

Herrman, William H. *Charge Account Banking*, New York: By the author, 1960.

Higgs, John, O'Connor, William, Simmons, Richard S. *Bank Credit Cards —Problems Under Regulation Z and Possible Problems as a Result of Future Developments Under Proposed Consumer Legislation*, The Business Lawyer: Section of Corporation, Banking and Business Law of The American Bar Association, Vol. 27, No. 1, November 1971, pp. 111-138.

"How Many People Use Credit Cards," *U.S. News and World Report*, May 23, 1960, pp. 137-39.

"Is Money Really Necessary," *Forbes*, Apr. 1, 1967, pp. 104.

Johnson, Herbert E. and Ricker, Charles S. "Economic Implications of the Checkless Society," Speech delivered at the Checkless Society Committee Meeting of the ABA, Washington, D. C., June 20-21, 1967.

Johnston, Robert, "Credit—and Credit Cards." *Monthly Review*, Federal Reserve Bank of San Francisco, September 1967, pp. 171-77.

Kasdan, Alan Richard. "Third World War—Environment Versus Development?" *The Record of the Association of the Bar of the City of New York*, vol. 26, No. 6, p. 454, June 1971.

Knauer, V. et al. "Symposium on the Uniform Consumer Credit Code," *Kentucky Law Journal*, Vol. 60, Fall 1971, p. 1.

Kolb, R. C. "Computer Vital Tool for Credit Card Operations, *American Banker*, June 6, 1966, p. 16.

Konstas, Panos, et al. *Money Market Instruments: Characteristics and Interest Rate Patterns*. Federal Reserve Bank of Cleveland, Ohio, 1970.

Larkin, Kenneth V. "Launching a National Credit Card," *The Pacific Banker and Business*, October 1966, pp. 23-24.

Lee, N. F. "What's This 'Checkless Society' All About?" *Financial Executive*, June 1967, p. 20.

Lindauer, John. *Macroeconomics*, New York: John Wiley & Sons, Inc., 1968.

Livingston, W. Putnam. "Banking's Role in a Credit Card Economy," *Banking*, September 1966, pp. 111-12, 118.

Lozowick, A. H. "Compatible Bank Credit Cards," *Bankers Monthly* (London), July and October 1967, pp. 28-29.

Lumpkin, R. Pierce. *Readings on Money*, The Federal Reserve Bank of Richmond, Virginia, sixth ed. 1967.

Magnis, Nicholas E., Jr., and Pickell, Barry, "Credit Card Banking," *Bankers Monthly* (London), Nov. 15, 1966, pp. 31-33, 45-46.

Mann, Maurice. *How Does Monetary Policy Affect the Economy?* Federal Reserve Board Staff Economic Study, Washington, D. C. 1968.

Marcus, Edward. "The Impact of Credit Cards on Demand Deposit Utilization," *Southern Economic Journal,* April 1960, pp. 314-16.

Martin, James, and Norman, Adrian R.D. *The Computerized Society,* Englewood Cliffs, N. J.: Prentice-Hall, Inc., 1970.

McLeary, Joe W. "Credit Cards—Can Small Banks Compete," *Monthly Review,* Federal Reserve Bank of Atlanta, February 1968, pp. 18-21.

Meek, Paul. *Open Market Operations,* Federal Reserve Bank of New York, 1969.

"Michigan Banks Launch Credit Card Cooperative," *Burroughs Clearing House,* January 1966, pp. 15-16.

Midwest Bank Card System, Inc. *Annual Report,* 1966–67. Chicago, Illinois, 69 West Washington Street, 60602.

Mill, John Stuart. *Principles of Political Economy* (5th ed.) published by Parker, Son and Bourn, West Strand, London, 1862.

Mitchell, George W. "Effects of Automation on the Structure and Functioning of Banking," *American Economic Review,* May 1966, p. 159.

Money and Economic Balance, Federal Reserve Bank of New York, 1968.

Monhollon, Jimmie R. *Instruments of the Money Market,* Federal Reserve Bank of Richmond, Virginia, 1970.

Nadler, Paul S. "Checkless Society: Don't Wait Until It Comes to Face Up to It," *American Banker,* Oct. 26, 1966, p. 12.

"New Moves in British Credit Cards," *Burroughs Clearing House,* July 1966, pp. 53-54.

"Next in Banking: Pay Bills by Phone," *Business Week,* Nov. 13, 1966, p. 12.

Nichols, Dorothy M. *Two Faces of Debt,* Federal Reserve Bank of Chicago, 1968.

O'Leary, James J. *The Dilemma of Government Economic Policy.* Publ. of United States Trust Company of New York, 1971.

Orwell, George. *1984.* New York: Harcourt, Brace & Co., 1949. In paper, The New American Library, New York, 1961.

"The Other Side of the Card," *Finance,* January 1968.

"Patman Would Restrict Credit Cards," *Banking,* October 1967, p. 28.

Patterson, Harlan R. "What Spells Success for Bank Charge Plans?" *Banking,* February 1964, pp. 53, 98.

Pickell, Barry, and Abouchar, Roger. "Look Before You Leap into Credit Card Field," *American Banker,* June 6, 1966, p. 16.

Poquette, R. W. "Bank Credit Cards Gain Popularity," *Mid-Continent Banker,* August 1966, pp. 54-56.

Practising Law Institute. *Credit Cards: Legal and Business Problems,* New York, N. Y. 1970.

Prather, W. C. *Credit Cards—A Prelude to the Cashless Society,* in "Consumer Credit: A Symposium," *Boston College Industrial and Commercial Law Review*, Vol. 8, Spring 1967, p. 387.

Pullen, Robert W. "Bank Credit Card and Related Plans," *New England Business Review*, Federal Reserve Bank of Boston, December 1966.

Pullen, Robert W., and O'Connell, Frederick D. *Supplement to Bank Credit Card and Related Plans*, Federal Reserve Bank of Boston, December 1966.

"Regulation of Consumer Credit—the Credit Card and the State Legislature," *Yale Law Journal*, April 1964, pp. 886-904.

Reich, Charles A., *The Greening of America: The Coming of a New Consciousness and the Rebirth of a Future*. New York: Random House, 1970.

Reistad, Dale L. "Credit Cards—Stepping Stones to the Checkless Society?" *Computers and Automation*, January 1967, p. 26.

Richards, Vern C. "The Credit Card Mania," *Western Banker*, October 1966, p. 318.

Ritter, Lawrence S. and Silber, William L. *Money*, Basic Books, Inc., New York, N. Y. 1970.

Ritter, Lawrence S. *The Political Arithmetic of Reordered National Priorities*, The Morgan Guaranty Survey, New York, N. Y., July 1971. p. 3.

Robinson, Joan. "Critique of Capitalism and the Mixed Economy," from Joan Robinson, *Economics: An Awkward Corner*. George Allen & Unwin, Ltd., London 1966.

Rosenthal, Albert J. "The Federal Role in Protecting Our Environment," *Harvard Law School Bulletin*, Vol. 22, No. 2, December 1970, pp. 14-19.

Russell, Charles T. "Should You Be in the Charge Card Business?" *Mid-Western Banker*, October 1966, pp. 24-26.

Russell, Charles T., and Dougherty, D. "We're in the Charge Card Business—Should You Be?" Based on presentations at the regional meetings of the Bank Public Relations and Marketing Association in Columbus, Ohio, April 5, and in Montreal, Canada, April 22, 1966.

Samuelson, Paul. *Economics: An Introductory Analysis*. 8th ed. New York: McGraw-Hill, Inc.

Smith, Richard B. "The Stock Certificate Revisited." *Trusts and Estates Magazine*, Vol. 110, No. 4, p. 290, April 1971.

South, J. G. "Credit Cards: A Primer," *The Business Lawyer;* Section of Corporation, Banking and Business Law of The American Bar Association, Vol. 23, p. 327, January 1967.

Sprague, Richard E. "System for Automatic Value Exchange," *Banking*, June 1966, pp. 117-20.

"State Street Bank Charts New Path in Marketing Bank Americard First Year," *New England Advertising Week*, Nov. 16, 1967, pp. 1, 4.

Theobald, Robert. *America II: An Alternative Future for America,* The Swallow Press, Chicago, 1968.

Theobald, Robert. *The Economics of Abundance: A Non-Inflationary Future,* Pitman Publishing Corporation, New York, 1970.

"This Could Mean Banking War," *Economist,* Jan. 19, 1966, pp. 220-21.

Thompson, John. "The Case for the Credit Card," *Banker,* July 1966, pp. 444-46.

Thoreau, Henry David. *Walden, or Life in the Woods,* and *On the Duty of Civil Disobedience.* (Reprint) The New American Library, Signet Classic, New York, 1960.

"Toward Universal Credit Cards," *Marples Business Roundup,* Oct. 1966.

Townshend-Zellner, Norman. "The Bank Charge Account Plan and Retail Food Marketing," *Agricultural Economics Research,* October 1960, pp. 85-104.

U.S. Congress, Senate, Committee on the Judiciary. The Credit Industry. *Hearings, Ninetieth Congress,* second session, pursuant to S. Res. 233, credit bureaus and reporting. December 10 and 11, 1968. Washington, U.S. Government Printing Office, 1969.

Vergari, James V. "The Credit Card—Input to the Checkless Society," in *Proceedings, The American Bankers Association National Automation Conference,* New York: American Bankers Association, 1967, pp. 55-57.

Vonnegut, Kurt, Jr. *Player Piano,* New York: Charles Scribner's Sons, 1952.

Ward, Michael, "Credit Card Delinquency," *Bankers Monthly* (London), November 1967, pp. 245-47.

"Washington Looks at Credit Cards," *Banking,* September 1967, pp. 63-64.

Webster, William H. "Bank Charge Cards—Recent Developments in Regulation and Operation," *The Business Lawyer*: Section of Corporation, Banking and Business Law of The American Bar Association, Vol. 26, No. 1, September 1970, pp. 43-57.

Werner, Walter, et al. "The Certificateless Society: Why and When," *The Business Lawyer*: Section of Corporation, Banking and Business Law of The American Bar Association, Vol. 26, No. 3, January 1971, pp. 603-630.

"When Money's Tight, Just Put It on the Cuff," *Newsweek,* Aug. 23, 1966, pp. 84-86.

White, A. N. "Cheques and Credit Cards: More Competition Between the Banks," *Bankers Magazine* (London), February 1966, pp. 85-89.

Whittle, Jack W. "Session on Toward a Checkless Society, Part I: The Credit Card Revolution—Introductory Remarks," in *Proceedings, The American Bankers Association, National Automation Conference,* New York: American Bankers Association, 1967, pp. 48-55.

Bibliography

Wilmouth, Robert K. "Credit Cards and the Changing World of Consumer Finance." Speech delivered at the 92nd Annual Association of the American Bankers Association, Oct. 23-26, 1966.

Woodley, Annette R., and Steele, H. Ellsworth. "Charge Account Banking in the Sixth Federal Reserve District," *Atlanta Economic Review*, November 1966, p. 3.

Yen, Harry S. C. "The World—and How We Abuse It," and "The Fragile Beauty All Around Us," *National Geographic*, vol. 138, No. 6, December 1970, pp. 782-795.

Young, Gordon, and Blair, James P. "Pollution, Threat to Man's Only Home." *National Geographic*, Vol. 138, No. 6, December 1970, pp. 738-781.

Zipf, A. R. "The Computer's Role in the 'Dividends or Disaster' Equation," in *Computers in Management* (Leatherbee lectures, 1967); Cambridge: Harvard University Press, 1967.

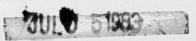